NIGHT DIVER

ANHINGA PRESS

NIGHT DIVER

BUCKY McMAHON

ANHINGA PRESS
Tallahassee, Florida 2008

Cover Art: *Night Diver* by Bucky McMahon
Author photograph, cover: by Tom Bennett of Exum Mountain Guides
Author photograph, page 238: by Heather Sellers
Cover design, book design, and production: C. L. Knight
Typesetting: Jill Ihasz
Type Styles: titles set in ITC Kabel; text set in Adobe Garamond Pro

Library of Congress Cataloging-in-Publication Data
Night Diver by Bucky McMahon – First Edition
ISBN – 978-1-934695-01-2
Library of Congress Cataloging Card Number – 2007938986

This publication is sponsored in part by a grant
from the Florida Department of State,
Division of Cultural Affairs, and the Florida Arts Council.

Anhinga Press Inc. is a nonprofit corporation dedicated wholly to the
publication and appreciation of fine poetry and other literary genres.

For personal orders, catalogs
and information write to:
Anhinga Press
P.O. Box 10595
Tallahassee, Florida 32302
Web site: www.anhinga.org
E-mail: info@anhinga.org

Published in the United States
by Anhinga Press
Tallahassee, Florida
First Edition, 2008

To H.B., the lovely one

Contents

Acknowledgments

Grateful acknowledgment is made to the publications in which these essays first appeared, sometimes in a slightly different form.

Tallahassee Democrat: "Lake Ella," "Ochlocknee, Dionysus, Pine Sol," "Newt New," "Hangover," "High School Football," "Barrel of Fun," "Wakulla: Mother of all Springs," "Tennis for None," "Toys R Us," and "Writing About Death"

Esquire: "Sea-Kayaking the Big Bend," "Montserrat in Ashes," "Percival Gordon," "Adrift on Gulf Stream," "Up the Grand," "The Moon and Danzel Cabral," "Adventures in My Bed," "Spearfishing with Captain Jojo," "Nicaragua Surf Camp," "This Ain't Boca, Baby," "Canyoneering," "Snowkiting," "Everest at Bottom of Sea," "Two Brothers, One Ocean, No Fish," "Searching for Madonna at Mahakumbh," and "Kayaking Waterfalls."

Outside: "Lord Long Arms, I Presume," "Armadillophobia," and "Suwannee River"

Islands: "Barbados Surf Diary," "I Was Dogman"

Scuba Diving: "Diving the Yonaguni Underwater Pyramid," "Journey to God's Well," and "Alaska Under Water"

GQ: "Night Diving"

Skiing: "SLYD"

My career might've been a different beast entirely if Bob Shacochis hadn't twisted some arms at *Outside* magazine to give me a shot. That opened a lot of doors. And, Mr. Bob wouldn't have been a "Barmadillo" reader if Mark Hinson, Zilpha Underwood and Janey Nelson hadn't made possible my weekly romp in the *Tallahassee Democrat's Limelight*. My sincerest thanks for the opportunities.

David Granger, *Esquire's* extraordinary editor-in-chief, threw me more than one life-line when I was treading tropical waters and showing signs of panic. Thanks for the faith. The mysterious, mercurial Mark Warren, *Esquire's* executive editor, traveled the world with inimitable child-like wonder — and then handed me the jewels he discovered. In similar fashion, Terry Noland brought his sharp eye and wry humor to the world of semi-crazy adrenaline sports for *Esquire's* "Restless Man," and sent me on some of the greatest adventures imaginable. Of course, that was just the beginning of our collaboration. Indeed, many of the pieces here were shaped by the discerning minds, demanding standards, and sometimes gentle cudgeling of brilliant editors, including Brendan Vaughan and Adrienne Miller at *Esquire;* and Hampton Sides, Laura Hohnhold, Elizabeth Hightower, Claire Martin and Leslie Weedon at *Outside.*

In their earliest avatars, these stories were often voiced as travel anecdotes, or worse, as complaints — about the fearsome blank page and the inexplicable recalcitrance of excellent material. True friends and fellow writers Steve Watkins, Pam Ball, Gary White, Lu Vickers, Susan Damerville and Diane Roberts heard a bellyful, sympathized and advised. Salut! The indomitably upbeat Dan Damerville heard it all and wisely philosophized court side. And as the melancholy Jacques observes, I'd have mortgaged my home to see another man's if Heather hadn't held ours together in my frequent absences, and through more hurricanes than is statistically probable.

Finally, this book wouldn't exist if Rick Campbell, poet, publisher, true bibliophile, had not believed it should. Special thanks to Rick, and to Lynne Knight and Donna Decker, for the care and craft they brought to this book.

NIGHT DIVER

Very carefully, and very professionally, that's the way to abandon ship, but even though I have all day, fair weather, a crew to help me, and a ship that doesn't really require abandoning, as soon as we begin to launch the raft things rapidly spiral out of control, like in a real disaster. First there's some debate about whether the raft stays in its blue canvas bag. There are pictograms on the bag, the sort of universal language you'd send out on a space probe, but nothing per se on the "in the bag or out" issue. Good thing we take it out or it probably would've sunk, or exploded! Then Scott Harrington, captain of the fifty-three-foot "Fish Hunter," and I heave the heavy, compressed block of canvas over the transom. Young Marcelo, the first mate, is keen to yank the inflation cord; there's a PFFFTT!! sound as the CO_2 canister pops, a puff of mist, and then the raft does this dramatically animated Transformer thing — "Fucking cool!" Marcelo says — and it is suddenly there, upside down, a pentagonal slab of black plastic fabric stretched between pontoons and quivering against the seas like the jelly between luncheon sausages.

All at once I'm awash with the bad sort of adrenaline, the fight or flight type, pulse-rate escalating. It's nothing like the raft I had in mind when I thought "raft." It's not Huck and Jim on the Miss'sip, kicked back on something stable, commodious, smoking pipes and watching the world drift by. It's more like an inflatable kiddie pool. It's hard to believe I'm about to take it for a spin on the world's fastest ocean current, the Gulf Stream. By doing so, I hope to explore the authentically gigantic through the lens of the truly sorry.

Marcelo, who is skinny and agile, leaps on to the raft to right it (see pictures on bag). As the raft comes over, dunking Marcelo, two smaller upright pontoons catch the wind, unfurling a light canvas half-dome like on a baby carriage. Captain Scott hauls to on the inflator rope and Marcelo springs out. "You going to be sick in there, man!" he says.

That's what everybody has been saying the past two days while I hung out in Miami waiting for the wind to lay down. I mean specifically the guys at Sea Tow International, proprietors of the "Fish Hunter," and experts in marine salvage and every other sea-going bummer. "Even the guys who never get sick get sick in those rafts," they all said, with theatrically raised eyebrows and disbelieving laughter at the idea of *voluntarily* submitting to that world of hurl.

As for mal de mer I chose denial, pretty effective right up to the present moment. I'm on hands and knees on the lurching deck of the real boat leaning out to tear open a sturdy plastic sack laced to the aft pontoon, the raft's guts. It's full of survival stuff — French survival stuff, to go by the labels — including the sea anchor, a parachute-like stabilizer tied to a hundred feet of rubber-band-bound strapping, which, immediately upon release, floats under the "Fish Hunter" and entangles the props — Hey, Marcelo! — and all of a sudden it's getting kind of late and the weather doesn't look all that great either.

On second thought ... Upon closer examination of the facts ... Gentlemen, my bad! My real identity is Jacques Lapine, an escaped lunatic from France with a harmless compulsion to hire boats ... But I have already clambered down onto the trampoline-like surface of the raft floor and captain and mate are passing me my considerable supplies: emergency communications and rescue devices, changes of clothes, water for a week, food for the rest of my life. Led by the rioting water jugs, everything topples, rolls, slides in a jumbled pile to the depression in the middle of the floor around my sunken feet. Ropes, rings, strings, packets — Jesus! — there has to be a bailer in here somewhere. The "Fish Hunter" rises on a swell, the raft drops down into the trough; down dips the "Fish Hunter," up bobs the raft. And so, in that see-saw fashion, politely bowing to each other, the two crafts begin to drift apart. I'm waving for a camera, bailing with a sponge, when I see the raft's instruction manual floating among the debris of hasty departure.

"Gardez votre sang froid," it reads. "Et votre bonne humeur."

Mais oui! I am fifty miles out to sea off the southern tip of Florida, on the far eastern edge of the Gulf Stream, in a rising wind, in a violently tossing raft. I find a couple of dangling electrodes and connect them, which turns on the little red strobe atop the dome. We're open for business, ye bogeys of the sea. Already it's deepening dusk, the sharking hour. In a very little while, it will be dark.

***

Off my starboard bow, to westward, where the horizon still eerily glows with the lights of the south Florida megalopolis (even at fifty miles!), there's a cruise ship lit up like Christmas. Harmlessly distant, but a reminder I'm smack in the middle of major shipping lanes with a couple of bath-toy paddles which would at most propel me in a tight frantic circle. In my pre-trip jitters, I imagined being rudely awakened by the prow of a container ship. Ahoy! — then blindly throttled, crushed with unspeakable force, and finally chopped up by the props. Raw superstition crept in, too — fear of monsters, and of discovering holes in the fabric of my soul. Of Bermuda Triangle types of doorways to other dimensions, like death. The Atlantic Ocean at night, in a raft, man. Fortunately, reality is proving less frightening, being more reliably real.

The reality is this: the raft rides a little rough in these two-to-four-foot seas. It slips no blows. It meets every wave head on and scrunches like an accordion. Bulges up at the midriff. Stretches out lengthwise as if to ingest the wave, and then passes it out under the shuddering aft pontoon like a four-foot fart. For sheer variety of motion it's the worst ride at the fair. I've given up bailing for the time being and so far have organized my gear mainly by repeatedly kicking it as far to the front of the raft as its varying properties allow.

On the plus side, the raft points reliably into the wind, thanks to the sea anchor, I think. And I've had an ace up my sleeve all along. I'm not in the raft. I'm on it — perched side-saddle on the leeward rail, left hand tightly twisted in the rope that rings the raft, right arm out-stretched for balance like a bronco rider's. Yee-haw! And I'm doing all right. Not a bit sick yet, thank you. Of course, I'm on "the patch" — Trans-derm Scopolamine — and it's fucking me up like a horse tranquilizer. Sort of centers consciousness about a millimeter off to the side, so that you're looking at yourself from outside yourself and thinking, "You'd like to puke, but you don't strictly speaking have to puke, so what's your problem?" Still, every time I crash through one of the bigger waves my spirits rise. Riding out the rough seas is a sport, at least, like white-water rafting a river without end.

Wind's getting a little *too* frisky, though. Snapping in the tent canvas. Freshening, as they say. This despite a spectacularly clear night, the sky a plasma of stars, glowing planets, blinking satellites, a few wayfaring planes. A poem or a pop song in every one of them. And me in a spotlight of glowing green, as every cresting whitecap ignites a world of bioluminescence, little green buggers that come up to the surface to fuck the stars. For them the weather is perfect.

Better not to look down at those glimmering universes. I had a fever-dream once, barely out of toddler-hood, back when my brain remembered being a blastomere. It was about the sizes of things. Terribly tiny things. Like atoms, only smaller. Things god-awfully huge. Like container ships. Only bigger. A lot bigger! Then I forgot about the maddeningly miniscule and the astoundingly huge; I rounded things off to the nearest whole integer. Sought the middle way. As Frost says of the beachcombers' watch, neither out far nor in deep.

But today at sea I've seen things: Miami's tallest skyscrapers shrunk to a delicate gray fuzz, till the whole thing would fit in a thimble ten times over — a world in a grain of sand, or vice versa. As soon as the cityscape faded entirely, about 14 miles out, it sprang up again — by persistence of vision, apparently — in a ring all around us, encircling us with an imaginary New Jerusalem, the City beyond the waves. By then we were in the Stream, which we knew from the blue-berry hue, and its heat, the "Fish Hunter's" digital water-temp gauge ticking upwards: 76, 77.3, all the way up to 80 degrees. We had hit the main vein of the Western World and I suited up in neoprene to be injected like one of the microbe-sized explorers in "Fantastic Voyage."

Wham! The raft takes one right on the snout. A real canopy crumpler. Never saw it coming. Slam! Jesus Christ!

This is space travel. Things abstracting, going blank. Yeah, sure, the sea, now and now and now, but with a Moe's repertoire of nyuk nyuk nyuks. Fucking ocean! The stars yo-yo-ing with the raft's rise and fall. I'm in a new zone of disengagement. No longer alert. So long as we're not going to capsize, then, okay: waves, wind, spray. Not a panic situation. Just hold on. Ten past ten by the glow of my watch. Five hours on the raft and a chill in the air now. Time to layer up: life-jacket off, wet-bag clinched between knees, sweat-shirt out, sweat-shirt on, fleece out, fleece on, life-jacket back on, wet-bag booted forward. Better now.

"Brandy, you a fine girl ...!" I sing.

A million thumps later — Midnight! Made it. Come on, twelve o one! The real night watch now. Everything done that can be done, which is very nearly nothing about anything. Sea, raft, stars. All is one. None. One. Nodding off for moments at a time on the rail. How idiots are separated from rafts. I watch the horizon. I watch the sky. Until *the stars thrown down their spears.* They really do. The last thing I see is a pair of vast figures hurrying towards me from the stars. "The Celestial Couple" I call them, slack-jawed, awed. They're as tall as cathedrals, but gauzy like wraiths of light. Kindly somehow. Kind of corny. Mamma? Daddy? Or was I already sleeping?

Time to assume the position — fetal, that is — on the flooded raft floor. Damn the container ships, and let the waves crash where they may.

I wake up astonished to have slept, but oriented at once by a bemused narrative voice: dude, you're in a raft! I'm shivering. Cold, but not *cold* cold. I mean, the water I'm lying in feels warm; I'm kind of warm myself. But shaking convulsively. Gentle convulsions. A pleasant sort of hypothermia. Best of all, it's no longer night if not yet exactly dawn, and the wind has slackened appreciably too. Seas still chuck the raft under its chin, hiss and seethe, but it seems the ocean wants to make nice after last night's squall.

When it's indisputably morning I climb back up onto the lee pontoon and look out onto a subsiding field of silver seas — two to three feet and confused. The seas, I mean. Guzzle some water from the nearest gallon jug. Munch a few Saltines. I don't have much appetite. More alarmingly, I have no saliva — severe cottonmouth another side-effect of the behind-the-ear sea-sickness patch. This is a blow. The loss of eating as a pleasurable activity opens a huge hole in my day. Off my feed? No likey that.

Better organize my shit. Rescue gear aft: a flare pistol and six shells to send arching across the sky. Half a dozen French hand-rockets that look like giant fire-crackers (I'd love to fire one off, though at the risk of my hands). An aerosol bull-horn. Whistles. A Sat phone. Hand-held GPS. VHF radio. Coast Guard Epirb in a James Bond-esque case. Great stuff that would have the normal shipwrecked person off a raft in no time. The paradox is that I'm not in trouble, so I can't be rescued. Or am I in such deep trouble that these things have sought me out, as this situation has done, to make that point?

"M'aiddez! M'aiddz! Have capsized and am entangled in rescue gear!" When I asked the guys at Sea Tow if there was one thing I should absolutely not forget to bring on the raft, the old salt Captain Joe said — no hesitation: "Yeah, a blonde!" Guy knows his shit or what.

The MRE carton got soaked and fell apart in the night, spilling plastic bladders of plastic wrappers of foil packets of carrion in carrion gravy. My tins of sardines? In my dreams. A sack of oranges — Arrrgg! matey — for the scurvy. All of you to the starboard rail. It's the rope for you water jugs. But, nah! I can tell it's the sort of task I just ain't got the Bligh in me for. Besides, how much better off will I be when they're bound? You see? And now for the bailing. That's what I've really been wanting to do, to be done and be dry.

It's like this, as I learned last night, when I didn't have the means to study the problem. The bottom of the raft being malleable, it collects water wherever it is weighted. When I kneel, I corral a couple of gallons of it — along with two hundred feet of yellow plastic rope, a flashlight, the raft's blunt-bladed knife, and half a dozen MREs — but I can't get the water that's right under me. The problem is Archimedian. And then no matter how much I sop up and squeeze out over the rails, the volume of the water in the raft never seems to change. Though that's hard to verify. Except by pressing down hard with my feet and collecting a new puddle, which I mop up with renewed, but not infinitely renewable enthusiasm, going so far as to poke down on the depression with one finger so as to mop directly under my feet. At last I conclude that somewhere between the pontoons and the floor there's a leak below sea level so that in effect *I'm trying to sponge up the whole fucking ocean!*

A small matter. A very small matter. The raft won't sink (if only it would!). But it means I can't change out of my neoprene into dry clothes. And since the zipper in this farmer john type wet suit only goes down to my navel, peeing into my pee bucket (you can't lean out to piss because there's nothing to hold onto) means a regular Bowflex workout of stretching rubber. Gotta kneel to do it, and in a damn puddle. Important to stay hydrated, though. The wind and the sun and the salt will wick the moisture right out of you. So I'm gulping my way through the jugs, and flinging repeated contributions over the rail.

Everything I see around me, and miles more that I can't, is the Gulf Stream, and what powers the current is literally everything in my present physical circumstances — those things that I can feel and those things I never can. The Trades. The heat of the sun. The tilt of the Earth's axis. The Coriolis Effect of the planet's eastward spin, driving water hardest on the western margins of all the ocean basins. All these factors, plus water's well known desire for its own level. The Gulf Stream plows northwards for the Arctic in part because the Arctic water sinks, being cold, dense, and very salty. Thermohaline circulation, it's called.

As annual temperatures have risen in the North Atlantic, and the Greenland ice cap has melted, the cold end of the Stream has freshened considerably, gaining heat while losing salt (the "haline" in the term), and beginning to lose the wherewithal to sink to the abyssal bottom and begin its slow creep to Antarctica, a vital part of the eastern side of the ocean conveyor. The gyre stills turns, but the falcon can't hear the falconer. Things fall apart. Ironically, though the culprit is global warming, the result will be a new Ice Age, triggered by the sudden failure of the Gulf Stream.

That's the worst case scenario, anyway, in an alarm sounded by an October 2003 Department of Defense report titled "An Abrupt Climate Change and Its Implications for United States National Security." The paper cites climatological studies from Greenland ice core samples which reveal that similar warming trends in the past have shut down the ocean conveyor, triggering centuries-long ice ages. The worse news is that when it starts to go, it can go fast. The consequences for six billion human beings, even in sober DOD-speak, sound Biblical in wrath and scope. Siberian cold in Northern Europe. Storms of furious magnitude. Drought and dustbowls and wild fires in formerly fertile croplands. Wholesale famine. The Haves bunker down, and the Have Nots sharpen sticks. "Given the choice between starvation and raiding, human beings have always raided," the DOD report intones in a Dr. Strangelove-ian passage.

Sounds promising in terms of employment for young untrained males. Welcome to the Global Smackdown. In the doomsday scenario, the Gulf Stream may still flow as far north as Florida, but it might be heavily mined. I'm seeing it while it's safe.

***

Can I feel the Gulf Stream hurtling me north at four knots an hour? Facing west into an east-southeast breeze, plopping and dropping, bending and heaving, can I feel a lurching, ratcheting progress to leeward? Maybe, maybe not. The Stream may be eighty miles wide here, as much as seven miles deep. And no fixed objects anywhere. Just a few toots of cirrus drifting across the sky. Lovely view, though. A whole fucking lot of blue water. So much that you have to serve it to yourself in great glittering slices, splicing together a circle of endless planes in order to take in the whole pie chart, of which you are the infinitesimal nub. For lunch, Fig Newtons. An indomitable cookie, the Fig Newton. Not without its chewy goodness though the world were ending. After lunch I'm thinking about moving to the other side of the raft.

Godzilla walks, and civilization crumbles! The water jugs topple and roll. The lid is somehow off the lone grape Gator Aide bottle, dumping purple into the puddle. By the time I climb over the medical kit and the MREs and my dry-bags and settle onto the hot starboard pontoon the raft is a shambles. Now my back is turned slightly more to the wind and the waves. And oh, man, it's much worse over here. How could I have thought it would be better? That's a mistake I won't make twice. It's better for fishing over here, though, maybe. Six casts of a spoon, and who do I think I'm fooling? Six thousand casts and I might get a strike. Because of the risk of mayhem, a rafter should never land a fish longer than the span from his elbow to his fingertips. These things you can learn from experts. If I caught a fish I would eat its eyes, because that is what rafters should do.

At last, mid-afternoon, I spot a container ship on the eastern horizon. I'm like, Bring it on, big guy! This after hours of uninterrupted vigilance, back on the lee side, seeing no other ships, no whales, no sharks. Just a fireball sun, the myriad glinting chevrons of its reflection, and the roving, crisscrossing scalpels of light with which it probes into the blue. Of sea-life, just three little frilly brown Sargasso fish (they're like toad fish), and a squid — the looker in that quartet. These are the first creatures to colonize the shade of my floppy hull. Survivors of real life-raft disasters, like Steven Callahan, author of the brilliant non-fiction book, *Adrift*, report that the undersides of their rafts become veritable oases of sea-life, being a precious something in the midst of so much nothing. First come the bait fish, then come the game fish, and the sharks, and if you're really in it for the long-haul, barnacles and coral. Callahan owed his survival over a nearly three-month ordeal to the practically amorous attraction to his raft of dolphin fish (Mahi mahi) which he was occasionally able to spear. So far I haven't yet felt any thumps on the bottom of the raft, which would signal the arrival of dolphin or cobia.

But my life as a floating ecosystem is forgotten with the arrival of the container ship. In the brilliant afternoon light it gleams wondrously white like an iceberg with telephone poles on it. In all this ocean it's making straight for me. What were the odds? Excellent, I always thought. But the big ship bears north ever so slightly and misses me by a quarter mile. There's not even going to be any wake-surfing. It's very disappointing.

It's going on twenty-four hours in the raft now, probably a hundred miles of drifting. The day has begun to subside. I still don't have my sea legs, which means I still have to steady my brains on the horizon line or I may puke. And once I start puking I'm afraid I won't be able to stop. Attention to that duty has become a burden like consciously monitoring my heart beat. Do it now. Do it now. Do it now. It's times like these when heroes of isolation write novels in their heads, arrange and re-arrange an imaginary collection of CDs, or conjure up a pair of all-time NBA teams and play out a seven game series in their heads. Such feats lie on the far side of boredom, and I'm just dipping in on the near side of the stream, listening to a horrible dial-tone coming from its depths. I've taken on the demeanor of a dullard, slumped on the rail. I could easily drool.

It's then that somebody calls my name. From maybe ten feet behind me. In a perfectly normal, conversational tone of voice.

"Bucky!"

Yeah, what? What?

Now I'm straining to hear the voice again, hearing only the wind. The gentle pishing and pshawing of seas. Plickle-plunk, tiddledee tiddledee. Captain Scott warned me about going to the edge: "You might fall through." He talked about finding an empty raft.

"Hey, Bucky!"

Fuck off! This is intolerable. It's like meditation with no omm in sight. Help! Help! My thoughts have twisted in an ever-tightening spiral until they've reached a point, and the point is this: the only thing to do on a raft is plot your way off of it. Paddle like crazy. Fire off a flare. Pick up the radio. Given the choice between raft and rescue, human beings have always reached for the radio. But not just yet.

It's night again at last. Done it again, I'm thinking. Reached my goal. That was sixty-seconds of sixty-minutes of twelve hours of daylight, and hardly a moment squandered on distractions. The sea is jealous of its wonders — its mythological-looking sunfish, its singing mermaids. Beginners cut their teeth on monotony. I did have my Star King and Queen, though. Seems ages since I saw them. I was a mere pup in life-raft years, and now I'm nostalgic for the man I was yesterday. More the fool, but with bonne humeur to spare. At least I've learned a lesson better than I ever thought I'd know it: that time may wait for no man, but it brakes for rafters.

Time for me to layer-up again: life-jacket off etc. Strobe light on. Open for business. Some awful long time later, brooding in the dark, sulky as Queequeg, I see something. There — on the south horizon — the White Whale! I snatch up the VHF. We've got a container-ship-in-the-night situation. Punching in Channel 16 I overhear Captain Scot on the case already.

"Captain of the north bound container ship, do you read me? Captain of the north bound ship, do you read? Son of a bitch isn't even listening to his radio! This is the "Fish Hunter," do you read? Better turn on your flashlight!" This last is directed to me.

I'm waving my flashlight, thinking about sending up a French hand-rocket. But then the poor devil might think he has to stop his barge and rescue somebody.

"Okay fisherman, what do you want?" It's the container ship captain, who sounds tired and bored. But Captain Scott apparently can't hear him. He keeps at the radio: "Do you read me? Do you read me?" This is bad. This is a breakdown of faux-survival rafting security.

The giant misses me anyway, sliding by like a city block on casters. Whew! A close call. But not that close. Still, it was somehow unnerving. But was it unnerving enough? Am I in fact unnerved? No. Nope. Not really. I'm really achy though, cramping up in the back from riding the pontoon for most of thirty hours. I really need to lie down in the bottom of the raft and sleep, but then I'd be soaked. And then I'd get cold. But I could get warm again. Or could I? Am I in extremis, or would I not know extremis if it bit me on the butt.

Reach for that radio, pal, and you'll regret it for the rest of your life.

Who said that? My better self, that hardass nutcase. I'll just check in, I tell my not-so-good self. To Captain Scott on the radio I say, "I'm having my doubts."

"I'm sure you are," he says. "Look, you don't have to prove anything to anybody. It's not like you're trying out for the Navy Seals."

But I'm always proving something to somebody, and that's exactly what I'm always trying out for. Tough enough to last on a raft? At least one more night? But then it will be day again. In the end it's human sympathy that rescues me, lifts me out of the time warp of confined isolation under simulated stress. A friendly voice.

"All right," I say. "I'm done."

And then — boom! whammo! alacazam! — the very next moment, or so it seems, not counting a nanosecond dragging the raft onto the stern of the "Fish Hunter," a brief chat on the flying bridge, a warm shower and a change of clothes, prone time unconscious on the sofa in the cabin — almost instantaneously I'm standing on a swank dock in Fort Lauderdale with my stuff back in boxes, waiting, with what felicitous ease, amidst all the riches of dry land, for a cab.

For me and Bathsheba — biblically-named beauty of a beach town on Barbados' wild Atlantic coast — it was love at first sight. A handful of homes hidden in the trees, a few modest guest-houses, a couple of bars, a little park of palms and grass, a ragged wind-chewed coast cupping a crescent of sand. Then sea to infinity. It was the world as I might've drawn it in my loose-leaf notebook back in high school when I was a surf-crazed kid with skinny legs and sun-bleached blond hair.

I'm writing this from the patio of the Bajan Surf Bungalows, sipping a local Banks beer, still mesmerized by the sight of Soup Bowl, Barbados' most famous surf break. From here, it's a cat's eye swirl of blue and white — dark blue swells, white foam and frothy rip current, all revolving with a point break's elemental symmetry. Framing the break are Bathsheba's colossal "Lord of the Rings" rock formations, green-topped and mushroom-shaped, more extravagant than anything I ever sketched.

A mid afternoon shower is moving in from the south, blurring the view to a sort of dreamy soft focus, but doing good things to the waves, smoothing and grooming them. Out in the water, da boys are killing it, everybody busting big moves on the Bowl. Me, I'm temporarily surfed out, sunburned and red-eyed from the offshore wind blowing spray back in my face. After two hours of rigorous delight — good waves; wonderful clear warm water; that lively breeze — my arms are limp noodles, and my ribs...can you break ribs just paddling a surfboard? Back in those high school days, when I first heard about Bathsheba and Soup Bowl (from a friend who nearly drowned here), I woulda, coulda still been out there, jockeying for poll position on the point. Shoulda been here yesterday, as they say in "Endless Summer." No. Better to be here tomorrow, and I will be.

There's talk of a big swell coming (though is there not always such talk?).

Yesterday I took two tours of the island, getting a handle on the place. I was staying on the south coast then, near the airport; I didn't think I could find Bathsheba in the dark, and in retrospect, I can see I was right. I've saved the scrap of paper on which I wrote down the way: "Left, Right, Left, Right, Left, Right, Second Left Past Mike's Mini-Mart. Then ask someone else for directions." One of the most densely populated islands in the Caribbean, Barbados is a crazy quilt of roads — primary, secondary, and "mystery" (those not on the map) — stitching together innumerable little neighborhoods of tidy homes and pretty stone churches. Not surprisingly, driving twenty miles across the island took me two hours today, in daylight, with half the island chipping in advice: yes, yes, Bathsheba, that's right, that dirt track through the sugar cane field, that is the way. Or one way, at least.

Anyway, yesterday I was up with the roosters that shared my address: Peach and Quiet, Inch Marlowe, Christ Church. Gem of a place, killer sea-view from the pool, and small enough that you meet the charming and helpful owners, Adrian and Margaret Loveridge. As for that delightfully Dickensian "Inch" in the address, it's "thought to be a corruption of the word 'peninsula'," according to Adrian, a dead-ringer for the actor Kenneth Brannagh, and a fount of local lore. He invited me to come along on a pre-breakfast walking tour with a group of mostly older British tourists. "Little England" and all that, I thought what better way to absorb some history than among elderly ex-colonialists.

Slathered with sunscreen, some of us dressed as if for desert warfare against Rommel, we disembarked our tour vans high on a cliff above Salt Cave, formerly a famous smugglers' den. There we beheld a sweeping view of sunrise on a sparkling sea. What we were seeing was, in fact, Adrian informed us, the longest sweep of open ocean on the planet: the nearest land mass due south was Antarctica. This isolation gives Barbados, the easternmost of the Windward Islands, some of the world's cleanest air. "When scientists tested the air quality, the first impurities they picked up turned out upon analysis to be bits of camel dung from the Sahara," Adrian told us. A little further on he called our attention to the waves foaming on the outer reef and explained that, thanks to this natural barrier which surrounds the island, Barbados was never successfully invaded, as compared to Tobago, for instance, which was taken forty-two times. "A great defense, that," Adrian deadpanned, "plus some seven thousand cannon."

So it went, Barbados fun-facts spiced with wit, along the south coast cliffs, racing clouds breaking up the brilliant sunlight. Quite hot! we all agreed, but nice breeze! We followed the old 1930s rail-line trail to the broad fields of the Garrison Savannah, where Barbados Defense Troops were lining up for target practice. There we were accosted twice by officers in jeeps, the first time to be directed to march quickly in front of the rifles, the second time to countermand that order. We scurried from the shooting range like a flock of quail. Beyond the Garrison, at Chancery Lane, we came to a wetland — "Careful, a bit squodgy there!" — unique in Barbados, a nesting area for frigate birds, but the proposed site — with potentially disastrous ecological consequences — of a 500 condominium health facility. "The man who wants to do the building, a gentleman from Lebanon," Adrian said, "has the distinction of having been that country's last official supervisor of stoning."

I loved that guy! (Mr. Loveridge, I mean, not the stoner.)

My second tour of the day was with Zen master Zed Layson of Zed's Surf Adventures. Zen master, I say, for whether the subject is the quality of the surf, or the meaning of life, he is much given to the irrefutable, "It is what it is" ("wha' it is" — something almost Cockney about the accent). He also taught me, in four or so hours, everything I needed to know about surf travel in Barbados. Among gems to remember: "All roads lead to Bridgetown," and "Don't eff with Smokey" (a Soup Bowl local with impulse control issues). At 33, Zed is still one of Barbados' best surfers — which is saying plenty because the Bajans shred — and like many top flight surfers, he's a compactly built towhead with the metabolism of a wolverine. When he wasn't in the water, he seemed to have one hand on the steering wheel and the other in a box of take-out chicken.

Zed had another client to pick up, and we saw quite a lot of the west side of the island getting to him. This is the lee side, the money side, of Sandy Lane fame — David Niven mixing martinis for Ari and Jackie Onnasis in the ab-fably elegant golf resort — the milky calm Caribbean side. With its bazillion restaurants and hotels, tasteful little mini-malls, it looks something like south Florida, with better everything, especially trees, and no ugly parts. The complete air-conditioned catastrophe, as we Luddite surfers say — but so nice.

When we got to the client's posh hotel, Glitter Bay, Zed said, to the liveried girl at the gate, "I've come to collect that white man." She did a little double-take — Zed being a white Bajan — then grinned back at him as she raised the traffic post. Labor versus leisure. Beyond were groomed lawns and graceful palms in rows, marble fountains, neo-Palladian columns, and "that white man" in a bathing suit and tee-shirt, waiting outside the open-air lobby with his surfboard. The client — Jeff, from the Jersey Shore — actually apologized, sort of, as we stacked the boards on Zed's racks, for being on the wrong side of the island, and for spending a fortune on luxury. Surfer-cool demerits. "It's really just for my wife," he said.

After that the three of us pretty much circumnavigated the island looking for surf. The lee side reefs in front of public parks and resorts were gently foaming, miniature versions of their potential selves; they won't break until the biggest winter swells sweep in from the north. The south coast was quiet, too, under its chalky cliffs, a few kite-surfers colorfully airborne over the outer reefs. As we drove over the hump of the wooded Highlands (minor-key echo of the hills of Scotland) in St. Joseph Parish, Zed wondered aloud about the success of Barbados: the clockwork arrival of gigantic cruise ships at the Bridgetown harbor, the tourist throngs from toney Port St. Charles to the St. Lawrence Gap bars. It's not the prettiest island, Zed said, not dramatically mountainous; though fertile and green, there are no real forests, no lovely waterfalls. It is what it is: stable, predictable, not much poverty, very little crime. Toss in rock-solid infrastructure, lodging for every conceivable budget, cuisine for every taste, spectacular weather and beautiful beaches and — mystery satisfactorily solved. And the surf?

By then we were driving down the hill to Bathsheba, where the surf actually was — what it was — which was smaller than today, but still head high, perfect for Jersey Jeff and me. Out in the Bowl, which boasts rideable surf a remarkable 300 days a year, Zed surfed like the star he is, slashing turns, smacking the lip, pulling off effortless floaters and nimble tuck-ins in the little tubes. The three locals in the line-up were all nearly as talented. Zed's ambition, he'd said, was to make a success of his tour business and sponsor a team of the best local kids, give them a chance to travel and compete. They need to see the world, and the world needs to see them, he figures. And after what I've seen in the water I believe it's true.

Tonight H.B. arrives, thank God. My loving wife will sympathize and massage my surfboard-bruised ribs. Meanwhile, I need to catch Melanie, the proprietor of the Bajan Surf Bungalows, and tell her we'll be moving out tomorrow. It's not that I don't like it here. I love the patio view, the honor system for Banks beer from the fridge, the international surf bohemian atmosphere in the evening. I'm surrounded by a swirl of foreign languages and card-playing camaraderie. I've met Israelis and Argentines, Southern Californians and even a couple from my own home town — not to mention Flop, the guesthouse dog, who's stretched out on the sofa watching surf videos. Soup Bowl is a renowned stop-over on the world surf tour, and Melanie's guesthouse is a cozy home away from home for the aquatic tribe. On the downside, my room is clearly meant for a single surfer guy, one who can surf all day and party all night, and just needs a place to crash. Myself, I like a night table for my books, little amenities of middle age ... of course I'll blame the move on H.B. Melanie will understand.

Melanie Pitcher's story is an interesting one. Born in Barbados (her family goes back ten generations), she moved to Miami when she was six. At twenty-one, she had just begun a career training horses. And then it was like lightning struck. "I heard the gods tell me to open a guesthouse at Soup Bowl," she says. And so, that's just what she did. Single, aged 22, she became the Wendy of Bathsheba, den mother for the Lost Boys. Her first guests, in '96, were pro surfers who stayed for a week and got perfect surf — and Soup Bowl and Melanie's Bajan Surf Bungalows got a big write-up in "Surfer" magazine. Married now, with a two-year-old son, she surfs nearly every day (she's traveled with the Barbados National Team), in all but the very biggest swells, like the day in September of 2001 when she looked out the window and saw a guy dropping in on a 30 foot wave, "tall as a telephone pole."

That's what Zed told me, too, that it gets huge here, tubes you could tuck a tour bus in. "And do the guys ride them?" I asked, naively. "They sure as 'ell do," said Zed. "Waaaay back in the barrel."

The dawgs!

H.B and I have moved, just a stone's throw up the beach, to the quirky Round House (Spanish-style stucco, very few corners), into Room 3, which Zed said is the best room in all Barbados because you can open the shutters and see Soup Bowl from the bed. This, I've found, is a mixed blessing. When you are lying in bed, a cold Banks beer sweating on your belly, you are wondering, *What am I doing lying in bed when I could be surfing? What is wrong with me?*

It's all over between me and Soup Bowl anyway, after just two days. There is a cruel economy of surfing. If there're four surfers out, and four waves to a set, the result is universal happiness. But with six surfers out, and five waves to a set, the result is misery for the weakest surfer. I was getting shut out by younger, fitter, more talented surfers. So I've switched allegiance to Parlors, the surf break south of the big mushroom rocks.

Also known as The Mother of All Walls, Parlors is a bigger wave than Soup Bowl, but mushier (no barrel, just a great big wall). This morning there were only two surfers out at Parlors (a husband and wife from New York City) and plenty of waves. Still, they were not especially happy to see me in the line-up (it's the surf economy, stupid). Later, though, when I blew a big take-off and somersaulted, still holding on to my board, we all shared a laugh, which seemed to break the ice. It's a big ocean out there, and lonely, especially with the swell continuing to rise. I hope to see the New Yorkers out there next time.

Midday today, after my morning surf (ribs better, neck stiff), H.B. and I set out for a power walk on the beach from Bathsheba north to Barclays Park and back, about a five mile trek. The entire way we passed only one couple, who were building a shelter from driftwood. "We do much nothing, and now this," they explained, with Gallic shrugs. This rugged windward coast is definitely not to all tastes, which must be why *everybody* is on the Caribbean side and *nobody* is here, and why there is no direct route from anywhere to Bathsheba. Long story short: You cannot safely swim here. Couldn't turn your back with kids in your care. No wading for the oldsters. "The sea has no backdoor," say the windward Bajans. It would just be rip, zip, and gone. Even Zed, life-long waterman, said he'd be hesitant to attempt a rescue among these rocks and currents.

The walk back, with the sun in our faces, was plenty hot, and so choosing very carefully where we went in, and wading in only so far, H.B and I were able to bathe, by God, if not swim in that turbulent sea.

H.B and I have moved again, for the last time, I believe, to the Sea-U Inn, which is south of Parlors and up the hill, about a five minute walk to my new favorite break. The New Yorkers are staying here; and a couple from New Hampshire, Chris and Caroline (especially nice); and Maureen, a Bajan school teacher (shy, very nice); Katrina, a novelist from L.A. who lives in St. Thomas (opinionated); and another couple, Mike and Matty from Cornwall (younger, sweet). We are a merry group at mealtimes, served boarding-house-style at a big table on a detached deck. The conversation often strays from surfing, a big relief for the women. You can't see Soup Bowl from the Sea-U, which I find I don't mind. The obsession nagged.

In Barbados, I've learned, you don't need to rush to get in your surf. No "dawn patrol" needed. Time and tide have little effect on the consistent swells. And so, forgoing my morning surf, we booked a dive with

West Side Divers in Holetown (not a "hole" at all, but Caribbean Vacation Central). Our itinerary called for an "advanced" dive on the wreck Stavronikita, but it couldn't have been easier-breezier: a ten minute boat ride, glassy seas, our descent to the bridge of the hulk at 100-feet chaperoned by a very responsible-looking barracuda. Our second dive was a leisurely drift over Bombay Reef, a very healthy coral garden populated by eagle rays, and morays and green turtles (the Holetown catamaran crews feed them, so they're always around). Then a quick zip back, the lee side looking leafy and lovely with its cabanas and clubs under gracious breadfruit trees.

On the way back H.B. and I braved the B'Town traffic, and scored major hot sauce purchases at the Cheapside Market ("Watch your purse!" the shop mamas warned H.B.). Hugging the coast, we stopped for a snack at an art deco hotel called Little Arches and ordered appetizers in the restaurant upstairs, La Luna. H.B.: baked brie cheese in phyllo pastry basket with red grape chutney (whole peeled grapes) and crispy onions — a culinary work of art. Me: marinated grilled peppers filled with goat cheese and pine-nut gratiné served on mesclun greens with raspberry vinaigrette. Yum, both! Being a big city girl at heart, H.B. was in heaven. She sent her compliments to the chef, who's name was Moo. Moo?

I'm beginning to see the advantages of this two-hearted, two-sided island. Once you know the routes (a driver-navigator combo helps) you can bounce from rugged to riches and back in a jiff. Even with a final excursus at Sunbury Plantation (check out the slave-era political cartoons framed on the parlor walls — shocking!), I still had plenty of time for a sunset surf.

This morning I carried my surf board down the hill — so steep I felt I might slide on my beach-toughened bare feet — to the sound of an angelic choir. It was Sunday and the faithful were piping joyous Anglican hymns inside pretty St. Alban's Church, right across the street from this man's place of worship, the ever-lovin' Atlantic, pumpin' a swell of pomp and circumstance. Big? Not the BIG it gets, those mid-winter freight-trains from the nor'east, but big enough to be nearly too much. I couldn't find the channel, the easy way out beyond the breakers at Parlors, and, battered by perpetual walls of white water, was nearly washed in onto the mushroom rocks.

However, far from defeated, I concocted an audacious plan. I went ashore, walked around those rocks, and put to sea at Soup Bowl, counting on its clockwork rip currents to carry me to the line-up. Now the

Bowl was showing its true character — smoking green tubular grinders, sucking hollow and pitching thick board-breaking lips. I paddled right past everybody to the primo take-off spot. Stares, glares, and who dares, from the uber-toreadors. It was like a jackal cutting in front of a line of lions. "Hey! Nobody over forty allowed on this side of me," one local quipped. But it's true: post position is a hard-earned privilege on a real Soup Bowl day.

"Just headed to Parlors," I said, and put my back into it. A long paddle but well worth the labor. I surfed all day (well, with a long lunch break), dodging monsters and riding monsterettes. I rode one last wave all the way into shore in the gloaming, lights popping on in the little homes on the hillside. A full moon had risen out of the palms. There was a strong scent of salt from the churning sea and of new-mown grass in the park. The high season was just kicking in, Surf Town primping for the pros. When you're finally feeling fit, must be time to split. Arms re-brawned, ribs ruddy but ready, neck limber at last, I kept looking back as I dawdled up the hill. "It's still just a little fishing village," Melanie Pitcher had said, "but surfing is what makes it alive." True true. Ah, Bathsheba. Love at last sight, too.

The Moon and Danzel Cabral

One Saturday night, after a certain amount had been drunk, I walked a little ways into the backyard to look at the moon, which was full again, a big orange harvest moon. I was indulging in a little blessing counting, I confess, under the piney woods of Tallahassee, Florida, with a loving wife, good company I could rejoin in a moment, and the comforts of music, wine and abundant food — a lifestyle granted to me due to vast historical forces and sheer blind luck ("You Americans have all the money," you once said) — and I heard your voice, Danzel, the castaway caretaker cook of French Louis Caye, reciting a tone poem of resonating pathos. "For tea," I heard you say, "we have fry fish, fry plantain, and johnny cake, and that is all. That is tea. For dessert we have nothing, and that is because Rannie too damn cheap, he."

The contagious Creole accent, the surprising emphases, the way you seemed to seize upon words and savor the character of them, the sauce of the sound and the soup-bone sense of them, it sang out so clearly in my mind that it jolted me back to that other Saturday night, my last night on the island. I was back again, five miles off the Caribbean coast of Belize, in the dark of the cookhouse, with its smoke and fish smells, and the empty bottle of rum on the old beat-up table, at the moment when you rose to your feet, and struggling to master your emotions, said, "I am not an educated man; I do not know how to address myself to you properly." How properly you pronounced that needless disclaimer, when in fact it was I who failed to address myself to you with the wisdom I must have missed getting at school.

As I write this several months after the fact, it occurs to me that you might not remember me at all, precisely because of that failure, but that doesn't matter much. I came out to the island in the last week of August, intending to stay a week, though I lasted only six days. The heat, you know, the isolation. Hell yes, you know. But I wasn't the usual tourist, or I would've had a mate, a help-meet, someone to help me meet the heat, bruddah man. I was on a solo mission — there to write about you. Your job was interesting to me, the outstanding badness of it, the peculiar combination of innocence and punishment, which is the caretaker's lot. I came at the height of the off-season when things would be their worst — my muse commanded it — and I was there when you quit.

You said, "Take these job and shove eet! I no work on these islan' no more."

In retrospect, I can see that you were working yourself up to escape velocity the whole time. I saw the seeds of conflict while I was riding out to the island in Rannie's boat. The sight of French Louis Caye, like a floating shrubbery on the horizon, made me anxious, and I shouted back over the growl of the outboard, "So how does the caretaker like his job?" Fucking fool, me.

"He doesn't have to like it," that sea-faring entrepreneur Rannie Villanueva said. He'd worked his ass off setting up the guesthouse out there, and you'd taken the job of cooking for the tourists and guarding his property when no one else was on the island. And right there you have the futility of your dispute with Rannie. He didn't have to call you every day on the radio and you didn't have to like it. "What else is he going to do?" he went on, a tough, practical imperturbable person in the Belizean business suit of faded swim trunks and shades. "Danzel's too quarrelsome to work on the mainland. But you don't have to worry about that. He'll get along with you because he doesn't know you."

Well, we did get to know each other a little in the days that followed, and we did have us a small quarrel on the last day, about proportionate to our acquaintance. Rannie knew his shit, but my sympathies were immediately on your side. I remember the first thing you said to me. I'd just got off the boat, taken in the whole island, really, at a glance. At the foot of the dock, almost in the hooped roots of the mangroves, was the little caretaker's hut — through the open door I caught a glimpse of white sheets, a night table with a stack of books lit by a shaft of sunlight, a real monk's cell. In the middle of the island the rough-hewn guesthouse stood on stilts, with the cookhouse slung underneath it. The dogs, your daggies, Lightning the lab-mix pup and Honey the golden Belizean potlicker (a breed you later told me was becoming extinct), had come pounding down the planks of the dock to greet us as if they held tickets for the next boat back to the mainland, which they didn't. Two females, they were on vacation from reproduction, as Rannie put it. Then you stepped out of the cookhouse, wiping flour from your hands on a rag, a shortish, plumpish, fiftyish fellow, barefoot in shorts and a Yamaha teeshirt, with wild wavy hair shot with gray and a grizzled beard and the haunted, harrowed look of a burnt out professor of cosmology. You'd been on the island ten months.

"How you doing, Danzel?" I asked.

"I'm going crazy, man. It too damn lonely. I talk to myself out here. I say, it's okay you talk to yourself, just don't answer back."

I said that sounds like an answer to me, and you said, yes, it does, and you laughed — heh heh heh. Then you showed me around the rest of the island, which you could pretty much do by turning in a circle and pointing. On a precarious little peninsula straggling south were three wooden outhouses of the shake and bake organic compost sort, and a rain barrel shower. Seven hammocks were strategically placed for admiring the sea or dodging the sun. "They're not as comfortable as they look," you warned me, in a classic Shakespearean aside. There was a wheel barrow without wheels beside a compost pile of coconut husks and fruit rinds and fish bones in which five ducks foraged, a dam and a drake with warty red faces and three buckskin colored ducklings. They wiped their bills in the mud, lifted up their feet like baseball players digging in to the batter's box, and then waggled their asses in unison a half dozen times the way ducks do.

"The first time in history a duck lives on an island and plays in salt water.

The first time in history," you assured me. "You come to French Louis Caye and you see it with your own eyes, bruddah-man. What we want is to raise a whole fleet of them. Boy, that would be so nice!"

And that was it, that was all, that was French Louis Caye — an escape for me from the softening surfeit of luxury, a place of profit for Rannie, and for you, you fantastical person, a dream of a fleet of salt-water ducks.

"Was the island always like this?" I asked Rannie, my third stupid question in a row. I didn't mean the guesthouse and other obvious improvements, but the little half-acre of shaded sand between the mangrove muck on the mainland side and the gritty coral edge looking out towards the barrier reef and open sea — the geography of the place. Rannie just chuckled ruefully. He had thrown a foam pad on top of the picnic table in front of the cookhouse and was lying on it wrapped in a sheet. With his almond eyes and ginger goatee he looked like the sheik of French Louis Caye. It was his island and he knew how to downshift to island mode; I wouldn't be surprised if he'd lowered his heart-rate like a yogi. "No, it had been different," he said with enormous patience. He'd started clearing the island eighteen years ago, he told me. As he described it, you couldn't walk from one side to the other but had to climb through the branches horizontally like a monkey. He'd hacked out the central clearing, a huge task, pulling stumps out of muck, and when he was done with that there was foot and a half of leaf-litter, the habitat of vast colonies of cockroaches and biting centipedes. But Rannie knew how to deal with them. He brought out chickens to eat the centipedes, and when the chickens scratched out the centipedes, he ate the chickens. He'd transplanted lizards to deal with the excess cockroaches.

"Lately we've seen an increase in lizards, and so can expect a continued decrease in cockroaches," he said, a man with his finger on the bottom line.

I remarked that there seemed to be no hermit crabs on French Louis Caye, which struck me as strange, since I'd been on other islands in Belize where there were multitudes. "This island produces no shells, so there are no crabs," Rannie said, which reminded him of the time, back when he was lobster diving for a living and waiting out bad weather on an island much like this one. "That island had too many crabs and not enough shells — a housing shortage. You'd throw a peanut shell to the ground and a crab would move into it. You ever see a crab change shells?" Rannie asked. That thought was vaguely shocking; it seemed to represent a lot of time spent watching crabs. "They do it very carefully," he said, and described in great detail the measuring of the new shell, the turning of the shell hole-side-up, and how, once satisfied of its superiority, they'd hoist themselves up like a little man doing a push-up, and swing their ass over and drop it in. Drop and roll. One motion, very quick. "They don't like the chill on their butt."

On the island of too many crabs, Rannie had spent some idle rainy hours fashioning shells out of tin foil, and pretty soon there were tin crabs crawling all over the place. "Maybe they are still there, though when the sun hit them maybe it wasn't so good."

Was he speaking in parables, Danzel? I think maybe he was. I'd brought along a single bottle of rum in case of emergency, and it seemed to me an emergency had just arrived with the thought of tin crabs cooking in the sun. I fetched the bottle and poured us all a round. That was noon of the first day.

The next morning Rannie was up before dawn and gone, and we began to find our routine. There were early pelicans circling the island like the delicate parts of some elaborate timepiece, and you would philosophize upon them. "After I die, I'd like to turn into a pelican," you

THE MOON AND DANZEL CABRAL

mused. "He no have to worry about clothes or money, only to find fish. Though sometimes they miss their aim and break their necks. Then the dogs get them."

I kicked around the reefs surrounding the island, the first of many laps, and hid under the dock in the hottest part of the day, up to my eyes with a mask and snorkel, orchestrating a school of silversides that would part and converge with the motions of my waving hands. And I watched you. Watched you pace the sand and watch the horizon. You kept threatening to rake the island, and I'm glad you never did. It didn't need it.

When it was cool enough in the cookhouse we would turn on the radio and listen to the news. Music you didn't want, sports was nothing to you: "Give me news! The news!" I never met anyone who loved news so much. I remember you were very much concerned about the potato. You'd heard a report on the Voice of America that a virus had infected the Irish potato, and then you never heard anything about it again. "Shit, man, the potato sick." Where did that leave you? Where did that leave mankind? I couldn't tell you how those things were sunspots, academic flare-ups that wink in the general interest atmosphere and fade as soon as seen. People like me have learned to discard reams of the stuff. Not so for Danzel Cabral. After more than forty years of fishing you were hungry to learn.

That was the week when Swissair flight 111 crashed into the sea. Not a sparrow falls, eh Danzel? You were on top of the story. "See! I tell you this happen!" you said. Divers were searching the frozen waters for the black box. "How they do that?" you wondered. "What the hell is it?" Why did the plane dump fuel before it crashed? Was that acceptable practice? Who? What? Where? Why? And it was the same for every story that followed. You seized the nuggets of knowledge that came your way, and vigorously questioned the vague void surrounding them. Clinton and Lewinsky? "Eet between the man and he wife," you said. "Let it go already!" Saddam and the U.N. weapons inspections? "The man fierce. He will be hard to beat." Famine in North Korea? "Where the fokk is that country?" The worst year ever for violent storms? "It because of the oil," you said. "You cannot take out the oil. The earth needs its grease. You can fill up the holes with water, but water not belong there. That's why we have these hurricanes and landslides and such sheet."

You were mostly right, I'd say, a pretty fair pundit, all things considered. Remember when I wrote down your name in my notebook, in big block letters — D-E-N-Z-E-L — (I got it wrong, and that is because I'm a fuck-up). "Yes," you said, "that is it, that is Danzel. I know my letters, but I cannot tell swiftly all the ways they can meet." Nor can I. Nor can I.

By then you'd told me a few facts of your life, and bruddah-man, you never caught a break. A sickly child abandoned by your mother to a Belizean state institution, you lost most of your teeth to bad medication, which has given you your wry, lopsided grin. Lost your childhood next when you were adopted, Oliver Twist-style, by a fisherman Fagin and put to work as soon as you could hold a line, filling up the live-well of a sailing ship with snapper and jack and yellowtail. That father robbed you of your education, but he kept you fed, "And I thank him for that," you said. Next, you were beaned in the head by a random pop bottle hurled by a careless teenager in a rowboat, which nearly killed you. You showed me the long pale scar under your grizzled beard; the kid never went to trial. Too many connections in the town. Long years of fishing the diminishing local stocks. "Fishing hard work, man. You bust a brain or two in your head. But the money good, the money good." A better job cooking on a banana boat, with Christmas bonuses, but you were plagued by false friends, "bad crows," you called them. A few harrowing years in Belize City, hounded by Bloods and Crips, more bad crows. "You got to be swift," you said. "They cut off your hand to teef your ring." But you were getting older, slower then. So you came back to Placencia, and started working for Rannie. "And he was already cheap."

"Rannie work hard for what he have," you said, always fair-minded. "He earn it. But he cheap, man." He was cheap, and he wouldn't call you on the radio, but as soon as he did we ordered us another bottle of rum. You insisted on buying. I said no no no, let me, I'll expense it. "You bought the first one," you said, and I'd already lost too many of those arguments in my past to start winning now. So when we had our Saturday night party, and toasted the moon, you were the proper host.

Remember? The moon was where our conversation started. Hardly surprising, with it shining through the rough-hewn window of the cook house like God's own flashlight. A great white stripe of light was slathered across the sea in front of us, and the sky fell down in lucent waves, as if the Milky Way were blowing perfect smoke rings which broke across our brows, wave upon wave. Few have ever enjoyed a better view of space, or had to make do with less turf to ride into it. You were an astronaut, my friend, and the cook house was your command module, with the tangled roots and limbs of the mangrove fringe behind you a leafy burst of exhaust, and the hard coral windward edge of the island in front of you cutting a significant swathe to wherever the universe was going.

"The man smart who went to the moon, he foking smart, he," you said. "How he do eet? How far eet?

It looked close that night, the old pocked rock. I thought, Jesus, I used to know that. Then, that it would be on the Net. Or that if we had a phone I could call my wife, who would know. But on French Louis Caye, there's no Net, no phone, nobody to ask. So I took a guess: "Maybe, a hundred thousand miles?"

"What?!!" you thundered, rocking back in your chair in shock.

"That far, mon, that foking far!" And then you chortled — "Heh heh heh" — you positively cackled like a miser up to your elbows in a pot of gold. There we were, there was the moon, and we had this, um, fact to contemplate, this marvelous amount of distance. "Boyee!" you said, and you beamed again, like a sports fan glorying in the fabulous stats of a favorite player. It was some moon, the moon.

"Where I would most like to go, in all the world," you told me, as we poured ourselves another round of rum and lime juice, "is to Florida, to the Kennedy Space Center. I would like to go there and look into space at the moon. But!" you protested, gravely, reconsidering. "I think God will lash the man for flying up in He face. If God had meant man to be on the moon, he would have put man there."

Then you reconsidered again, the sign of an open mind if ever there was one. "I'm not saying we shouldn't go." And you know, I felt an absurd little jolt of rum-fueled optimism at your change of heart, as if we might just go there if we could get off the island. "I say it's all in the manner in which we go," you said. "We must go gentle, with respect."

Everything was silent then, the island bathed in cemetery moonlight, palm fronds drooping like icicles, the vast nimbus of the moon feathered and furred with infinite darkness. Everything still, except me swatting at the flies, the no-see-ums you stoically endured. A single plane described a slow arc south across the sky, a comet full of earnest citizens bound for Tegucigulpa, maybe.

"Why don't you get married, Danzel?" I asked, the obvious intrusive question, considering that was what French Louis Caye was all about, what it was for, when you got right down to it. I mean, come on — who was French Louis if not some legendary stud of the islands? Guests came from all over the world, you told me, from the First World, and nearly always couples, to spend a night or two naked to the annihilating sky. They would lean out of the guesthouse windows, bare feet on the plank floors, right above the cook house, and watch the silent heat lightning flare above the Cockscomb Mountains on the mainland, which resemble the teeth of a dragon. We are living right in the teeth of a dragon. You see that clearly on French Louis Caye. It is a hamburger machine, monstrous large, and none shall escape digestion. As the poet said: Ah love, let us, for it is too fucking much! Talk about howling at the moon! You must have heard some real caterwauls in your nights on the island.

What about a wife, then, a flesh and blood woman instead of your cruel lover the moon?

"A woman do me bad," you said. "I blame all woman. It a long time I no want to live with woman."

Why? What? Where? When? What did she do you? I asked, and you told me, the saddest tale of woman and liquor I ever heard. She wiped your shot glass on her what!!? I said. My turn to rock back in my chair, shocked.

"I tell you, I smell it, mon!"

You smelled it, but you hadn't seen her reach under her skirt to do it, so you brought the glass to your lips, and the bad crows, raucous, squawking, roared with laughter.

That's when you stood up. "I'm not an educated man; I cannot express myself to you properly!" And what did I say? Such bad behavior, who can account for it? Forgive and forget? Move on, for God's sake? Some other platitude I don't remember? I remember that it was late, and I dragged a foam pad out to the end of the dock and tried to sleep, watching the moon march across the sky hour by hour. And it only occurred to me months later, in light of the events that followed, that the rest of that night might have been your agony in the garden, and I was the sleeping apostle.

The next morning you seemed happy. I was happy — I'd decided it was time for me to go. I had my story, as we say, the secret of the hermit of French Louis Caye. All that was left was to take some pictures. You posed in the cookhouse, looking out the window to sea. Then you got up and wanted me to follow you outside. "You got to take the ducks!" And I shot the ducks. "You got to have a picture of the dogs!" I shot the dogs. "And the beans!" you said. You hustled back into the cookhouse and stirred the pot, lifting up a spoonful of beans to the camera's lens and laughing. Were you making fun of me? I think maybe you were.

"When you write these book about the island," you said. "Maybe good things come." "It's just a magazine article; you can't expect much," I told you. "Maybe this magazine article help me to find a wife."

I said I hoped it would, and would you call Rannie and tell him I'm ready to leave? "He should call me," you said. "I work for him, he not work for me. He should call me. I could be lying down dead here and nobody know." You're right, I said, but would you give him a call? Then things went really wrong.

Chalk it up to Sunday afternoon, a problematic time anywhere, doubly so on French Louis Caye. I decided to take a kayak and paddle to Laughing Bird Caye, which I'd been meaning to do all week, though you'd told me not to — "Eet too far, man!" It took all afternoon and it crushed me. Back when Rannie first brought me out to the island he'd trailed his hand in the water and said it was getting too hot, that the coral bleaching was getting worse. "Glabbawamma," he said. I'd smiled and nodded, "Glabbawamma?" "No, global warming," he said, in clearest unaccented English. And it did seem to be the hottest week in the history of the world, as if we, the behemoth to the north, were cooking you, the little countries to the south, with our aerosol sprays and our internal combustion engines. I oozed towards the horizon in the little plastic boat; I crawled, melting, like a paramecium on a microscope slide. When I finally pulled into the shade of the mangroves on Laughing Bird Caye, I looked up and saw a pelican, hung in a crook in the branches, its bill open wide in final derision. Some last laugh that was, some joke. I thought, man, I got to go home.

I made it back to French Louis, barely, all burnt up, and you were in the cookhouse sending out an SOS of existential urgency. "Kitty's Place, Kitty's Place, this is French Louis Caye, do you copy? Kitty's Place, Kitty's Place, this is French Louis Caye, do you copy?" Over and over, until finally somebody broke in and said, "Shut up, you bloody ass!" You came storming out of the cookhouse, furious. "You hear that?" you said. "That man call me a bad word! He lucky I not know who he are!"

"What would you do?" I asked, mercilessly.

"Why, I tell him not to call me that, not on channel 16. That is a public channel, man. You not supposed to curse."

"And where you go?" you asked me. "I tell you eet too far, but you not listen."

Back into the cookhouse you stormed, back to the radio.

Next thing I know — it's a couple of hours later — Rannie shows up with two new tourists, a young couple this time, the usual thing, backpackers, badly sunburned but full of play and fun, and a new caretaker — this one tall and slim and quiet, but looking decidedly nervous as he began to stow away their food.

Rannie put you off the boat on the beach at Placencia with all your belongings, which seemed to consist of just your radio and two big bundles of refundable soda bottles. You hadn't said a word the whole way back, and I couldn't think what to say. The last I saw of you was your back as you trudged up the sand under your burden, into a very uncertain future.

Which is why I am writing this, the way I'm writing this, making the letters meet this way and not in some other, and not very swiftly, either, I assure you. It's in the hope that some day somebody might read it to you, maybe some tourist if you go back to French Louis Caye, or far better, and my fondest hope for you, a good woman who has seen your picture in a magazine and wonders, "Who the heck is this Danzel Cabral?" I'd say he was the cosmic Maytag repairman, ma'am, doing the heavy mental lifting of moving the moon across the sky. A thinking man, and a Christian. "I obey the commandments and treat people good, and that is a Christian," you once said. Let that be your introduction; I could never write a better one. There's this groovy theory, Danzel, of the Cognoscienti, obscure men, wise and good and true, who keep the earth rolling on its appointed rounds. Oil where the oil belongs, water where water goes.

Those things you know. Possibly nobody has ever told you this before, but you are a great man, and at the very least an all right guy. Not cracked, not fucked, not finished. Just don't move into any tin shells, and look out for things falling from the sky, and maybe you'll be okay. I hope so. "If you cook, you're going to get burned—and I just did!" you once said, and said it with a grin, that Danzel grin that takes a stubborn side-long bite at the world and veers to the side with it like a front-end with bad alignment, but always towards something kind and good. And that is the whole point of Danzel Cabral—de hool fokking pint, mon!

I Was Dogman

"Honey, I'm going down to the beach to check on Penny," I said, oh, about a thousand times during the two years we lived above Pools Beach, the prettiest little cove in Rincon on the west coast of Puerto Rico. Penny, our Irish setter, was hopelessly enthralled by minnows, the gaily colored tropicals that darted about the coral pools of Pools Beach. If you've been to a lot of beaches you've probably seen one or two of those specially touched dogs, sun-burnished as old club tennis pros, but with a look of gaga joy in their eyes, pouncing and wagging, biting a mouthful of sea, wading, wagging, pouncing, all day long.

At first it worried me a little that she was unsupervised down there, though she didn't have to cross any streets to get to the sand, and it worried me a lot that I was up in the house instead of on the beach with its pools and its fish and its happy bathers whose laughter floated up to me the whole day long as I worked (when I could) like a siren's song crying, "Come play with me! Come play!" So I made about a dozen trips a day, down fourteen steep and wobbly concrete block steps and under the banana trees, down to the beach—ah, there! — leaping onto the deep sand.

"Penny! Hey, Penny!" I'd call. "Where's the fish?" And she'd look up, as if pleased at last to find another believer: Don't you see? There they are! They are everywhere!

Usually, along with the tiny fish in the pools, there'd be a few of the beautiful people down there, young trustafarians, sometimes with little tanned and naked babies crawling on big beach towels; and sometimes our neighbor Myrtle, and guests from her guesthouse with their kids employed at making fortresses out of the rough sand and the ever-available driftwood from the creek that emptied into Pools Beach after the biggest rains. Always Myrtle's speedy dog Johnny would be down there cavorting from beach blanket to beach blanket; and our friends David and Wendy and their dog Suerte; and maybe a few other surfers and their dogs; and maybe a couple of characters from town with a bottle of rum and a dog or two; and in the winter high season a volleyball net and a beery day-long match to conclude with a bonfire and a lobster roast; and during the summer lots of Puerto Rican families having a picnic meal of many foil-wrapped courses. And always there was music and laughter and voices whose apparent joy and mysterious import were only magnified by distance. How could I stay away?

I was a surfer and H.B. was a boogie-boarder, and that was a big part of why we'd rented a house at Pools Beach. So another perfectly legitimate reason to go down to the beach at Pools was to check the surf (*Hey, Honey, I'm going down to check the surf*), and if, from the prospect of Surf Check Rock, any doubt arose that it might be better around the bend, to scout further down the coast. This meant a stroll along old Spanish Wall, where the beach steepened and the water deepened and the surf often disappeared entirely, only to reappear at Crab Rock, surging and crashing over the lava mesa where crustaceans scuttled in the intermittent waterfalls. Nobody surfed Crab Rock, but you could clamber from it onto the rubbly limestone coast road and after a few hundred yards arrive at Domes, the defunct nuclear plant overlooking a broad, prefect crescent of sand. Now Domes was an excellent surfing spot, but it was local turf, often muy ocupado with adolescent boogie-boardistos. And anyway, just beyond Domes, past the lighthouse — El Faro — was The Point itself, the real deal break that put Rincon on the beach sports map.

Frequently a thorough surf-check ended at The Point — it was hands down the best wave in typical conditions — but plenty of times The Point would be too crowded, and then it was prudent to drift a little further south, down to Dogman's. When the surf got serious, overhead or bigger, and the waves started breaking boards, then The Point crowd went pro-time, tolerating only high-performance, pedal-to-the-metal surfing. But even at those times, when the swell was spinning gorgeous green translucent tubes, Dogman's was just for fun, and the crowd at Dogman's just fooling around. Frankly it was something of an underachiever's break; there was something, well, dog-like about surfing there, hanging on to the margins of the action, picking up scraps. After awhile, out of sheer lack of seriousness, I just naturally gravitated to Dogman's and it became my regular break.

After whom was Dogman's named? Nobody quite remembered. Some gringo surfer from back in the 60s — 70s maybe? — had a lot of dogs? Who knew, really? Well, I found out, before too long. Soon enough, I came to understand a lot about him, how he spent his days, how his mind worked, what his weaknesses had been, and just how he had acquired all those dogs. Once I picked up a pack of my own I knew all there was to know.

I figured the original Dogman, if he ever actually existed, and wasn't simply a composite of all the gringo flaneurs with a soft spot for curs, was a lot like Penny, really, our minnow-mad Irish setter. I imagined the sun had bleached his hair yellow and spun it into curls, as it had done to Penny's red locks; like Penny's his muzzle was grizzled and his eyes wild. He hunted that same flash of quickening life at the water's edge, and saw it always receding ahead of him in the shine on the wet sand, the way the light shatttered and crazed under the pressure of each footfall. He was a beach walking fool, was Dogman, in no hurry but toting up the daily miles all the same. He was a surfer, *fer sure,* but after a few years the game just grew to be the sea itself and the whole of the shore and the way it was born every second, was always new after each new wave, and he came to feel an urgency always to be there, present at the drama of its birth, scrolling the scene underneath him with his feet. Because he moved at predictable times, when the light was most delightful and the air cool, the dogs moved with him.

Dogs, of course, are banned from many mainland beaches. This is a shame, because all the canids are great players in the sand, great loungers on it and bounders over it and great burrowers into it after crabs. They appreciate a cooling dip every bit as much as we do, and alternating wet and dry, hot and cool, can beguile a whole beach day in idleness, even without the benefit of novels. On islands like Puerto Rico, there are always lots of dogs on the beach, and they are always on the lookout for someone to lead them in a caravan to the next oasis.

"Honey, I'm going down to the beach to check on Penny," I'd say, and there would be a couple of fanatics waiting in the sun outside our gate and more of the faithful at the bottom of the fourteen steps — poor pathetic Mama Dog, displaced pedigreed Goldie, Lionhead the chow, the mongrel Monkey Dogs, to name a few. Penny, seeing the sheer weight of numbers milling in anticipation, would cast a last wistful look at her fishes, and come bounding out of the pools. And then we'd move out, en masse, the whole damn pack of us. By God, we had to.

We were too many by then for the popular Point, so I led them off the other way, past the Tamboo Tavern to Second River, a couple of miles of deserted coast highlighted, one odiferous season, by dog nirvana, a half buried beached whale. We would stroll, strung out in a quarrelsome phalanx until we espied and threatened to engage with our rival from the next town, the Dogman of Aguada and his pack of feral terriers and chihuahuas. That ancient herdsman would suddenly appear atop a dune, weight planted on a staff, his fiesty little curs spilling down the slope. Always I would sound the retreat, knowing we were no match, my dogs bristling and barking defiance over their shoulders as they trotted away. The Dogman of Aguada had a secret weapon my troop feared and loathed: he had a goat.

Yes, for a season or two, I was Dogman; not the original, not the best, and surely not the last Dogman of Rincon, but merely an incarnation, destined to move on, as ephemeral as the fish of Pools Beach. How could I leave my pack? With multiple and mixed regrets and a fifty-pound bag of Alpo, which I poured into little honorific mounds at several canine strongholds along the shore. We packed our personal dogs into crates and left Puerto Rico and Pools Beach before I became so idle that we had to move onto the sand, into one of the palm-thatch lean-tos that camping surfers built, which is probably what the dogs had been hoping for all along.

Two Brothers, One Ocean, No Fish

Laborious as it is, "tossing out" has at least all the advantages of entropy, of the tendency of things to leave you, to pour away into the sea, that bottomless pit of property lost over the side. "Hauling in," on the other hand, has against it all contrariness. Line loves to snag, to snarl, to snake into fabulous knots, and then break. All reels — and the massive mainline reel of a long-liner is no exception — are inveterate sinners given to wicked backlash and untimely jamming. Add to these villainies the brute forward momentum of a thirty-ton boat, the constant sideways suction of the current, and the eternal ups and downs of the seas. And if you're lucky, and the moon and tide and wind and water are all propitious, you'll have fish the size of buffalo with broadswords growing out of their heads coming through the stern gate. For all these reasons, there's tremendous potential for entanglement. Of lines and tempers and destinies. Which is why long-liners like the Soares brothers look out for each other, why they have to stick together.

Life-long fishing companions and partners in the *Argus III*, a forty-eight-foot modified motor yacht out of Anegada, British Virgin Islands, Mark and Dean Soares complement each other perfectly in the two-act play of tossing out and hauling in. Dean is the baiter, the one with the grim patience for the assembly-line task of fastening hundreds of squid to the hooks as the mainline runs out over the stern. Mark has the skill and the dash and the optimism to be the hauler, the one who coaxes the line back in at the starboard rail. Now, in the lilac light of dawn, with sooty clouds dissolving into day over an oily eight-foot swell, Mark steps up to the hauler's station, just aft of the cabin gangway, and seizes the hydraulic throttle. The big reel groans, and the thirty-mile length of the quarter-inch-thick monofilament mainline pulls furiously tight and begins to come aboard. Younger brother Dean stands aft about three paces back, sea legs akimbo on the rolling deck, his gaffs and truncheons at the ready in their rack.

Since ten o'clock last night, when the *Argus III* drifted free of its burden of snares, the longline apparatus has been dangling 350 hooks at the end of 350 individual leader lines. Each line was rigged with a disposable chemical light stick, clipped on about six feet above the bait so that the tendrils of a dead squid would wave in the green nimbus of the glow all night. A longline is a fever dream of fishing, a whole highway of illuminated baits sunk down 140 feet in the nigh-infinite dark, enticing God knows what.

With his left hand fingering the toggles and levers of the auxiliary steering station, Mark powers the boat forward alongside the mainline and controls the speed of the reel as it ravels in. His right hand weighs the line just in front of the tackle, feeling for fish. The hauler's job is like playing a high-stakes video game with one hand while working out on a Nautilus weight machine with the other. Mark is an unflappable and genial big man, of medium height, stout and hard-bellied, with massive arms from hauling line most of his forty-one years. His face is bronzed but not weathered, with prominent round cheeks, a strong Portuguese mustache, and close-set, amused eyes. He loves this boat — you can tell. Back in 1992, Mark traveled to Groton, Connecticut, where his uncle Al had found an interesting-looking wreck. She'd been driven aground, her hull staved in, her cabin raked off by what would become known as the Perfect Storm, the devastating nor'easter that struck the New England coast in October 1991. The Soareses paid twelve grand for the hulk and would sink another hundred thousand dollars into rebuilding her inside and out, and now fate has made Mark her captain. He loves the power her twin 250 horsepower diesels transmit to his will; he loves his skill at fishing her. He has thumbed a load of Captain Black's tobacco into his pipe for this moment and puffs it contentedly.

The first leader comes into view, dangling from the mainline. Mark grasps the steel snap connecting it to the heavier line, squeezes, and snatches it off. Nothing there. He passes it without comment to Shaba, the salaried crewman, an athletic twenty-nine-year-old from St. Vincent. Shaba walks it back two paces to Dean, who hauls in its 140-foot length hand over hand and begins to rewind it onto the leader reel, putting it all back together to toss it out again tonight.

If Mark is the jolly big man, Dean is the dark and mysterious gnome, the seafaring Rumpelstiltskin. Dean is just a baseball cap taller than five feet, with a remarkable hirsute growth of sable whiskers. Skin burnt nearly as black as his beard, wizened eyes squinting through the smoke of a cigarette, Dean looks more exaggeratedly maritime than any sentimental painting of an old salt I've ever seen. That he's achieved this look in just thirty-six years astonishes me.

"I stopped growing so I wouldn't hit my head on the boat," he'd joked on shore earlier. Seeing him drop into the hold to tinker with the ice machine when we are beating against the falling swell of a mid-February storm and everything on deck is rushing to collide with anything it can, I half believe him. He, too, has the oversized arms of the lifelong fisherman and his father's bandy little legs. In the age of the schooner, when the Soares family was already renowned on Bermuda as shipwrights and whalers, a man with such a build could brachiate among the top riggings with the ease of a gibbon. Yet for all his adaptation, Dean seems sunk in gloom. "Ain't gonna be no bed of roses," he warned me from the start.

He's been right so far — cousin Jeff Soares, the other amateur aboard, and I have been tossing out every bite we've been taking in while Mark and Dean and Shaba have been fueling themselves with challenging foodstuffs, such as jalapeno-pepper-Cheez-Whiz and peanut-butter sandwiches.

The *Argus III* bashes along the line, and the reel shrieks and moans and grinds in thirty more empty leaders. Then one comes in taut. Mark snatches it off and pumps it twice, weighing. "Something small," he says and passes the line back to Jeff. A sturdily built union iron-worker down from Pennsylvania on a working holiday, Jeff is crazy about fishing of all kinds and hauls in like a sportsman, playing the fish carefully. Dean meets him at the stern gate with a gaff and snatches the catch aboard. It's a little swordfish, stone dead, about four feet long and half of that sword — a perfect miniature.

"A rat," Mark pronounces, with what I take to be comic disdain until he explains that *rat* is the designation of any swordfish under fifty pounds; *pup* is the next weight up, to one hundred pounds; then *markers*, double, triple and quad in increments of a hundred. The biggest swordfish the brothers ever caught weighed in at just under five hundred pounds, a quad marker. The *Argus III* has a seven-thousand-pound capacity hold, which, their last two times out, the brothers filled in five days, the take from ten days of fishing totaling about $50,000, minus considerable expenses. Mark, who handles all the paperwork — permits, record keeping, finances, and taxes — estimates he and Dean will clear about $30,000 each for the six-month swordfishing season. Evenings at sea, when Mark goes visiting electronically via the single-side-band radio, the other captains he contacts are amazed at how small his boat is.

They are usually on ships twice the size and triple the crew. The *Argus III* is about as streamlined as you can get, part of the reason why she's the last long-liner still working the waters of the Anegada Pass.

A few more empty leaders and then Mark eases off the hydraulic throttle, cuts back the engines, and gives a thoughtful tug on the main-line. Something big coming in maybe. He unsnaps the leader line and passes it to Shaba. Shaba is a skilled novice, in Mark's estimation, with the bad habit of sometimes letting loose leader line bunch up in his hands. Mark knows of a fellow longliner who brought a thousand-pound marlin to the boat and got himself tangled in the line, and when the green fish saw the boat and spooked, the fisherman was jerked overboard like a rag doll tied to a truck. "The last anybody saw of him was the bottoms of his sneakers," Mark said.

This fish turns out to be a good-sized tuna. "Big-eye," Dean says when it resolves into view, showing its bullet-shaped silver sides as it makes weak runs. Dean stands by with the gaff. Suddenly, the tuna thrashes, turns tail, and vanishes, and Shaba drops the line, cursing, rope-burned through his cotton gloves. Dean snatches up the leader and hauls hand over hand with deliberate and blinding speed, making that tuna skip across the seas like a bit of trolling bait. Jeff gaffs it, and they yank the quivering fish through the stern gate, and Dean brains it with an iron rod. He slides it alongside the scuppers of the starboard rail with the dead "rat."

The *Argus III* plows on like a truffling hog and brings up a trash fish, the escolar, or oilfish, a famed diarrhetic, and then a fluttering bat ray, a creature like a slab of liver with a tail, which Dean expertly dispatches by slitting all around its jaw and pulling the hook out with the whole gorge. The next leader arrives in loose loops around the mainline, a major snarl, indicating something large and frisky has been on the hook awhile, fouling the gear in its attempts to escape. Mark shuts down the reel and shakes the mainline hard, slinging the looped leader line off it while tickling the steering toggles and bringing the bow into the seas. Dean, meanwhile, has snagged the leader line with a gaff and is bringing it into the boat. The great thing about fishing with Dean, Mark told me earlier, is that he always knows what Dean is going to do at any given time. He's going to do the right thing and do it fast, which is why the brothers have all their fingers.

The fish is a heavy presence, evident in the straining line and the knots in Dean's forearms, but evanescent to sight, staying down about twenty feet and steadily working its tail. It's a sword, a marker this time, its long pallid image broken up by the seas. Mark shuts down the engine and the *Argus III* drifts in silence. The brothers don't have to say anything. There's no sound except an aluminum rattle as Mark removes the long-staffed gaff from its holder and Dean stalks the deck, trying to turn the fish, which is making a play to circle the bow. Mark and Dean communicate by the merest flicker of eye contact, maintaining a relentless triangulation with the sword until Dean wrests the head up out of its swimming plane and it breaks the surface, fins splayed and sword slashing. "Stand back," Mark orders. "You don't want to be anywhere near a green swordfish on deck." Mark gaffs it, and with the fish three quarters of the way through the stern gate, Dean passes the line to Shaba and reaches for an ax-handle club. He beats the fish on the bony plate of its skull — smashes it in systematically, like a mason demolishing a bit of wall. He heaves it alongside the rail, where it lies dying, its great plate-like eye going dull, sleek skin flashing its farewell colors, the aurora borealis of the pelagic depths. It is magnificent even in death, one of evolution's triumphs of muscle and speed. No creature has ever been more certain of its direction — straight on ahead!

With three fish at the rail, Dean takes up his butchering knife and starts on the marker. He prunes off the fins, then slices around the gill plates, breaking the spinal column in his bloody hands and kicking the head free with the toe of his rubber boot. The knife flashes into the body cavity and the viscera tumble out. These Dean scoops up and tosses over rail. I swear that swordfish's heart is still beating when it hits the water, and the sea closes over it and rolls on.

The *Argus III* is quietly adrift, the hauling in done, when Mark radios home to report on the day's fishing. Vernon Soares picks up. Mark and Dean's sixty-six-year-old father has lived the sort of heroic life that casts a long shadow down the generations. The year he turned twenty-one, his own father lit out in his cargo ship, and Vernon became the head of his mother's household, charged with the care of his eight younger siblings. In classic Horatio Alger fashion, Vernon left Bermuda with two dollars in his pocket and his hand-built boat, the *Argus I*, determined to build something that would last, that he could pass on to his children. "Stay with me," he always promised them, "and you'll have something."

By 1967, he'd saved enough to buy land on the leeward coast of Anegada, the northernmost of the British Virgin Islands. "The Drowned Island," locals call Anegada, because on that barrier island there are only dunes and mangroves to hold back the sea. There were no roads and no electricity when Vernon moved his family — wife Julie, Mark and Dean, and daughters Linda and Sheila — to his Anegada holdings. A lantern on the beach was all they had to guide the boat in after a day's fishing. Cement came before bread, and the family lived in tents for three years while they built the seawall, and eventually, over the decades, Neptune's Treasure, an inn and restaurant that Julie ran while Vernon fished. The brothers lived a boy's adventure story before they were old enough to fish with Vernon full-time: Mark the captain of the dinghy, manning the outboard, Dean his mate, standing in the bow, knife clenched in his teeth, ready to dive overboard and deliver the coup de grace to a green turtle, a marine reptile many times his weight. For twenty years the brothers fished with Vernon and added on to Neptune's Treasure, building a dock, a big freezer, modest homes for their own families as they came along. Until Julie died of cancer and Vernon decided that fifty years at sea was enough. His heart wasn't in it anymore, and he passed the *Argus III* on to his sons. *You'll have something.*

Now, on the radio, Mark talks to Vernon about the weather — which has turned gorgeous , if still bumpy: big cumulus clouds, bright sunshine on the hard blue water, the easterly swell stacked like steel corduroy. And they do the fish count: ten swordfish, mostly rats and pups, one marker; one tuna; and three dolphinfish — about six hundred pounds total. "The line must've drifted during the night," Mark speculates, a possible explanation for the poor catch. "Well, tell everybody we're getting ready to toss it out."

"How's he sound?" Dean asks.

"About the same as usual," Mark says. "He has his tea and tuna. Linda's looking after him."

Next Mark calls his wife, Pam, who answers at her bakery business, which she runs out of an extension to the front of their house.

"Not so good," Pam says about the catch. "What's going on out there."

Mark tries to sign off on some positive note. "We're gonna try and stay on that good water tonight. I'll call you later, about nine maybe? All right?"

But Pam won't bite on any bait; the general sentiment she leaves him with, unspoken but unmistakable all the same, is that Mark is the father of five and had better bestir himself and find some fish. Dean's heard all this before. The brothers conduct a good deal of their marriages over the single-side-band radio within each other's hearing. "All right, then," Mark says. "We're gonna toss it out."

We're all seated around the little saloon table, which is heaped with tackle and the remains of dangerous-looking food, smoking and eating and murdering the art of conversation in its very cradle. Mark and Dean, I suspect, communicate by telepathy. There's no question of "catching up" with each other; after all, they live just a clothesline apart; their wives see each other every day; their children play together in a communal yard. Where one is, there is the other. Saba, too, is silent at the table, working a green toothpick between his frowning lips. When he smokes, he plucks out the toothpick and impales it dead center in his hair, which he wears in a six-inch cone like a fez. Cousin Jeff passes the time rummaging in his tackle box, occasionally showing off lures to Dean as if they were talismans of great and ineluctable medicine. I ask Dean if he ever thought about leaving all this, you know, running away to land, to the States, say. But he just shakes his head. "No, unh-uh, never did."

Dean pushes up from the table, and he and Saba and Jeff begin to struggle back into their foul-weather gear, the slick yellow overalls making them look like firemen getting ready to go out and extinguish the sun, which is expiring outside the smoky cabin with great fiery fanfare.

"Red sky at night, sailors' delight … they say," Dean mutters, planting another cigarette in the middle of his whiskers. He's ready to toss out.

On the tracking screen, where differences in temperature of a few tenths of a degree register as a jagged EKG of biotic potential, Mark has sniffed out likely water again. Now he'll try to hold the *Argus III* on course along the seam of the thermocline while the crew tosses out the immense line of hooks. The deadweight of the first highflier — the heavy, radio-beacon-equipped buoys that link the longline — and the seven-knot boat speed will keep the mainline humming out of the reel.

Dean sits hunkered down with his back to the stern, a plastic laundry basket of squid beside him, as the mainline, thick like surgical tubing, comes off the reel — howls off, I should say; there's fury in it — and as fast as Saba can pull the gear off the leader reel, Dean baits it and attaches a light-stick. The oil-drum-sized reel sets a maddening pace, groaning as the *Argus III* labors up a sea, screaming as she plunges down into a trough. After sundown, the boat is lit up by its running lights like a little puppet theater lurching through a world of dark surprises. Dean's face is weirdly illuminated by the light sticks the crewmen all wear around their necks against the mischance of a man overboard, but if he were snagged by one of his hooks, we could only watch. He'd be jerked backward over the stern and dragged underneath the mainline, where he'd flicker in the black water as he spun deeper, like an ember falling down a well.

But he takes care. He slips the hook under the mantle and sews it snugly and invisibly with a double stitch. And then he holds the bait out away from himself, as if demonstrating to an audience that he's not in any way attached to it: not hooked here, not hooked there. Then he tosses it out — brilliantly, I think, the gesture verging on oratory: Take it, sea, this is yours, this we give you, away! The squid sails over the rail, and Dean lets the leader line pay out to the snap at the end. He reaches up with the snap the way you might reach up to feed bread crumbs to avenging angels, reaches up and snaps it to the furious mainline gingerly. That baby's hot! He does it the same way each time. His life depends on it.

Mark, meanwhile, brews coffee for the crew, and prelights cigarettes three at a time and carries them aft in his mouth like a tailor with needles. He bends to offer the cigarette, and Dean lifts his face like a communicant to receive it. Mark comes rolling nimbly back to the cabin and sees me gazing mournfully at the crew. Tossing out strikes a landlubber like me as something close to motion-sickness martyrdom, like pulling a factory shift on a carnival ride.

"As for why Dean's back there while I'm up here ... " Mark begins to explain. "As to whether or not it's fair — or right — I just don't know. Dean is certainly capable of captaining his own boat. He knows the sea as well as I do. We've talked about getting a second boat, having Dean run another crew. But Dean has always been shy of responsibility. Even when we were kids, I was always in charge. But I can tell you this: If I could choose any crew, pick anybody in the world as my right-hand man — it would be Dean."

Mark shuts down the diesels, and Dean wrestles the terminal high-flier over the rail. It's as tall as a basketball goal and weighs as much as a truck tire filled with cement, but little Dean can toss it. It hits the water with a smack and begins at once to sway like a metronome as it bobs away on the seas. With that, the tossing out is done, and the boat drifts free of the longline.

"What do you want for dinner?" Mark shouts back at Dean. "Beef or chicken?"

Dean hooks his thumbs under his armpits and waggles his elbows.

"Chicken it is, then," Mark says.

It's 2 a.m. aboard the *Argus III*, the middle of my watch, and I'm praying, sort of. There's nothing to see but the green radar screen and the shadowy forms of Mark and Dean asleep, feet to feet on the cabin bench. The wind is rising. I can feel it on my face through the cabin window; I can see it in the moon, being violently dribbled through the sky by the rocking of the boat. After four days of being sea-sick off and on, I've just about got my sea-legs, but precariously so. I'm praying that the coming storm won't plunge me back into green hell.

I was three days in Anegada while we waited out the previous storm front. I took long walks on the windswept beaches of the north side, scavenging among the wreckage of ropes and buoys and worrying about being sea sick on this trip. All the rest of the time, I was listening to Vernon. "Everything I got came off the ocean," he told me. "I put it here." His story left me like the wedding guest in *The Rime of the Ancient Mariner* — a sadder and wiser man. Or oddly depressed, at any rate. His victory — Neptune's Treasure — impressed me, but his tragedy harrowed me, and left me more confused than ever as to which life mostly is. Vernon did it for his family, but mostly he did it for Julie, and then she died, as we all will. She died, Vernon quit, and the boys took over the boat; in that chain of events, as in all bereavement, there was more of tossing out than of hauling in. On the sea at night, you can see it more clearly than on land: something stately, massive and annihilating behind all things.

Somewhere out there, the longline lies below us, but I don't think so much of its catching powers anymore. A melancholy aura surrounds it, for me, anyway; in my mind's eye, I now see a lost and lonely highway through a wasteland, where tiny chitinous gargoyles flutter around its dim streetlights. An endgame, it seems.

What could he do? What is the work of grief? That's what Vernon asked me when he showed me the sign he'd made for Neptune's Treasure — a painted plywood treasure chest overflowing with gilded seashells. "I made that for her," Vernon said. "Now what am I supposed to do?" And I wonder if maybe Mark and Dean are doing the work, if by cleaving to family they kept death on the line, knew where it was at least and felt its strength all the time.

Seas are coming over the rail with firehose force, but Mark just puffs away and steps back — Ole! — into the shelter of the cabin bulwark. Mark is grinning like a devil, toggling the controls and weighing the mainline. All he needs is someone shooting at him to complete his pleasure. Dance, amigo! Ole! Haul line and damn the torpedoes! His work is more athletic when the sea turns snotty on him; there's more to grapple with, more tangles, more breaks in the mainline. The rats and pups keep coming in.

"It's pretty bleak when you're just catching juveniles," Mark has to admit. "You know the end is coming." But he loves fishing too much to quit. His oldest boy, Aaron, is away at school in the States with his sisters, and Mark knows they'll all see a lot more of the big world than just Anegada. Maybe Matthew, his youngest, four now and the last still at home, might want to fish. "He likes to be with me," Mark said. "Which is good." The boy already follows Mark like a shadow, from house to dock and boat and back. "But you can't predict with kids. You can't make those decisions for them."

As for Dean, he doesn't even have to love it. He is the bloody thing. With his gaffs and his truncheons and the grit of his sinew, he is the master of any fish. The harder it gets, the more he glowers and digs in like a bulldog. Vernon told me this story about Mark, how one time he found a quarter in the street, and Vernon said to him: "Did you earn that?" No, he'd just found it, Mark said. "Then you take it right to the church. You don't get nothing you don't earn." It was a lesson aimed at Mark, but it seems to have struck Dean right in the heart. Maybe that's true of all Vernon's lessons.

To the north, the gathering gale broods over the horizon like a vast, purple bruise, and the famed white sheep of the sea are grazing in a frenzy. The mainline grinds a dozen empty leaders and then another bat ray. Nobody's even watching when it happens: Saba poking with his knife at the wriggling beast, and then roaring with pain. In an instant, the ray's barbed tail has pierced his glove and driven through his pinkie finger and right on into his ring finger.

What happens next transpires in a heroic blur of action. With Saba laid up in the cabin, Mark and Dean and Jeff carry on with the hauling in, at double time now. Through high seas and salt spray, routine tangles and frequent breaks in the old mainline — which sound like rifle reports and delay the brothers only a moment while they splice — with rats and pups to be butchered, the brothers haul in. Now more than ever, there is that silent communion between them, carried out in the merest flickering of the eyes. In just under four hours, they have all the gear stowed aboard.

Then Mark spins the wheel and points the bow toward Anegada. "We've got to get this man to medical attention," he says.

The whole extended family meets us at the dock. There's the patriarch, Vernon, still dapper with a full poll of silver hair and blue, twinkling, storyteller's eyes. One moment those eyes are moist with pride in his boys; the next, they flash and turn critical. "Mooring line's too damn loose," he says, but mostly to himself. There is Cindy, Dean's wife, and their three daughters; Pam and little Matthew; sister Linda and her husband, Randall. After Saba is trundled away by taxi to the airport, where he'll catch a charter flight to the hospital on Tortola (already arranged by Mark over the radio), the scene takes on the emotional tone, for me, of the post-dream end of *The Wizard of Oz*. I look at Dean, nuzzling his baby daughter, Kia — and grinning! — and I think I recognize him for the first time. He was so fierce tossing out, like a lion! And Mark, hauling in like a madman, a juggernaut spewing clouds of Captain Black's! When no one is looking, I drop to my knees and kiss the wood of the dock.

Due to our unexpected return, I've been bumped from my room at the inn, and Mark offers to put me up in his house that night. We all sit on the couch, Jeff, me, Mark, and watch Mark's favorite movie on tape. "Not *The Rock* again!" Pam moans, but she's only teasing him. She's relaxed in an easy chair next to the couch with her legs thrown over Mark's and Matthew in her lap. Matthew clings to what looks like the shreds of some old rag, and therein lies a story. It's the last of his crib sheet, Pam explains, and there's hell to pay if he's parted from it. Matthew will watch while it tumbles in the drier; he'll wait under the clothesline for it to dry in the breeze. Once , on one of their driving vacations in the States, they misplaced the relic, and Mark had to pull over and empty the station wagon looking for it. Of course, now it's about to come apart into dozens of strands.

"Let me see what you've got there," Mark says, and Matthew shyly hands over his treasure. Mark holds the strings of fabric in the palm of his hand and says, "If you'd like me to, I'll tie them together into a fishing line."

"Dude, you wouldn't believe the day I've had," Jack Ucciferri tells me, steering the mud-splattered Land Cruiser through the airport queue of dilapidated taxis onto the highway leading out of Managua. The road is cloaked in an eerie orange-colored smoke, out of which suddenly appear ancient creeping ox-carts or buggy rigs drawn by some of the world's scrawniest horses, and I'm thinking, *Dude, I would.* Poor Nicaragua, the sprawling capital still — *still!* — reeling from the 1972 earthquake (not to mention Ronald Reagan and Ollie North, which I promised myself I wouldn't). It's a place where word-of-mouth directions often begin with "donde fue" — where something used to be — as in back before the quake. That's just plain sad.

But we're headed for the Pacific coast, where a breeze of optimism — I gotta believe — blows offshore all day, sucking in that most coveted demographic: affluent males between the age of 14 and 29. The surfers are coming, in a kind of recreational Manifest Destiny, drawn by that reliable all-day offshore wind — a wave-sculpting freak grace of massive Lake Nicaragua — plus the long swell-season, and the rock-bottom real-estate prices. After ten years of relative stability, all of a sudden Nicaragua has ocean-front property, a primo morsel of which is Giant's Foot Surf Tours in the tiny fishing village of Gigante.

We're lucky it's still there, though, after last night, Jack tells me. Barefoot in board shorts and T-shirt for the airport pick-up, the twenty-five-year-old surf entrepreneur looks like an exhausted otter, as if he swam all the way to Managua. Last night the rainy season commenced with a vengeance, he says, a storm that was like nothing he'd seen in his three years in Nicaragua. Non-stop lightning and thunder and just a flat-out deluge of rain: "It was coming down so unbelievably hard and for so freaking long that we just knew something was going to be destroyed."

In the morning the surf camp's menagerie of dogs and cats and poultry were found to have survived, all except one of the turkey chicks

— drowned — and the boat — where was the boat?! The camp's 22-foot panga (canopy-topped, with padded seats and hardwood grilled floor), moored in the bay, had filled up with rainwater and sunk. Just the tip of the prow poked up from the becalmed bay. It took all day, and Herculean labor, but, with some local assistance, they'd muscled the Vale La Pena ("Worth the Trouble") to shallow water and bailed her, and had set about over-hauling the big 115 hp outboard motor, again with a little help from a couple of village fishermen — one young guy, sober, and an older dude, not so much so, who, within the cloak of invisibility of the very drunk, was pilfering the camp's tools.

The young Nicaraguan called him on it.

"Ladron!"

"Hijo de puta!"

Out came the knives. Time for Ucciferri, who studied International Relations at the University of California at Santa Barbara, to practice conflict resolution. Just then his business partner, Zach Baker, came sprinting down the beach brandishing a machete and somehow a blood-bath was averted.

Cool. Boating disasters. Knife fights. When do we get to the Hole in the Wall, and will Butch and Sundance be waiting up? An hour or so later we exit pavement to lurch in and out of mud-bogs on the long sketchy dirt road to Gigante. It's dark as a tunnel, giant jungle trees arching overhead, the Cruiser bucking like a slow-speed mechanical bull. Sometime after midnight we roll into the pitch black, seemingly deserted village, just a humble assemblage of shacks along the waterfront, and on to the end of the road and the surf camp — where suddenly there's light, music, surfers. Everybody's still up, but winding down, sprawled in hammocks or kicked back in deck chairs with the last beer of the night, puffing reflectively on stogies. The nightly poker game has just broken up, they say. I'm bombarded by introductions, instructions on how to make myself at home in the ramshackle brick and timber bungalows, everybody so friendly, so welcoming, it feels like I've arrived at a sort of surfers' after-life — except that everyone is young and, of course, still alive.

"And how are the waves?" I ask one of the campers, Casey Fox, a genial giant who's stopped off at Giant's Foot during a two month trek through Central America.

"Dude, the waves are excellent," he says.

Felipe, the camp rooster, awakes around four-thirty. Everybody else sleeps in. Dawn patrol at Giant's Foot is more like nine o'clock — thanks again to the all-day offshores. Plenty of time for some of Carol's banana pancakes. Carol Starr is the camp's accountant, sometime chef and chief bottle-washer. Pretty and adventurous, she lives with Zach at the camp, and keeps the testosterone from boiling over into Lord of the Flies territory. That morning I offer her yesterday's New York Times and her eyes go wide. I'm her new hero, she says. Beaming, I help myself to another pancake.

When everybody's good and ready, Chapin Krueter, the full-time surfing guide, paddles out to the Vale La Pena and fires her up. A boat ride is the best way to get into surf — a short boat ride better still. We motor south around the nearby dramatic crag known as El Pie de Gigante (the eponymous "Giant's Foot"), and then cross a brief open stretch of deep water to another rocky point about a mile distant, where Chapin steers in towards the cove. He cuts the engine and we wait, our suspense palpable in the sudden silence, to see what the swell will bring.

Water plashes sonorously against the fiberglass hull; the tide surges and burbles in the rocks at the base of the cliff, darkly glistening in the early morning mist. And then: "Here comes something!" one of my surf camp-mates says. I all but wolf-whistle as we watch the set peel off perfectly from the point to the deeper water of the channel. These are just the sort of mellow puppies I can ease into after an unintended year's lay-off.

Everyone else is pretty skeptical. "You want to give it a try?" Chapin asks us, scratching at his mariner's beard. My camp-mates, five skilled and surf-seasoned twenty-something Californians, decline. This left point-break, known as Manzanio, can be world-class, the guide assures us, and, of course, a whole lot bigger. "Swells missing it," Cap'n Chapin says, and guns it back north. In about ten minutes we're in an entirely different world. The sun has burned off the mist and glitters brightly on a wide-open field of play. In front of us is the dependable beach-break, Rio Colorado. Here the swell is hitting straight on, hoisting up the panga so we can admire the mile-long stretch of white sand, the tawny hills behind just perking up with the new rains. About a half dozen earlier-bird surfers share a couple of take-off spots, dropping in and disappearing behind muscular walls.

"They're going to be bummed to see us!" says Eli, a spectacularly tattooed drummer from L.A.

Yeah, but sometimes you're the bummers and sometimes you're the bummees. That's surfing in the global village. We storm the lineup and within fifteen minutes two of our company have broken their boards — one crumbled from just duck-diving an eight-foot guillotine, the other spat out of a barrel in two pieces. The swell keeps rising and we keep moving back, back, into deeper water. After a couple of aborted take-offs, I find my niche at the edge of the pack where I can sneak into a few of the smaller set waves. Meanwhile, Chapin has dropped anchor and joined the fray. The twenty-five-year-old guide, a veteran of Hawaii's North Shore, and a former UCLA soccer star, is the morning's standout surfer, flying out of barrels into wheeling cut-backs, just killing it.

We play in that semi-serious stuff (it isn't really big enough to hurt you, much, probably) for hours till hunger and thirst drive us back to the boat and the shade of its canopy, where a cold drink from the cooler really hits the spot. Chapin organizes our leisurely departure: tie up the boards and we'll just head on back to camp and see what Zach and Carol have for us for lunch. My first session in Nicaragua and frankly I've been outclassed by the surf. It doesn't matter (okay, it stings a little, in the old adolescent pride); I can already tell I'm going to love surf camp about as much as Ol' Br'r Rabbit loved his briar patch.

The whole experience takes me back to age fourteen when I all but moved into the Burns brothers' beach-front garage-rec-room. All I'd wanted that summer was a convenient place to stash my board, play a couple hours of ping-pong, leaf through old surf magazines and raid the fridge at will — was that asking too much? It was, in fact, for Mr. Burns. And though at Giant's Foot Surf Tours I'm paying for the privilege of surfing, loafing, eating, loafing, surfing, playing ping-pong, loafing, surfing, leafing through old surf mags, the camp somehow recreates that golden age of boyhood indolence and camaraderie with stunning authenticity.

Credit the gregarious Jack Ucciferri, who stumbled upon the tiny fishing village of Gigante at the end of a 2002 surf trip through Central America. Enchanted by the untapped potential of Nicaragua's Pacific coast, Jack called his friend Zach Baker, a rock climber and sailor with a mechanical knack (they'd met aboard a training schooner in the North Atlantic), who invited his girl friend, Carol (they'd met through another friend of Jack's). Jack, meanwhile, had married a Nicaraguan woman from the nearby town of Rivas, Susan Caldera, beautiful, multi-lingual — and thus the camp was staffed: two dynamic couples in their twenties, plus burly, laconic Chapin Kreuter, the Rowdy Gaines of the outfit — creating a business in the middle of nowhere (though in the quietly booming world of Nicaraguan surf travel, little Gigante may turn out to be at the epicenter of everything, the picturesque sheltered cove closest to some of the best breaks).

Along with a ton of fun, it was grueling work. Advice from the locals was mostly about holding onto their stuff. Wood pile next to the fence? Very bad. Passing banditos would help themselves. Chickens running loose? Very bad. Banditos would pick them off one at a time. Chickens in a coop? Ah, no, banditos would steal them all at once. Each basic necessity presented logistical and diplomatic challenges. Water, for instance, they fetched a bucket at a time from the village well, until Jack negotiated a deal with a guy who would haul water by ox-cart and fill their tank every Saturday. Only, not *every* Saturday. Finally, calling upon his wife's connections, Jack got the Rivas fire department to come out and fill the water tower the gringos built themselves, with plumbing of their own design, about which they are justly proud.

What Jack wanted was some real world experience to back up his degree. You maybe knew somebody like Jack in college, part Jay Gatsby, part Milo Minderbinder, who knew everybody you knew plus a hundred others. As an undergrad he represented U.S.A. Youth at a W.T.O. summit in South Africa, where he met Nelson Mandela, became inspired. But Gigante has been frustrating, the community all but impenetrable. His idealism has been … adjusted. Some people are drunks, and some are thieves. And some are both, with knives.

There's not even a whiff of trouble for us campers, though. We leave our boards in the boat and swim the short distance to shore, wolf down lunch, and chill on the patio where we watch Zach's dog Nica and Jack's lab pup Ed chase a pig from the premises. We have Bob Marley on CD, Jack Johnson's surf flick "Thicker Than Water" on the DVD, and the week-long ping-pong tournament is underway — John Renkin (a photographer, friend of Jack's from UCSB) vs. Casey Fox (an organic farmer by trade, and an outspoken advocate of the avocado, another friend of Jack's from UCSB — the place sometimes seems like a branch of the college). There'll be another surf session in the afternoon, and poker that night at the Griffs', the little cantina up the beach run by a colorful ex-pat, Keith Griff and his Nicaraguan wife Maria, whose father — according to local legend — had secured his fortune by helping the U.S. marines escape from Ernesto Sandino in the 1930s.

It's a small town of a country, and everyone is entangled in the web of its history. But this is surf camp, and we're all abuzz about the visit of

Yvon Chouinard, the Patagonia CEO and surfer who dropped by with his posse looking for rooms. Giant's Foot Surf Tours is booked, though. Which leads to a story about the Ranch, the fabled Big Sur surf break where Chouinard has a home. And then to other surfers who'd made it big, or flamed out due to drugs or drink, or drowned in this gnarly break or that, and on and on until Carol, sitting back with the kitten Gallito on her lap, finally calls us on it.

"You guys, there's just no end to it, is there? It's worse than Hollywood celebrity gossip." Momentarily stunned, we just stare at her a second and then go right back at it.

For the next three days we surf our brains out, catching Panga Drop multiple times in gorgeous overhead and glassy conditions. While not exactly a pussycat (it's named for an incident in which an unwary fisherman, chauffeuring surfers for a few extra bucks, got caught by a clean-up set and was flung over the falls in his panga), Panga Drop is more forgiving than Rio Colorado, more of a great rolling wall than the nearby top-to-bottom breaking A-frame. It's the beginner's break for these parts, and I start to get my chops back, dropping in comfortably early and carving long satisfying turns. I ride one all the way to shore — a little stall, a little nose ride — working my big yellow fun-shape as if I've never been away from the game. Faced with the choice between paddling back out to the boat or hoofing it three miles back to camp, I take the hike. It isn't a choice, really; my spaghetti arms have no more paddle in them.

By the time I make it back, the wind has switched to onshore — which it never does. What's up with that? Jack, who's been to Rivas to check his e-mail, tells us about a message from a friend: "How are you guys doing with that tropical storm?" Hmm … what tropical storm? While there's a big-screen TV with satellite at the Griffs' (we'd been keeping up with the NBA playoffs during poker), who ever reports Nicaraguan weather?

The onshores keep pushing clouds in from the Pacific and that night it rains like a cattle stampede on the roof. In the morning the bay is looking ugly, whitecaps haystacking to the horizon. "One boat in the water," Eli comments. "Belongs to a gringo. That's not good."

Jack and Zach and Chapin are watching in horror as a mass of white water bears down on the Vale La Pena. It couldn't sink twice in one week, could it? It fucking-A could. The wave smashes over the port side, she wallows, founders and goes down — all but the tip of the prow. At that point all of us campers spring into action, plunging into the hurricane seas to salvage the floating detritus, more an act of bravado than anything else since it would've all washed in anyway. An hour or so later, after ruminating a bit on the rainswept beach with a bottle of rum, Jack and Chapin swim out with a rope and cut the mooring line.

Then something wonderful happens. The whole village turns out, every able-bodied man and boy over eight, to heave-ho on the line. The village strong man, a bull in a beret, takes pride of place at the head of the line, the rest of the community arrayed according to subtle rules of status. They muscle it in, the boat submarining through the surf, all the way to shore.

The canopy struts are twisted like pretzels and the engine cowling is smashed, but Zach thinks the motor will be all right. They'll have her running again by the time the surf cleans up. The Giant's Foot crew buys beers for all the village at the Griffs' — Maria spreads the word — but most of the men are too embarrassed to go there: it's the gringos' place. True enough, we gringos are there that night as usual when the hurricane finally knocks out the power. But Keith Griff, that wily old operator, not wanting to miss the chance to take our Cordobas, fires up his generator, serves a fresh round of Jamaica Roses, and the game goes on. The only worry is the blustering wind, which threatens to blow over our down cards.

Lord Long Arms, I Presume?

In nearly thirty years of surfing, I've never seen a shark. At least I don't think so. There was one time many years ago off the northeast coast of Florida — the Hansen Superlight had just come out, that proto-short board with the delicately stenciled feather on the deck — when I saw something that looked like a small U-boat cruising towards me in a big gray wave. Whatever it was, I pinwheel paddled out of there, thrashing a wake like a cartoon motorboat, all the while, oddly enough, laughing like Curly of the Stooges — nyahh-ah-ah! — in nervous hilarity. My friends, who hadn't seen anything, followed close behind, likewise half amused, if only a quarter terrified. Safe on the beach, nobody really believed me. Besides, the waves were pretty good, so we all went back out.

Dozens of times I've suddenly seen the dorsal fin of a dolphin or the black wingtips of a manta ray, every sharky simulacrum jolting the brain back to its reptile core. Every time a surfer kicks something that gives, something slick and living, it's an immediate psychic hotfoot: adrenaline floods; you achieve maximum positive buoyancy, nearly brief yogic flight. One day — I remember the board I was riding at the time, a beautiful new six-foot eight-inch Midget Farrelly — I rose over an oily chop and dipped down into the trough and saw the pale hand of a drowned man reaching up to me. Turned out it was just a sunken latex glove full of water. But I remember that day. A low pressure day. Sickly yellowish light. The waves not big, but misaligned and crumbling treacherously like rotten cake. A real sharky day.

There were lots of sharky days when I was little. Younger surfers, closer to their dreams, closer to the heat and vapors of the oedipal engine, see most of the sharks that aren't there. In moments of doubt, the sea becomes haunted by cannibal ogres and *vaginas dentatas*, and the thing under the bed becomes the thing under the board, your worst suspicions about life confirmed. The fear of weakness and the worst possible consequences of helplessness shrinks you then, contracts you tightly. You occupy your limbs in a remarkable way, your toes twiddling with identity, calf muscles packed with consciousness like taut fruit. You've cast off all lines to father and mother, friends and school. You're a straggler. Mother Nature's child. It's you, little dude. Just you. And the shark.

But most likely not. You survive, of course, not necessarily by being the fittest. Through no particular virtue of your own, you ride through with the herd, untouched by Lord Long Arms, favored by an average fate. With the years you grow to like your odds. But every time you enter the sea you join the food chain a notch below the shark; you are knocking on the door of a terrible possibility. But millions of others are also knocking on that same door. You're pretty sure you'll always get the lady. Somebody else gets the shark.

On July 1, 1991, at a remote reef break near Davenport Landing, 15 miles north of Monterey Bay, a Santa Cruz surfer named Eric Larsen became that somebody else when a 15-foot great white shark rose slowly below him and took his left leg, from thigh to shin, into its mouth. It was just tasting him, chewing through the neoprene of his wetsuit, sampling the qualities of his blood. Larsen, a 32-year-old software designer and a seasoned athlete, kept cool and used his arms to pry his leg loose. But like a terrible Tar Baby, the shark shifted its grip to Larsen's arms, chomping down. Pinioned again, Larsen had to rip his right arm out of the jaws through serrated teeth that scraped into the bone. He pummeled the shark with his fist, and suddenly it let go, vanishing as abruptly as it had appeared. Alone outside the lineup, Larsen climbed back onto his board, paddled toward shore until he could catch a wave, and rode it to the beach. Thanks to his own first-aid training, a quick call to 911 by a Davenport local, a life-flight to a Santa Cruz hospital, five hours of surgery, and 400 stitches, Eric Larsen survived. He had lost half of the blood in his body.

On November 5, 1992, at Keaau Beach Park on the Leeward Coast of Oahu, 18-year-old Aaron Romento was bodyboarding with some friends in the shore break when he became somebody else, too. A large tiger shark passed up closer targets to attack Romento from behind, biting him once on the thigh. The next day's *Honolulu Advertiser* headline read: "It Should Have Been Safe." Indeed, the attack happened on a bright sunny morning in four feet of clear water within 150 feet of shore. Despite immediate aggressive first aid, Aaron Romento bled to death on the beach.

These two attacks, so different in setting and circumstance, involving two very different species of shark, were the most horrific in a series of frightening batterings and close calls over the last five years as shark attacks, first on the West Coast and then in Hawaii, have been on the rise. Between 1982 and 1987 there was a total of 20 attacks; in the five years since, that number has jumped to 33. What's got shark experts puzzled and the surfing community nervous is that 79 per cent of those attacks have been on surfers; in the previous five years only 25 per cent of the victims were surfers.

The surfing press called 1992 the Year of the Shark, and in fact the five attacks on surfers that occurred in Hawaii alone represented a very bad year. Yet in perspective, the odds *against* being attacked by a shark are overwhelming. The five surfers in Hawaii, for example, were among six million divers, swimmers, boardsailors, and snorkelers who played in the islands' waters last year.

Numbers, however, never reflect the growth in fear in a genuine shark scare. The reaction in the surfing community — escalating dread, panic, then calls for vigilante justice — mirrors the paradigm established in Matewan, New Jersey, in the summer of 1916, when three men and a boy were killed and another boy was badly mauled by sharks during a twelve-day heat wave. For the first time in America, the shark as monster made national headlines, and the shark attack, that peculiarly awful mode of death, loomed large in the collective imagination. Like the shark itself, the fear has never gone away: It lurks just below the surface, awaiting some extraordinary event to summon it forth.

Never mind the numbers, then; like all irrational fears, this one counterbalances some weird wish to know the worst. Our morbid fascination with shark attacks, our delicious fear of being eaten alive, seems deeply rooted in a reverence for infinite brute power, and our love of — or rather our faith in — wildness itself. It's our oldest faith, the prey species' belief in the bigger beast, and all our eschatologies are mere footnotes to death by devouring. Collectively, the suspense is unbearable. And yet many bear it, regularly, pursuing their sports in waters frequented by big sharks. "I've seen fins, and I've felt the surges of big sharks passing under me," a veteran surfer told me. "But I haven't felt teeth yet." To feel teeth — that's hard knowledge at last! Shark attack victims go down into the heart of frenzy like holy initiates and expire like saints in the throes of ecstatic vision — the hard-wired prey response, and the hardest lesson of the old, old animal world. Or so we might comfortably hope, here in our armchairs.

And therein lies the difference between the masses who stick close to their armchairs (or beach chairs) and surfers. For surfers, the shark has always been a desired part of the cutting edge, one more difference between the committed waterman and the chuckler on shore. It's the surfer's nature to seek out wilder, sharkier waters. The language of surfing reflects the wilderness metaphor: Surfers hunt "rogue" waves with "guns"; dangerous waves have "toothy" lips; where the big waves crack like cannon fire, the curl is the "jaw" — the tube the maw. The nature of the sport itself is to survive, with grace, in the belly of the beast. Yet lately, as the big sharks have been scaring surfers and scaring them bad, they've had to ask themselves new questions about the sea: How safe do they want it? How dangerous can they take it?

The shark scares in Hawaii and California have taken the surfers' measure, both as risk-seekers and as environmentalists. The return to the inshore lineup of the apex predator, the large tiger sharks and the great whites, seems to herald a new, more hazardous era. Hazardous for the sharks, too, as backlash against the big fish may propel them ever more quickly towards the "endangered" category. As conservationists — often surfers themselves — push these popular, populated surf zones toward a more pristine ideal, the waters have taken on a problematic identity as playgrounds and game reserves, like a Glacier National Park with its grizzly bears untagged, unmonitored, and all but invisible, until they bite.

The heroic bronze statue of a surfer standing with his flaring deltoids turned to the inside break of Steamer Lane marks a kind of Mecca for the central California coast. Surf City Santa Cruz remembers back before the Gidget and Moon-Doggie days to the dawn of the surfer as iconoclastic ironman, outlaw-athlete, one-in-million, one-of-a-kind. He's not such a lonely boy anymore. In the early 1950s, there were probably as few as 1,500 surfers on the entire West Coast; the figure is now closer to half a million.

Just moments ago I watched as a local surfer took off under a cliff, charged right, banged an off-the-lip, pulled a floater (unweighting in midair, getting behind the breaking curl, and riding it back down on the edge of the inside rail), cranked a bottom-turn, and set himself up for the tube — then got stuffed by an inconvenient surf-kayaker competing in a contest. Naturally, the surfer deftly stepped to the back of his board and shot it out from under his feet, point-blank, right at the kayaker's head.

This motivated the announcer for the World Surf Kayak Championship to spark up the PA again in yet another attempt to mollify and clear the water of noncontestants. "Our local surfers here," he said, "truly some of the finest athletes in the world, sometimes — ahem! — get a little bit territorial."

A bit gladiatorial, too, you could say. There's an intensity down there that I could watch all day from the natural amphitheater of the cliffs of Lighthouse Point. But I have an appointment with a conservationist to talk about the impact zone where man meets shark on the shark's turf.

I'm browsing through the Surfing Museum at the end of the point, running a finger along the jagged crescent of bite marks on some surfer's unlucky board, when a stocky, freckle-faced beachboy in knee-length board-shorts comes in talking sharks a mile a minute and handing out literature on the great white to the museum's cashier. When Sean Van Sommeran, operations director of Santa Cruz's Pelagic Shark Research Foundation talks about sharks, it's a rapid-fire kinetic account full of love of information and enthusiasm for the big fish. Before we're out the door he's described six conservation projects the foundation has going and recounted highlights of the recent White Shark Symposium, which brought experts from around the world to Bodega Bay last March to discuss, among other issues, the shift in great white shark attacks away from swimmers and divers and onto surfers.

"Investigations," Van Sommeran calls the recent attacks on the central coast. "They spit people out."

With the lyricism of a privileged witness, Van Sommeran recalls scenes of great whites feeding. He tells of watching several of them swimming into the body cavity of a partially beached whale, nibbling on the tender organs. He remembers another beached whale, buried by public officials, washing back into the surf, the sodden mass like a tea bag for the sharks.

Van Sommeran's business is counting sharks, and he shares with shark experts the belief that the great white remains relatively rare in West Coast waters. But he also believes that further white shark attacks on surfers are inevitable now that crowding in the safer zones — like Steamer lane, where no surfer has ever been attacked — forces more and more surfers north, towards Davenport and Pacifica and Half Moon Bay, towards the seal rookeries of Año Nuevo Island, the bloodiest zone of the central coast's famed Red Triangle.

"It used to be those northern waters were surfed only by an elite cadre," Van Sommeran says. "Now no place is remote."

From where we stand in the little park on Lighthouse Point, the whole California outdoor scene — backpackers, twirling in-line skaters, betighted cyclists, paddle-crafters toting their rigs, and a constant traffic of arriving and departing surfers — seems to be swirling around us. Just about everybody in Santa Cruz is into something active, semi-dangerous or downright life-threatening. And of course the crowd isn't all local. From San Francisco south on U.S. 101, through Palo Alto and San Jose, west to Santa Cruz and Monterey, then north up Highway 1 and back to the Bay area, the human tide flows round and round in restless circulation.

"Look," Van Sommeran says, "we have a real problem just with people falling off the cliffs." (This is true; there's a cliffside warning sign nearby: Don't Be The Next Statistic). "People who surf Davenport and Año Nuevo are taking a real risk. The elephant seals themselves are very dangerous. Those places are like the Serengeti."

With that Van Sommeran excuses himself to go tag some sharks. Over his shoulder he tosses a final thought. "Maybe it's just natural selection at its finest."

Down on the beach at Davenport Landing, about a dozen surfers are enjoying some extra elbow room in the very spot where Eric Larsen was mauled. I'm thinking about a story that was circulating at the White Shark Symposium. Witnesses claim to have seen a shark, somewhere in the Mediterranean, hit a diver with such ferocity that he literally exploded from the impact. At any moment, I wondered, could one of these surfers simply blow up, blasted out of the water as if torpedoed from below? There would be no warning — the best thing about white sharks, surfers say, is that you never see them (though if you see a seal fly out of the water like a cruise missile, that's considered a strong indicator). Indeed, the portrait of the shark that emerged from the White Shark Symposium is that of a magnificently evolved predator. It rockets up in ambush, its bulbous snout wrinkling back, jaws bulging out, teeth snapping off as much as 50 pounds of flesh in a bite. One of the stars of the symposium, renowned animal behaviorist Peter Klimly, analyzed some 250 white shark attacks on marine mammals around the seal rookeries of northern California's Farallon Islands, 133 of which he'd documented on video. In one shot, an energetic white shark leaps clear out of the water to snatch a seal off a rock. But in most attacks, witnesses see neither seal nor shark, only a sudden explosion blasting spray 15 feet high, then a slick of blood on the surface. Often the seals and sea lions are beheaded. The shark will sometimes wait for the mortally wounded prey to drift away from others so as to not alarm the rest of the pinnipeds.

They sound like real bad shepherds, keeping watch over their flocks.

Like other species, the great white has sensors, small jelly-filled pores on its head, the Ampullae of Lorenzini, which can detect minute electrical fields. "They're so sensitive," Van Sommeran told me, "they can tell if a seal is wounded, if a seal is sick."

The great white shark also has enormous optic nerves, thick as ropes, which means it sees extremely well. And for a fish of its bulk, it is astonishingly fast, with the design specs of a six-foot speedster like the blue shark or the white-tipped reef shark, but scaled up to 20 feet and 3,000 pounds with no loss of efficiency. With that kind of overkill, it's no surprise the great white is a highly successful predator; in the 133 attacks videotaped by Klimly, only one victim got away.

These facts led the experts at the White Shark Symposium to wonder about a perplexing inconsistency: So far on the West Coast there's been only one fatality in 25 great white shark attacks on surfers. If the white shark is a man-eater, why does it eat so few men?

Klimly argues that our flesh must be repugnant to them. "Seals are like shark PowerBars," he says. "They have a fatty, energy-rich layer that we don't." So the shark takes a bite of us, decides we're not its ideal prey, and declines to finish the meal. Then again, says John McCosker, director of San Francisco's Steinhart Aquarium, the human will to live must run counter to the white shark's hard-wired assumptions. "They seem to bite once and wait for us to die." Which would work well enough with those marine mammals lacking a tradition of emergency medical treatments and major surgery.

McCosker also subscribes to the mistaken-identity theory. The idea that when sharks bite us, it's because they're mistaking us for their usual food has been around for as long as scientists have been trying to figure out why sharks sometimes attack but decline to eat people, but McCosker and a colleague decided to throw a surfboard into the hypothesis. They put wet-suited dummies ("Can't use grad students," McCosker says) on shortboards off the southern coast of Australia to try to entice white sharks to attack. The sharks proved quite willing to oblige. Shark-eye view photos show a provocative silhouette: the shortboard's shape a seal-sized hydrodynamic torso, the dummy's limbs providing little flipper appendages dangling like hors d'oeuvres.

****

As little as we know about the great white shark, one thing is increasingly clear: California's pinnipeds may, sooner rather than later, need the sharks to kill them — to keep their populations in balance. Nowhere is this more graphically apparent than at Año Nuevo State Reserve, about ten miles up Highway 1 from Davenport. From the visitor center on the mainland, you can look through a telescope at a city of seals, more than you can imagine, slithering like slugs on the shore of Año Nuevo Island. Harbor seals and elephant seals, California sea lions and Steller's sea lions, have completely overrun the abandoned lightkeepers's house (a ranger once found a dead sea lion in the upstairs bathtub). Seals have thrived since the passage of the Marine Mammal Protection Act of 1972; 2,000 elephant seals come ashore here each year to sumo-wrestle each other, stab each other in the chest with their canines, and make more seals.

Out on the island's dunes, some bull elephant seals, 5,000 pound 15-footers, lie face-down in the sand. These malingerers, late for their migration, either have never had sex or have had so much it's almost killed them. Nearby, a heap of 300-pound pups, the color and shape of a great basket of dinner rolls, lie on their backs with their little forelimbs patting their overstuffed bellies like peasant gourmands in the Land of Cockaigne.

This is serious food for the serious eater. Experiencing an elephant seal colony at close range, hearing their bawlings, taking in a nasal blast of their stink, thinking of the bloody battles for dominance, of the bulls and their harems, of the life knit together by sex and suckling, hot blood and chummy bunchings, you just might intimate a few things about the x-factor, the jumbo predator Nature employs to balance her equation: the unseen white shark.

They are far older than the mammals; older than the rocks, it seems. Expressionless, mechanistic, solitary; cold and lonely as death. Buzz-saw-jawed agents of dissolution. Time itself with teeth. Swimming open-mouthed in close collusion with the sea, they swallow whole the projections of our most primordial fears: the fear of water and the fear of being devoured alive — birth fears and death fears.

But food was never meant to think too long or hard on the teeth that ate it. The white shark eludes hyperbole just as it eludes research. There may be hundreds of white sharks in these waters; there may be as few as ten. So far scientists have succeeded in tagging only two with an ingestible sonic device that adheres to the stomach lining. When a trophy fisherman working the waters off the Farallons in 1982 caught four whites in a day, attacks on marine mammals recorded at the Point Reyes Bird Observatory dropped nearly 90 percent. Since then the Farallon shark watchers have identified 18 individuals on the basis of nicks and cuts and other abnormalities, and the same sharks seem to come back each year, from wherever it is they go. It's still a true wilderness out there.

Recently, the great white shark has made some new friends, among them the United Anglers of California, the Friends of the Sea Otter, and anybody who values fish and would like to limit the sea lions' consumption of them. Whites aren't on the list of endangered and threatened species, and in fact no shark species is, though the federal government recently posted strict shark-fishing limits for 39 Atlantic species. The California legislature is considering a bill that would declare great whites protected, should commercial or sport fishermen desire to target sharks. That bill is expected to pass this year without much opposition, even from the surfers who might join the sea lion in the food chain. Which makes you wonder whether the white shark's environment might include the beach towns, the cafes and bookstores, and maybe soon the gift shops, where it may claim its place with the seal mugs and the whale sweatshirts as an icon of the wild.

Down on a wink of sand called Loser's Beach, sulking grounds for defeated bull elephant seals, I wait to talk to two surfers who've been braving the white sharks. I've been chatting with their girlfriends, two UCSC students who are heavily New Age in their outlook on a haphazard, violent death by shark. They trust their lovers' good karma to bring them back alive.

The cold damp wind is really whipping now, shoving the swell into a sloppy mush. The surfers finally come in, blue-lipped from the cold, and towel off briskly. Now these are some hardy action studs, shouldering aside the elephant seals and the great white sharks for a crack at this frigid and thoroughly mediocre surf; these are surf martyrs, in my opinion. They loom as large as the bronze statue back in Santa Cruz. And naw, they don't worry about white sharks. They're mostly worried I'll give away their secret spot.

"It's a smorgasbord out there," they say. "The sharks pig out on the seals. Tell 'em it's real sharky."

They confidently slip their boards under their arms and trot off to join their girlfriends. Today, these guys get the ladies.

The surfers on Oahu, however, seem to like their odds less and less. They have come here to the world-class breaks of the North Shore to make their mark in the surfing world. It can only be done here. California, Florida, South Africa, Australia — everywhere else is local; the

North Shore alone is a surfing universal. For this reason, a shark attack on the North Shore seems almost a violation of the sacred, a profanation of a nearly religious trust. The faithful here have focused their lives in the water, and the shark they have to share it with, the tiger shark, has been doing some very bad things in their church.

Like the white shark, the tiger shark can see contrast, and therefore surface prey, very well. Unlike the white shark, the tiger shark seems to deserve the reputation of man-eater. It will eat people, and does so under a variety of unpredictable circumstances.

When a tiger shark in the 12- to 16-foot range — hefty enough to swallow a man whole — bit a chunk out of Gary Chun's surfboard, from rail to stringer, on December 23, 1992, Chun became the fourth Oahu surfer to be attacked by a tiger shark that year, the third on the North Shore. Suddenly the mood on the five-mile stretch of precious reef was as starkly paranoid as that of a small town terrorized by a serial killer.

This was peak season, when the whole surfing world was in town for the Triple Crown of Surfing, and professional surfers and photographers were trying to make careers out in the impact zone. After the attack on Chun, people started talking about the young bodyboarder, Bryan Adona, who had vanished on February 19, 1992, at dusk at a North Shore break called Leftovers. His board had been found the next morning at Waima Bay with a massive bite missing from the nose; his body was never found. Then there was Rick Gruzinsky, who lost a big piece of his board to the jaws of a tiger shark on October 22 at nearby Laniakea, just a mile or so up the beach from Leftovers. Then in quick succession came the fatal Romento attack on November 5, and now the attack on Chun.

Clearly the North Shore had a tiger shark problem on its hands, but why now? Had the big sharks always been out there, cruising the reefs, looking up at thousands of kicking limbs of surfers and bodyboarders? If so, what had made them suddenly turn nasty? Or had they only recently arrived, like a new plague?

Some thought all the attacks might be the work of a single rogue shark, a Tony the Tiger (the phantasm had already earned a nickname), a territorial fish, perhaps injured, which had decided that people were easy prey and was systematically whacking them. Some blamed the commercial fishermen for upsetting the balance of the food chain, starving the sharks of their natural prey; others turned that theory upside down and blamed the Endangered Species Act for protecting the green sea turtle and so surfeiting the sharks with an over-abundant near-shore food supply.

Still others who knew their shark history figured it was just about

LORD LONG ARMS, I PRESUME?

time. More than 20 years had passed since the last major shark eradications in the islands, in which nearly 400 tiger sharks had been killed — plenty of time to grow a bumper crop of big new tiger sharks. In early 1992 a bill to start up a new eradication program had been pulled from the floor of the state legislature. But by Christmastime a lot of people wanted the state to get back into the business of killing sharks.

In the small-town atmosphere that is Hawaii, a bitter argument raged. Native Hawaiians, fearing a shark slaughter, evoked the tradition of *aumakua*, the belief that ancestral spirits manifest through animal forms, including *Mano*, the shark. The North Shore surfers invoked their right to a reasonable degree of safety. Shark experts fretted about the dangers of manipulating the environment. Eradication, they argued, had never worked. In 1969 and again in 1971 the state had sent out boats and staff to fish for and then to kill as many of the big fish as they could find. Thousands of sharks of numerous species were killed, yet not even a month had passed after the 1971 eradication when a new attack occurred. Shouldn't the state have learned by now not to tamper with things it doesn't understand?

Although many might argue about its effectiveness, the state does have an elaborate system designed to protect people from sharks and, consequently, sharks from people. The first step is to distinguish between unconfirmed and confirmed sightings. Many sightings, in fact, are of imaginary sharks. But if a sighting is confirmed — by a lifeguard, an expert, even a quorum of rational people — and the shark isn't too large or menacing, it's "monitored." If the confirmed shark is eight feet long or longer, or if it acts like it wants to bite somebody, it's closely monitored. Jet-skis are brought in to harass it back to deep water, rescue craft are summoned, megaphones and vehicles are dispatched to warn swimmers, and fire department personnel may be brought in to help. If the shark won't go away, if it's still breaking bad, then the State Shark Task Force — a committee of public safety officials, scientists, and Native Hawaiian cultural representatives — is called in. They may decide to monitor it with extreme prejudice. That's when the Task Force calls in the hunter.

With an irony that embraces all the contradictions of the tiger-shark debate, the Task Force's chief tiger-shark hunter is also the tiger shark's most outspoken advocate, Steve Kaiser, Curator of Fishes at Oahu's Sea Life Park. As a naturalist, a scientist in the fine old sense (he's conducting a tagging project at his own expense), a longtime Hawaiian, a fisherman, a surfer, Kaiser's sympathies have been painfully divided. But the true tragic figure, in Kaiser's view, is the tiger shark.

Through the plate glass behind Kaiser's desk you can look right into the park's Hawaiian Reef exhibit, see the rays wing by, watch small sharks bump the glass and swim on in their lapping of the tank. More so than the other fish, they seem to be looking for a way out.

Kaiser, a big man (about 260 pounds, a longboarder by necessity), speaks tenderly about a young female tiger shark he caught last March and brought back alive to this tank. "She was just a beautiful, graceful creature," he says, one he'd hoped would prove helpful in his colleagues' research on tiger-shark maturation. When its health declined rapidly (they don't do well in captivity) Kaiser released it. The capture and the release both made news, and there was talk of a lawsuit if the tagged juvenile shark grew up to be a man-eater.

But Kaiser wasn't about to let the small female die. Most of the tiger sharks he'd seen lately had ended up dead. Kaiser was part of the Task Force's first action, when he captained the boat sent to kill the shark that had killed Martha Morrell, a Maui resident who had been attacked as she swam near her home on Maui in 1991. His crew landed a 12-foot tiger shark but found nothing in its stomach, possibly because the tiger shark can extrude and flush out the entire organ under the stress of capture. On the North Shore and off the Leeward Coast, Kaiser and crew have taken out eight more big tigers. Kaiser has accepted the necessity of hunting problem sharks, but he regrets each kill.

"They're the jet fighters of the sea," he says. "They fly through the water, zero to thirty in a split second, and turn on a dime." And they're smart fish, he says, "real intellects." Kaiser has watched a tiger shark nudge a piece of bait for 20 minutes and then swim away. He says some tigers learn to eat the bait around the hook.

Kaiser and other Task Force members worry that the work they've done on the North Shore in the name of control and safety may not have been of any use at all. In fact, a real vigilantism has sprung up in the islands, as local fishermen have taken it upon themselves to hunt sharks in areas where families and friends surf. By conservative estimates, locals have removed about 25 sharks in the last two years — almost double the number killed by the Task Force — enough that biologists fear damage is being done to the ecosystem.

Moreover, says Kaiser, "Fishing 100 hooks off the North Shore won't prevent an attack. In fact, bloody baits could attract sharks. If somebody was fishing for sharks where I was surfing, I'd be pissed off."

Kaiser suspects that the root of the tiger-shark controversy in Hawaii may lie in the way the problem itself has been perceived. "When Marty Morrell was killed," he says, "there was a real feeding frenzy."

"By the sharks?" I ask, wincing.

"No, by the media!" Kaiser says. He stalks to a filing cabinet and brings back a tabloid with the headline, "Terror in Paradise!"

Who is protecting the tiger shark, Kaiser wants to know, and why, in a world that tolerates so many other horrors — muggings, murders, car wrecks — does everyone have to crack down so hard on the shark?

There is, he allows, something unusual going on in the North Shore area around Laniakea and Leftovers. He'd love to figure it out. He has an idea about the markings on the rails of the attacked surfers' boards. "They're identical. You know the mistaken-identity theory? I know that a lot of people don't believe it, but the fact of the matter is it's a good theory."

And then there's that old culprit again, human population, always pushing the boundaries and the odds. Kaiser remembers surfing Hawaii in the sixties, when ten was a crowd. Now there are 70 or more surfers in the lineup at Sunset Beach. Every little break has somebody in the water. Attacks are inevitable under such conditions, he says, and every new attack is another nail in the tiger shark's coffin.

"People have all of a sudden become unwilling to accept the risk that they could get bit," Kaiser says. "We have a real problem with people thinking the state has to do something for everybody.

"I'll be real honest with you," he says. "If we find out we have a shark problem we should do something, but until we do, I don't think we should go out there and whack them just because it makes somebody feel good. What is this? Retribution?"

Agitated, Kaiser rises out of his chair. He seems amazed at his own involvement in the Task Force's attempt to control something so little understood, and disgusted that they've had to resort to such crude tools — cables, hooks, guns — when what's needed is insight, a few facts.

"I don't know if you believe in God," he says, "but when you're called, you're going. I could be attacked by a shark. But I'm not going to blame the shark. My daughter could be attacked by a shark, and if she was, I'd be really sad. But I'm not going to blame the shark. I'm just not."

As this was being written in mid-March, another surfer, Roddy Lewis, was attacked off Maui. The Task Force decided against hunting the shark, but two surfers went out and killed the tiger shark they believed had mauled Lewis. It was Hawaii's first shark attack of 1993.

Note:

A decade later, the "mistaken identity" theory remains plausible but unproved — and perhaps unprovable. An interesting companion theory is that the keen-eyed Great White makes few mistakes, but, confronted by the novelty of a thrashing great ape, indulges in a bit of "investigatory biting" to learn more about the potential meal. Whether the result is a crunched surfboard, a bad scare, multiple stitches, or a sheered off limb may depend on just how hungry the shark is at the time.

At any rate, following the summer of 2001, referred to thereafter derisively as "The Summer of the Shark," the media has been much more restrained in its reporting of attacks, and there has been little complaining about sharks from American bathers. Surfers, in the meantime, have continued to proliferate disastrously.

LORD LONG ARMS, I PRESUME?

Percival Gordon, King of the Howlers

"Listen, mon! Listen!" he said. "You hear them?"

Percival Gordon cut the outboard motor, and we drifted between green barricades of wild cane. Beyond that tangled picket line, from somewhere miles up Monkey River, deep within the jungle, came distant dinosaurian roars.

"Sounds like Godzilla on fire," I started to say, coughing out clouds of smoke and passing the mighty Mayan spliff back to Percival. The Maya grow all the best herb in Belize, the guide had told me, and their smoke was good for conjuring all the apparitions of the jungle, real and imaginary.

"Listen," Percy Gordon said, holding up a hand.

The river burbled under the boat, and the harsh, guttural shrieks came again and again, regular as a bombardment. Black howler monkeys, maybe several troops, sounding their morning territorial bellowings from the treetops. *Alouatta pigra*, just twenty-five pounds max, is the earth's loudest land creature; the alpha-male monkey's high-decibel kiss-my-asses can be heard from as far as three miles away. The monkeys called again, and Percival chuckled, probably because he had just then figured out the monkeys' true tree address, somewhere in the seemingly limitless bush of the Toledo district of southern Belize. "Ya, mon, what I tell you, we find lots of monkeys, for true." He tugged the starter cord and the Honda 50 grumbled to life, and we sped off in pursuit of the outrageous roars.

Seated on the stern with his arm slung over the throttle, Percival Gordon assumed a heroic pose — Moses, the tiller for tablets, or Lorenzo de' Medici on his tomb — utterly relaxed, sufficient, as inevitable to his boat as rider to horse. I sat below on the middle bench of the twenty-five-foot open fishing boat, Laocoön in fogged reading glasses, struggling in the coils of microphone cords and camera gear. I was taking my first baby steps to videotaping wildlife, but it was turning out to be more productive to shoot Percival Gordon — jungle genius, beastmaster, ace jungle-river guide — especially when the mood struck and he channeled his flamboyant alter ego, Barracuda Billy.

"Up that creek, there, called Black Creek, I killed a jaguar," Percy said, throttling down the Honda until it was just a background harmonic for his narrative mood. I sensed a Barracuda Billy moment coming and shot him in close-up.

"I was huntinin'," he said, his Garifuna dialect giving the word a double gerund. (Fishinin', huntinin' — they double up on the best things.) "Not in this boat but a dory." He meant the little dugout canoes that the Belizeans sometimes still use. "There was a great big tree fall across that creek, so I lean way back to get under it." He mimed the backbend tilting back his bearded face. "I look up and there's this jaguar, right above me on the trunk of the tree, ready to jump. And he jump! He go for me, brah! But I always have my gun ready. I'm falling backward from the jaguar and shooting at the same time. I paddle like hell away from that place, mon. When I come back, real quiet, sneaking around, I see he dead, all right, shot right here." He touched a finger to the center of his forehead and winked — hey, why shoot a leaping jaguar in any other place?

Carving a hard starboard turn, Percy coasted the boat silently into the overhanging brush. Vampire bats (impossible to video in their camouflaged clusters) thrived in the perpetual dusk of the thick brush at the river's edge. A brief bushwhack took us to where the jungle opened up and there was room to walk and gaze up at the high hollow places in the hundred-foot canopy. It was the rainy season, so the jungle was flooded in spots. We slogged through mocha water up to our knees, Percy slashing with his machete (two syllables here in southern Belize: *ma-shet*), me staggering behind, video-taping, trying to keep him centered in the LCD display, which was a little like backing a car through shrubbery using only the side-view mirror. With each zig and zag, the howler whoops intensified. The alpha males must've known we were coming by then. Wherever you looked, there was the monotony of a million wading trees, like botanical wallpaper on a planetary scale. The mosquitoes were ferocious if you slowed down. It was slog or die.

"Percy, you ever have to save anybody who was lost here before?" I asked.

"More than a few," he said, slicing a vine with the machete. "More than a few."

"They must've been very grateful!" I yelled. We had to shout now to be heard over the howlers, and about then I started psychically wincing, flinching on the level of my autonomic nervous system: *"How ya like being shouted at? Huh? Don't like it, do ya?! Huh? Huh!"* Oh, Jesus, no, I never have liked being shouted at. It seemed we hiked under a weight of vibrational admonition unknown since the last moments of Eden.

"Whup, whup, whup, whaaa!" Percy suddenly shouted. At that, the monkeys went ape-shit — literally — shat and pissed at us en masse. Percy allowed himself a muffled little chuckle from his safe position a few paces back. But finally, by following the descents of their contemptuous droppings, I caught a glimpse of many dark, furry bodies rustling the leaves. Now, to really push his buttons, Percy started slapping the trunk of the alpha male's tree with the broad side of the machete, belting out his challenge at the same time. Whack, whack, whack! "Whup, whup, whup, whaaaa!" That pushed the alpha male right over the edge.

"Here he come! Here he come!"

And here he came, rumbling down the limb, posturing like crazy, strumming at his chest as if playing some sort of pain-releasing air-guitar. On the charge, alpha monk shaped his mouth into a big black O, and, with his throat expanding like the bell of a trumpet, he aimed his wrath at us and gave us hell. It was the primal scream at the primal scene, how great Nobodaddy Himself might sound as he came roaring out of the celestial sheets of the firmament, his coitus with the cosmos interruptus: *"Can't you give us some fucking peace, you little shits?"*

Wild ferocity is something you don't see much of anymore, and nowhere else that I know of will you see such a sustained barrage as the one provoked by Percival Gordon. It resonated with me in a place of great infantile vulnerability and thwarted oedipal competitiveness. Now that we'd stopped, the mosquitoes caught up. They lined up along my fingers as I tried to hold the camera still. One at a time, they bit the end of my nose, and two by two they climbed into my ears like jet pilots revving the turbines of my nervous system.

Percy orchestrated a couple more shouting contests, during which I thought the howler might simply blow up. Instead, he abruptly concluded his tirade and wandered back up the limb, and they all — wives, children, the one-day successor to the throne sulking among the ladies — departed for another tree, their languid brachiation making a great show of having meant to move all along.

"You get the shots?" Percy asked. "I look one time you got the shot right on his balls. Heh, heh, heh."

Well, that was thematic, anyway. But my best shots, I was sure, were close-ups of Percy issuing his challenge, standing up to that monkey braggadocio, laughing — Barracuda Billy at his best.

We were two hours up the river from Percival Gordon's village, also called Monkey River, and we made it back in time for lunch at Miss Alice's Restaurant, where his mother, Alice herself, served us spicy Creole-style fish and rice and fresh avocado slices. I had to keep reminding myself: Miami International was just three hours away. Hell, Placencia, a growing beach-resort town, was only forty minutes away, though by a tricky water route over shallow reefs and through a maze of mangrove passages. Closer still, on the north side of Monkey River, about a mile apart from each other, were two beach-front micro-resorts, the terminal tentacles of the encroaching universal middle class, offering complete comfort and fully stocked bars. Both take Visa. But Monkey River village, on the far side, was still floating free, for good and ill, of all that.

It's the kind of place where not long ago a local looked up from his TV and saw a jaguar peering in through his window. Where, obeisant to their own obscure schedule, ants periodically enter the village, billions of them, a great licking tongue out of the bush, and there's nothing you can do but stay out of their way while they take whatever they want, which fortunately is just tiny particles of rubbish. They just come right in and clean house.

A generation ago, Monkey River thrived as a banana town. Freighters from Great Britain anchored offshore near the river mouth, and men paddled dugouts laden with fruit out to the ships, men who were giants of strength and labor, who commanded intimate knowledge of sea and jungle and were wise with the perennial wisdom that stretches all the way back to the first men, and that is everywhere being lost. Then a fungus struck the banana plants, and the work moved inland and north, and Monkey River's population began to dwindle, from several thousand down to its current 189 souls.

"Too much bush!" was how Alice summed up Monkey River's crisis. "They've forgotten us in Belize City, and now the jungle take over."

She said the young people didn't care to know the jungle anymore. They'd rather make some money lobstering, or guiding, and stay away from the bush. Percy did some lobstering, partners with two of his brothers, and guided, of course, but he was still a hunter, and that more than anything else, I think, made him the best guide. He still had a real relationship with the bush.

Out on the river, he was a fount of bittersweet Rastafarian homilies on the bush, that praised as much as they described. "That iguana," he would say, amused, congratulatory, his voice gone all syrupy with the sheer leisureliness of bush life at its best, "is gonna just eat those good morning-glory flowers or look for some figs or plums that he likes. Right now he's just enjoying the sunshine, warming himself up, eatin' a little, lookin' aroun'." He appreciated all the animals' abilities to make themselves comfortable, to work their gigs as copacetically as they could, and then chill out somewhere, in nooks and crooks and fine lookouts, and savor the sweet flavor of passing life.

And wasn't that a lot like life in Monkey River? Hardly anybody had the kind of job where you had to be somewhere at a certain time or answer to a boss. The lobstermen would blow off work whenever they weren't in a lobsterinin' mood. There were no police in Monkey River, though there was a dilapidated jailhouse that nobody had ever been locked up in except the former policeman himself, who'd briefly gone giddy with power and rum and made an ass of himself at a village dance. The community locked him up, then he quit, and there was no replacement on the way.

There are no cars in Monkey River. The streets are all of grass. They'd been newly mown when I arrived. Shredded candy wrappers were blowing around everywhere, attesting to all the kids with a sweet tooth, and to the two little general stores where their cravings could be appeased.

"You can go anywhere you want here, do anything you like," Percy had told me when he first brought me ashore. And so it had seemed to me a place of great peace and leisure. I woke up every morning with the roosters at around 4 a.m. and looked out the window of my room in Enna's Hotel — ALL NIGHT ELECTRIC FAN, the hand-painted sign advertised — and across the grassy alleyway my neighbor would already be up, sitting on his stoop. And though I would go back to sleep, when I awoke again hours later, he would still be at his meditations, a real Zen master. By first real light, Alice would be in the restaurant kitchen setting great cast-iron pots on low heat, where they'd simmer all day. I'd hear the *shh! shh! shh!* of Alice's slippers scraping along the hard-packed dirt outside the restaurant and know the kettle was on. By eight in the morning, there'd be a considerable stir of extended family and visiting neighbors in the cool covered space under Alice's house on stilts, where they would talk into the afternoon, maybe chop a bit of coconut, do some laundry by hand.

In the heat of the day, many of the women gathered under the shade of a palm and played hours of bingo. From anywhere in the village, you could hear Shirley, the great bingo caller, crying out, *"O niney-one! B tree!"* By the river, on the other side of town, a block away, the men assembled around a bench they called the Base and bragged and smoked and gossiped the day away. With a little effort (though also with considerable skill and knowledge), the people of Monkey River could, from the sea and the jungle, satisfy all their needs — except perhaps a certain sort of ambition, and frozen margaritas.

It was in search of the latter that Percival and I crossed the river that Saturday afternoon and dropped by the Monkey House Resort, where we met proprietor Martha Scott, a former oil-rig environmental technician from Texas. Monkey House had a computer, which was kept covered in plastic, and a Web site, and since this was just after the Love Bug virus, we talked about that and other online menaces. Percy had told me great stories about the monsters of the bush — Mama Le Teytey, a female vampire that flew in a ball of fire; the Duende, a backwards-footed dwarf who wore a great hat that hid his face; and even Barracuda Billy, the archetypal Belizean wild man, the local Paul Bunyan or Pecos Bill, who was a monster of indigenous competence, a wooer of lost women, too true, too much dude. So I told Percy about some of the north's goblins — computer crooks, identity thieves. One had recently got hold of my wife's credit-card number and was buying airline tickets out the wazoo. Not that we were going to have to pay, but still. Scary, eh?

Was Percival Gordon impressed? I guess I was hoping so.

Then Martha, Percy and I headed up the coast to Bob's Paradise for a couple more rounds. Bob's setup was a lot like the Scotts' Monkey House — a few tastefully appointed rooms, a palm-thatched beachfront bar. His partner, Blanca, brought out chips and salsa, and we drank beer and watched the pet chicken lay an egg between Coke cartons behind the bar. Entertaining at a certain level of intoxication. After a few Belikins, Bob told us how he'd come to be Bob of Bob's Paradise, how he'd survived a series of meretricious ex-wives and grueling sixteen-hour shifts as a pastry chef working for alimony money and emerged miraculously from the concrete hell of south Florida, big-bellied and bald as a baby, new-born in Belize. "Where I don't have to do a goddamn thing I don't want to do ever again!"

By this time Blanca had put on a rock'n'roll tape, and she and Martha were dirty dancing with each other behind the bar. I challenged Percy to a game of horseshoes, and, with Bob loudly cheering against me, I kicked Barracuda Billy's butt in match after match. (He'd never played before; I have a pit behind my house.) And I was on, baby! I'd been in Percy's territory all week, following his lead; now he was in mine — clang! clang! — piss-artist that I am. I was merciless with the shoes.

But I don't think it was losing at horseshoes that Percival Gordon minded. No, more likely it was the whole week of having the camera in his face and just the steady abrasion of two men in a small boat that got him worrying about what we were doing with the camera and what it might mean for him and Monkey River, if anything at all.

Then it was my last day; we were just prowling the river, and Percy talked about one of the best times he'd ever had on Monkey River.

He'd been hired as a guide for researchers from the University of Calgary who were studying the howler monkeys, and they'd recorded his howler calls along with the real thing. "The machine was fooled," he told me. "It couldn't tell a difference." One day he shot an antelope for them and roasted it, a feast for everyone, and one night, taking some of the grad students out in his boat for a cruise, he caught a four-foot croco-dile for a joke. He told me how he ordered everybody out of the boat, so that they gathered round him, up to their thighs in the water. And then, when everybody was real quiet and close, he goosed the croc.

"It goes, 'Bwahh!' Just crazy, mon, trying to get away, and I look around and they all piled in the boat, everybody just jump in the boat and everybody laughing, freaked out! I make a fire that night on the sandbar, and we have these good bottles of rum, and one of the girls, she say, 'You Barracuda Billy, all right. You wrestle crocodiles and drink jaguar blood!' "

Percy's mood changed after he told me that. Maybe he was thinking — though I'll never know — that if chance had willed otherwise, he'd have been one of those university kids. He was smart enough, but in Monkey River the sea served for high school, the jungle for college. And maybe he'd fallen a little in love with that coed who'd called him Bar-racuda Billy, that cool young thing from the U of C in the great frozen north.

"If I had the money, I'd be out of here like flash, *bwah*!" he told me.

I was shocked. What a waste that would be — Barracuda Billy work-ing to pay his mortgage in some suburb, like me.

Then he said, "Listen. When you gone, they gonna come to me. These people that you taken their picture, they gonna come to me with their shit."

I knew what he was talking about. The guys at the Base, the gossip group. I could imagine the sort of envy that might arise in a tiny community where everybody knew absolutely everything about one another. And there I was, mercifully oblivious, wielding that little camera on a stick all week as if it were a Car Vac and I was sucking up all the authenticity from every corner of the place — worse than the damn ants. And there was Percy helping me to it, the "star" of something suspiciously like TV, probably making a lot of money while nobody else got anything.

But there was nothing I could do about that. Except become extremely paranoid for a little while. Percy had talked a lot about hunting wild boar in the swampy jungle bottomlands, how they traveled in herds of a hundred or more and you could hear them from far away, the gnashing of their tusks like cicadas. "You got to have your shit, mon! You gon' hunt the boar, you got to have some balls, bwah!" And he'd talked about shooting the gibnut, a rodent the size of a suckling pig, easier game (also known as the royal rat, because Queen Elizabeth had eaten one on her visit to Belize). Now I got hung up on that word — gibnut, geebnut, give not. I was the give not! Barracuda Billy was gonna fucking shoot me.

And then I had a moment of inspiration. Percy had just spotted a basking crocodile, just a six-footer, and since I'd blown it the last time we'd found one — couldn't get focused in time, didn't anticipate its slithering retreat — I handed over the camera to him. "You've got better eyes than I do. You shoot it."

Of course, I was getting the better end of the deal again. I got to drive the boat, which I'd been dying to do all along. Percy shot the croc, and he shot Percy Jr. on the prow, chip off the Barracuda Billy block. He was the auteur now, and I was the kibitzer at the stern, saying, "That's a good shot there, yeah, shoot that," as he'd been doing to me all week. And he shot me at the tiller — a lot — flipping the LCD display around so I could admire myself in miniature, as I'd done for him, to him, plenty of times. "Cool!" I said. There I was, sunburned, twitchy, nervous, uncertain about the boat, uncertain about the river, uncertain about everything except that whatever it was we were doing, we were finally in it together.

Montserrat in Ashes

You couldn't tell from the northern half of Montserrat, where everybody lives now, that just on the other side of that hill the earth had cracked open like a boiling egg. And it was still cooking. The rumor on the ferry over from Antigua was that the volcano's dome was building at a rate of one VW bus per second. I imagined one of those coiling serpents of ash sold as fireworks, times one hippie van per tick. Big. Bigger. Bigger'n ever. Too freaking big. The rumor was, it was going to blow.

But did any one really seem concerned? No. No one at all. Not on the ferry, which was full of festive weekenders. Not on the dock at Little Bay, which looks more like a smuggler's cove than a real port of entry. Not the customs guys who somnolently stamped us through their shed at the foot of the rugged northern cliffs. Definitely not the man who worked the customs queue like a boisterous politician, crying, "Welcome to Montserrat!" in a booming voice, shaking hands, bowing, laughing maniacally. "Welcome! Welcome!" He was catching the ferry leaving the island. He wasn't concerned. But on the cab ride up to the hotel, the first pedestrian we passed was stark naked except for a sandwich board that read: REPENT YE IN DUST AND ASHES! He had besmirched himself with ashes in example. *He* was concerned.

Just the opposite was Jadine Glitzenhirn, general manager of Tropical Mansion Suites, Montserrat's only hotel. The Mediterranean-style hostelry commanded an incredible view of Little Bay and the whole northern end, which looks a little like the scrubby parts of Marin County, California, though in much need of millionaires. You could see all that there was in the north so far: along the waterfront at Little Bay, new shops and bars had sprung up, many of them miniature reincarnations of businesses that had moved farther and farther north — some of them two or three times — one step ahead of fire and ash.

Beginning on July 18, 1995, when the Soufriere Hills Volcano awoke from its millennia-long slumber, the island had been rocked by a series of devastating eruptions. The capital, Plymouth, was plunged into daytime darkness and evacuated twice, the second and final time in April '96. The Plymouth government had staked out its new barracks-style headquarters near the new settlement on a dramatic cliff overlooking the sea. And inland on the Silver Hills, the "Immediate Housing" communities — tiny, spanking-new wooden homes laid out in a grid, a Caribbean Levittown — were taking root, their residents beginning to beautify their plots with gardens.

The grand hotel, opened that December as a symbol of confidence in the future and no doubt to try to kick-start tourism in the north end, is by far the biggest building on the island now. "We're hot, but we're cool," Glitzenhirn said. Professionally friendly on top of just being nice, she was upbeat despite having lost her previous livelihood, her airport gift and dress shop, called Just Looking, when an exudiate of mud took out the terminal and three quarters of the runway. "We don't have the south anymore, but we now have a very interesting volcano, which people should come see," she said.

That was just what I wanted to hear. Enjoy the volcano. Somebody. Please.

And really, what other attitude can anyone take toward an exploding mountain? The Montserratians who stayed have become amateur volcanologists, like Cecil Cassell, whose office in the government barracks above Little Bay was my first stop. A mountainous man with a deep bass voice, Cassell has developed a rich ambivalence toward the volcano. On the one hand, he'll have to hire a surveyor to locate his house under the mud once it's safe to go looking for it; on the other hand, he's seen wonders. "It's such a beautiful sight to see pyroclastic flow traveling along the water and just boiling it. The thing is so beautiful," he said, "you cannot know it is happening and not look. I strongly recommend that persons go on top of Garibaldi Hill. From there you have a magnificent panoramic view of the volcano."

So that's where I was headed by motorbike, puttering along the coast road, a beautiful ride high above the far-flung fathoms of the sea, and then down into deep, shady "ghauts," as the stream-cut valleys are called. Then up through a couple of tiny villages, which explains why hardly anyone lived in the north before the eruptions — because man is not a goat — finally, after about twenty minutes, the road dropped down into a broad valley and disappeared under ash. A metal pole blocked the main fork; another lane seemed to lead past a big EXCLUSION ZONE sign. That was the road across Belham Valley, former site of George Martin's Air Studios and of Montserrat's beloved golf course. The valley is now a ruin of mud and broken trees and car-sized pumice boulders. I held my breath through ash drifts up the axels, and then the road re-emerged from the dust and began to climb switchbacks up Garibaldi Hill, a steep ziggurat with expensive, abandoned villas built into its flanks.

From the top, I could see the whole Montserrat disaster, like something out of Dante. To the south lay Plymouth, the formerly graceful capital city, most of its buildings buried up to the eaves in mud, its once-lush foliage scorched to ragged stumps. Looking back north, I could see how Garibaldi Hill itself had diverted a tongue of the mudflow through Belham Valley. Looking inland and up, I could at last see the Soufriere Hills Volcano, squatting athwart the island like a giant ogre, its sloping flanks a stubble of ash-coated snags, its head brooding in the clouds. You could imagine easily enough the mountain's previous generosity, how it had conceived the island long ago in violence and then mellowed for a millennium or two, its shoulders softening as they aged. The old evidence of birth by fire, the deep ash, turned to fertile dirt, and the people came. It was a people trap, a cannon aimed at a picnic basket, the kind no knowledge will help us avoid because it's so intrinsically what we need and want — beauty and food at once. As creatures, we'll take our goddamn chances every time. And we'll adapt.

Soufriere had divided Montserrat in half, as if with a sword of fire, and what was left for habitation was the geologically young part, beautiful in its own right but too steep and rocky to be easy. The luxe life was lost, if not forever then for a good long while. There was this beast to contemplate, though, and the ghost town, Plymouth, the new Pompeii, which seemed unspeakably beautiful. Even in its ruins you could see the artifice, the instinctive proportions of the tropic port done just right, on a simple, human scale, made all the more poignant for its lost charm. That was the landscape, anyway, postbellum — post-nuclear-bellum; the comparison was inescapable and sobering.

I came back to Garibaldi Hill every day, knowing that at any moment, with a tremendous sonic boom, Soufriere might launch a mushroom cloud of fire and ash thirty thousand feet into the air, and that at the blue-black base of the billowing smoke, dark thunderclouds would lash the mountaintop with bolts of lightning while it glowed and spat burning meteors and loosed pyroclastic flow that would boil the sea. Soufriere is a window on the geologic truth of life on this planet: We live, precariously as hell, on a thin, shifting crust above molten fire.

On my last trip to Garibaldi Hill, the trade winds were blowing a gale, kicking up a dust storm in the deserted streets of Plymouth, with clouds of ash a hundred feet high. All was flowing down in the exclusion zone, muted, smudged like an old photo, from the base of the volcano to miles out to sea, where the pallid cloud, like a dusting of pastels or the scales of a butterfly's wing, subtly blended with the blue of the sea and sky. At last the wind had stripped Soufriere's peak of its clouds and I could see the jagged crater, the caliber of the gun. Suddenly I was disinclined ever to witness the big show of an eruption. Frankly, I was *concerned.*

I was headed back to the hotel at top motorbike speed, passing through the village of Salem, the surviving settlement closest to the volcano, when a figure in rags waved me down. "Donkey Ears, my long-lost brother!" he greeted me. "I knew you in Babylon," he said, and a great deal more, full of biblical references, grinning implication, and finally a merry blessing that I be safely on my way. Okay. Thank you. But Donkey Ears? Well, maybe they had grown a little, listening for that boom that never came. And surely my donkey ears were pricked when I boarded the ferry and it pulled away from Montserrat, and the whole way to Antigua while it dwindled out of sight. I am listening still.

This Isn't Boca, Baby

In the end, it was the plumber, Don Jose Rivera, who unhoused me and drove me from Rincon. I call him Don Jose because he arrived, like a true caballero, mounted on his backhoe, which he steered with plump, magisterial dignity. And no conquistador could've ridden more rough-shod over my corner on the tropical oceanfront of Rincon, Puerto Rico. Not that the Don was alone in offense. Rather, in the reckoning we kept of how pleased we were — or not — to be in Rincon, his was the first stinging blow to hit me and not my wife. As for H.B., for months she had been teetering right on the brink of rising up from wherever she was reclining in near-despair and debilitating boredom and screaming, "I can't stand this place a moment longer!" She was just waiting for me to set the date. I was waiting for Don Rivera.

It was the February of our second winter in Rincon, and tourist surf-ers still sped up and down its hills in rental SUVs whose rooftops bristled with quivers of high-performance surfboards. But they were studies in futility, these gambling surf travelers from the megalopolises of El Norte. They were all testosterone and adrenaline fizzling and popping on a be-calmed coast. Most had entirely missed the big show, the twenty-foot swell that had hit the west coast of Puerto Rico like a four-day earth-quake. But we expatriates, we gringo locals, we hadn't missed it. As far as waves went, I never missed a ripple from my Nick Carraway niche on the very point of Barrio Puntas, a jungle-covered limestone land's end that protrudes into the Caribbean like the thumb of some misguided hitch-hiker looking for a ride back to Miami. Most of us had passed through there to get here and couldn't have been more pleased with the contrast. Miami was a sweltering plain of concrete, fake beaches abutting a dead sea; here were undulating hills dipping down to lively waters, leopard-spotted with coral coves. From my surf-check rock, I often spotted pods of humpbacked whales shouldering the swells of the famously turbulent Mona Passage between Hispaniola and Puerto Rico, and whenever the surf topped two feet, I was on it.

Only now my priceless lookout was very much imperiled, and not just by Don Rivera. H.B. had rock fever — bad. Normally effusive and hyperactive, she seemed bewitched by a Voodoo spell of torpor. Her seasonal work as a massage therapist should've been peaking, but the phone lines were down again. She had time on her hands instead of aching muscles. Time to brood on how the greater world was flowing on without her. Her culture was calling her, her family was calling. And the fucking phone (for H.B. it was always "the fucking phone") was dead again. Plus, our plumbing problem was rising to a head. When I'd told our friend David about the crisis of morale, he just grinned and said, "That's it, then." He'd seen it a dozen times. When the woman turned, the dude was gone, or divorced. "Face it," he said. "You're finished as a surfer."

And Rincon *was* all about surfing. Flash back thirty-odd years, to a skinny kid on a Styrofoam belly-board, pin-wheeling out into the mush of Jacksonville Beach, Florida. See the kid leap to his feet and trim that $3.99 piece of crap along a crumbling curl. You weren't supposed to be able to stand up on a board like that. Surely, you couldn't turn it; it didn't even have fins. But, you see, the kid had talent. Hell, not much talent. Just a niggling, nagging amount, the sort that creates everlasting doubt that maybe, just maybe, in the right place, at the right time, with the right confluence of forces — love, luck, will — that talent would hold up on the face of a significant wave. A dangerous wave. A blue, spewing monster cracking like thunder under whose bone-snapping lip the kid would draw the one perfect line. For one reason or another, I'd kept missing that showdown. I'd been a day late on a trip to Costa Rica, out of shape at Ocean Beach in northern California, out of my league on the North Shore of Oahu. Then circumstances conspired to give me my shot: I turned forty, landed a regular writing gig with a scuba diving magazine, and married an adventuresome woman who wanted a change of pace from managing non-profits. We tossed a dart at a map and — nice shot! — it happened to hit Rincon, where I could stake out a stretch of coast and wait for the best and biggest surf east of the Mississippi.

And now it all came down to Don Rivera. I needed another winter in Rincon, another go at a Tres Palmas twenty-footer, which meant another year's lease on our house, which we were due to re-up at the end of the month. But to have a chance at that, I believed, somebody had to fix our goddamn plumbing problem pronto. Or H.B. was going to scream. Scream and then leave, with or without me.

Foul odors wafted up from the little grassy mound in our backyard,

THIS ISN'T BOCA, BABY

where I whittled at a piece of mahogany while I waited for Rivera. It was a smelly lookout but an advantageous one from which I see could a little of everything that I liked about Rincon. Forward and westward, I could keep an eye on the sea and the sea-state. Behind me rose the green hills of Puntas, shaded by hundred-year-old mango and avocado and fiery flamboyant trees. On dry days, I could watch a little yellow tractor, driven by a nouveau-riche-boomer-surfer turned developer, gouging a new road up the limestone promontory, carving access to the jungle hillside he'd bought to subdivide. Surfers from the Sixties heyday had dubbed the formerly steepest road in Puntas "Bummer Hill," local wags were calling this new champion incline "Dumber Hill," for its promised impracticality. Still, the dude was living large, living the dream.

My dream was just a daydream, really, easily toppled, and I feared the Don, who was coming to tilt with it. I heard Rivera coming down the narrow hillside road through the traditional Puerto Rican section of Barrio Puntas, where the houses were all convivially cemented together like pastel barnacles. Rivera's backhoe echoed and was amplified by the cavernous carports in which little dogs behind wrought-iron grilles were going ballistic. I heard him long before I saw him. He had stopped, predictably, right in the middle of the road, blocking traffic of already-frustrated surfers while he exchanged pleasantries with beer-drinking cronies seated at the little plastic tables at the *colmado*. I heard the backhoe rumbling, dogs barking, horns tooting — it was a fiesta, a celebration of obstruction. Typical Rinconia. And then he rolled into view on the final sweeping turn on the gringo-fied seaside, where the stucco palazzo were spaced as far apart as the owners could afford. All around me were other *norteamericano* surfers, most of them East-Coasters, living among the local people's cattle, whose pasturage they were quietly buying up in a kind of beach-culture manifest destiny.

That February, it still wasn't too late to get in on the ground floor. There were still long stretches of empty beach-front where cattle stood on the dunes, ruminating over the surf. I was of half a mind to stake our claim (the half that fantasized it had the money) — buying a few scrappy hillside acres and living in a tent while I taught myself carpentry, wiring, plumbing — plumbing especially — and building codes and Spanish and general citizenship, overcoming my suburban know-nothing heritage. That was what our forerunners had done here back in the sixties and seventies — homesteaded like frontiersmen and women in a place that wasn't particularly under populated but that presented an aesthetic gap to exploit. In those days, the Puerto Ricans didn't surf. Up till the mid-eighties they even disapproved of bathing suits on local women. They preferred turf to surf, raising their pretty Paso Fino horses and *corriente* cattle and practicing the old vaquero arts, which was fine, only that Caribbean cowboy shit didn't sell in the States. But surfing would. Oceanfront real estate — neglected by the hill-dwelling Rinconenos and going for a dollar a square yard — *that* would sell. Big time, as we gringos say. It just might take a while, surfers being surfers. From the start, Rincon was a boomtown in a very laid-back real estate gold rush.

To the early gringo surfer settlers, hard-core alpha-male chargers who had outgrown home breaks from Cocoa Beach in Florida to Montauk Point in New York, the geographical genius of the place had been obvious at a glance. It was the surfers' equivalent of Aspen. The westernmost tip of Puerto Rico is a peninsula of serried points that protrude like the teeth of a circular saw into the immensely deep waters of the Puerto Rico Trench. Without a continental shelf to grind them down, storm swells marched in fast, steep, orderly processions into such classic point breaks as Middles, Maria's and Tres Palmas. Whenever a nasty Canadian cold front pummeled the East Coast, howling gales blowing frost down to the Florida orange groves, then Rincon would bloom its winter fairest (cool enough at night to snuggle under sheets) and host another volley of long-traveled waves, sculpted by the warm trade winds. For those of us who lived there for the surf, who'd wake up in the middle of the night to the artillery of its arrival, a new swell was like entertaining beloved out-of-town guests whose welcome never wore out.

But for H.B. (as for most other gringas shanghaied by surfers), once the novelty wore off, once the unadulterated pleasure of informing everybody that you were leaving the U.S. for the simple life of the islands had devolved into dealing with the reality month after month, the boredom and the narrowness and isolation — I'm afraid the only equivalent pleasure was entertaining *actual* human guests. H.B. was happiest when our friends came from the States and she could show them the beauty of the mountains and beaches and describe to them the quirky local culture, within which, or despite which, and without much help from me, she was good-naturedly wresting a measure of domesticity for us. She had plenty to be proud of on that score. It was she who had battled the bureaucracy of Rincon, which had learned its chops under colonial Spain and the pope in Rome, where authority is infinitely transferable upward like the smoke of incense. She battled by phone, when she could find a fucking phone that worked, and in person for the honor of Electricity and Water and Cable TV — commodities routinely bought and sold elsewhere but still jealously guarded in Rincon and often arbitrarily taken away. Just paying a bill sometimes required an exhausting war of nerves, like competing with an autistic child in a game of Monopoly. Of course, she was the one who had phoned and re-phoned Don Rivera, a chore I kept putting off and then forgot about completely when the swell arrived.

It had been a huge, high-season swell. Hundreds of surfers had been down from the States. The whole town went a bit crazy as it did for every swell. All day long, there would be a general scramble on the roads as surfers followed their hunches about the best break for the size and angle of the waves, the tides and wind conditions. Puerto Rican locals had long since embraced surfing; every kid ten or older owned at least a boogie board, and they would kick out to the takeoff zones by the dozens, a laughing, hooting, high-spirited mob. A Maria's Beach, the consensus best break in town, the cow-pasture parking lot filled up with old vans and beach buggies and rust-bucket sedans. The wooded point, shaded with palms and grand old mangoes, curved into a natural amphitheater for a show that lasted until long after sunset. By then the crowd at the Calypso Café would be overflowing into the street, surfers still streaming seawater, knocking back happy-hour beer and bragging about themselves and their buds. There would be pretty girls on horseback come to flirt with the gladiators. Bonfires on the beach. A sportsman's paradise.

And yet, perversely, I believe that in years to come, when nostalgia for Rincon waylays me on blustery winter days here in the efficient North, it will be for the times between major swells — the *smallish* days, when clean, well-mannered peaks swept in early in the morning, often to be gone by the afternoon; sneaker swells, when you might share the usually crowded break at Domes, offshore of the defunct nuclear plant, with one or two equally surprised and pleased locals; or evenings when Maria's looked iffy, but the waves turned out to be head-high and gorgeously back-lit by the setting sun. On those serendipitous occasions, there was no anxiety that your carefully selected un-crowded peak was about to be overrun by the next carload of surf-rabid *turistos*. No nagging fear of failure in the water when the swell maxed and the horizon humped up like a malevolently furrowed brow and you had to paddle for survival. No fear of drowning, to baldly state the fact. The time between — which was most of the time — when there was surf but not *serious* surf, and then the rest of the long tropical day to fill with some chosen form of idleness — that's what I'll miss.

Rivera Day was a day like that, and I planned to spend it — a golden coin from a diminishing stash — after my morning surf in front of our house at Pool's Beach (where the waves were small but pretty, nearly perfectly transparent, shaped by the coral of which I knew every knob), on top of the stinking hill in our backyard, under the shade of our coconut palms, in a long meditative session of wood carving. I was pleased with the piece, a little boat carved from a salvaged bit of actual boat, brutally studded with ten-penny nails, which I'd left in the wood, gradually exposing them until the thing looked martyred, penetrated from all directions. It was phallic, and, like all boats, feminine — an allegory of marriage. I called it *Bonheur*.

As I whittled away I could hear the old duffer next door wielding his machete, hacking at the growth that had rebounded in his absence. Our neighbor, the Texan, had the genteel gardener's puttering urge, which can wax rabid in the tropics. He would patrol his property line, harrowing down the shady nooks, and then, with his domain denuded down to punji stakes and browning banana leaves, he would retire to his hammock with a drink and his cell phone.

But I was at peace with Texas. He had done the harm that his sort will do. He was a fait accompli, an already exploded bomb. Congenitally unable to leave well enough alone, Texas had tossed up a pink, two-story rental unit between his place and ours, blotting out three quarters of our view. But a little jungle trail through the empty (for how long?) lot across the street led to the excellent lookout rock, a sunrise surf-check spot, which was my knight's move response to Texas' attempted mate.

More worrisome was the Texan's hired hand, the One-eyed Catman. I could see him skulking about under the pylons of the pink-stucco monstrosity, pretending to be doing some work. The One-eyed Catman had been among the first Rinconenos H.B. had met. I must have been surfing the time she had been returning from town on her bike with our first backpack of groceries and the One-eyed Catman had come up behind her, also on a bike, with what sounded like a tomcat in croker sack. The furious tom kept up a horrible yowling protest, so H.B. slowed down to let the man pass, to get that cat home or take it wherever he intended to finish strangling it. But he wouldn't pass, and the cat continued to howl. So she stopped. He stopped. H.B. looked back. No basket, no cat. The One-eyed Catman touched his groin. *Mowrr*! he said.

Since then, he had, in a sense, sexually imprinted himself on my wife. He intended to have sex with her, or beside her, or over her, certainly without her permission and with or without her knowledge. The One-eyed Catman, we later learned, was a notorious bushwhacker. These

THIS ISN'T BOCA, BABY

slinking, semi-public masturbators are a product of Old World sexual mores, which have the dual effect of sheltering local girls within a strict Roman Catholic purdah, while reducing gringas to the status of walking pornography, irresistible provocations for a spontaneous wank. The second time H.B. saw the One-eyed Catman was while she was sunbathing on our deck. Some shadowy premonition caused her to look up, and he was standing on the stoop of Big Pink, trousers at his feet, his T-shirt pulled over his head (his child-like way of hiding), having a go at One-Eye.

I hardly approved of the nuisance, but on a philosophical level and on practical grounds, I tended to see bushwhackers (unmarriageable rogue males with too much time on their hands and no talent for drinking) as symptomatic of other island traits that I liked: the complete reliable indifference and indolence of the police, for one (which went double for the sort of badgeless busybodies who so plague North American neighborhoods); the local tolerance of nearly everything, especially foolishness, up to and including imbecility, for another. A certain overall slovenliness and lackadaisicality and neglect. Litter on the beach, for instance, which you could train yourself not to see — picnics with paper-plate settings for twelve, pickets of rum bottles, chicken carcasses, foil-wrapped remains of rice and beans, and the inevitable loaded disposable diapers — the entire enterprise abandoned above the tide line with a Pompeian abruptness and a complete faith that the next hurricane would sweep things clean in a year or two. Also, there were the comatose rummies, the dead-drunk drivers, and the dew-lapped cattle wandering loose on the streets. This definitely wasn't Boca. I couldn't afford Boca Raton and wouldn't live there if I could. This was Barrio Puntas in Rincon, Puerto Rico, a tiny gringo surfers' colony grafted more or less peacefully, still more or less idyllically, onto a traditional village, a backwater even by Puerto Rican standards. I saw in the local refusal to get its shit together, to clean up and square away, a kind of noble passive resistance to the winds of change. Hey, if the place weren't fundamentally fucked up, if it were clean and things always worked, anybody could live here. Certainly, more people would come. And more people *were* coming anyway, from far away and with big bucks, buying up those oceanfront pastures, while I — I knew it already — was on the brink of being dispossessed of my lookout on the surf. I was holding on by my fingernails.

Which brings us back to Don Rivera and my little backyard rise, where I had set up a salvaged cable spool under the shade of palms and where I liked to beguile the time — between surf sessions and a modicum of real work — watching the world stir lazily around me. It seeped, my hill. It seeped a little, and it stunk somewhat. When the breeze was offshore (excellent conditions, if combined with a swell, for surf), the odor would waft indoors and bother H.B., bother her a lot, and she would call a plumber. The first plumber she called advertised "American plumbing," which meant that if a gringo phoned, he would eventually come and plumb. But American Plumbing could only scratch his head and chuckle. Gotta call Jose Rivera, he said.

You see, my promontory wasn't exactly a natural feature. It was more in the category of an ill-advised expediency. The original builder, perhaps daunted by the rocky soil, had simply placed the septic tank on a high point behind the house and buried it there. Oh, years ago. Of course, it eventually seeped. It gradually turned the driveway green. In the outside shower room at the foot of the hill, it produced a froggy, dismal, miasmic air, not ideal but indefinitely tolerable, I thought. And I feared Don Rivera. Feared all change, any threat to the delicate inertial symbiosis between the long-semi-broken and the one-day-to-be-fixed that a local man with heavy machinery might bring. But Don Rivera wouldn't come and wouldn't come and just wouldn't, despite dozens of phone calls over the course of half a year, in which H.B. would plead and he would shout (so she might better understand his rapid-fire, idiomatic, local Puerto Rican Spanish) until she had tearfully exacted *una promesa* that he would surely come tomorrow. And then he wouldn't come. This I secretly admired in the Don. I mean, would you want to come dig out a septic tank on a sunny day in February? I wouldn't.

But Don Rivera did come, came tooting his horn down that sweeping curve to the oceanfront.

Our street had no name, but he found it; and our house had no number, but Don Rivera knew it, since prior to a San Juan architect (our landlord), it had been owned by a local woman who had shot her boyfriend in it. It was a famous little house — famous, once, for its view. When Don Rivera arrived, he aimed his mount at our gate, which I had thrown open for him, shimmied his broad backside a little on his seat, and then backed up into our power pole. The streetlight came clanging down onto the asphalt. Live wires popped and sizzled. The dead phone line drooped like limp linguini. And the TV cable snapped loose, coiling and retreating into the brush like a beheaded snake. H.B. had just settled into the sofa with the curtains drawn to watch a Hitchcock movie on Turner Classics, and just as she was reaching for the popcorn, the TV went *boink!* And the fans died with a sigh. She came out onto the deck, assessed the situation at once — Don Jose looking up sheepishly at the teetering pole and the skewed fixtures, the One-eyed Catman sidling up to admire the disaster — and turned on her heel and went back inside.

What did the Don do next? He left nothing green standing. He gouged a deep pit in the old drainage field, then carted the greenish sludge across the street and onto the last of our view and dumped it. Dumped it and rolled over what he had dumped and went back for another load and another until he'd built a mud mound to rival the Texan's stucco low-rise. That was our new view. Don Rivera also flattened the little jungle, flattened it and buried it under crisscrossing tread marks in the sludge that hardened overnight like fossilized dinosaur tracks, which promptly convinced the pissed off owners of the lot to put up a fence and a locked gate. Checkmate on my favorite surf-check rock. Death of a niche.

Don Rivera worked for a week putting in a new septic tank, and when he was done we were living in a sea of mud and the surf had gone dead flat. Within a few days of the Don's departure, the new tank had begun to leak, though in a different direction. It now seeped into the Texan's domain. I saw in the this a metaphor, not entirely hopeless, for how things would play out in Rincon in the next several years. It would muddle on from rural backwater to semi-upscale resort — "From a Way to a Scene," as one old hipster surfer put it. The days of gated spa communities would come, but the spas would leak. From my niche I'd been watching prosperity come to Rincon, hoping it would arrive gently, seductively — new restaurants, a real library, whatever — in a way that would entice H.B. to want to stay. At the same time, I'd hoped it wouldn't come at all, that nothing would change. It had been like watching a horse race in which you had bet none of the horses would win.

And then there was the matter of that last big swell, and a couple of giant waves. The first had had my name on it. It was huge, it was perfect, it was going to break precisely, predictably, though on the grandest of scales. I'd been in the exact right spot to catch it, too. But I'd let it go by with a shiver. The next wave, the one behind it, was even bigger and already curling over, fire hoses of spray shooting skyward from the thick lip. I'd pushed my board away and tried to dive under, but it had come down into the dark deep water after me, as if to deliver a bit of advice with its hammering mass. That had been a perfect day in all respects — bright sunshine, light offshore winds, orderly if monstrous sets of waves, just a few fellow contenders in the lineup — and I wasn't likely to see a better one. But I'd been paddling for my life the entire time, taking extreme evasive action until that clean-up set finally caught me. Cart-wheeling along the coral bottom, engulfed in the deafening roar of near-drowning, I heard the message clearly enough: Not in this lifetime, kiddo.

No regrets, Rincon. In two years I'd caught a lifetime's worth of excellent, if not significant, waves. I'd had my shot at glory, and now the Don had offered me something like an honorable out. A face-saving excuse, at any rate. From my flattened backyard lookout, I surveyed Mount Rivera, heard the whisper of a surfless sea, sensed the summer doldrums coming, and said, "Ah, hell, let's leave, then." And H.B. said, "How soon?"

"Please insert coin."

The electronic voice speaks to me with authority, as if I were a child. But if I were a child would I be operating this dangerous machinery?

"Please insert coin."

All right, already. The coin slot is down there somewhere, down and under, where a child might stick a wad of gum and an adult find one.

I've wedged myself into this plastic egg of a helicopter game, Air Inferno; I've read the instructions and understood them poorly; found the coin slot and slid in two 25-cent tokens; located the start button and prepared for take-off. Now the engine is screaming like a Cuisinart on puree, the rotor blades thup-thupping, conceptually overhead.

Already I've had enough of this. Ahead through the windshield I see the wretched landscape of inexpensive computer generation — depressing de Chirico perspectives, ochre boulevards bisecting purple rectangular warehouses — a world I have little desire to visit and less hope of escaping, at least in this craft.

Who needs the world reduced to pixels? Those who cannot afford it otherwise. Reality is already badly diluted by the human brain (or so we strongly suspect); cut the phenomenal world again by the thinning agents of limited imagination and technical restraints and it's a very small world after all.

"Move up!" comes that commanding voice again.

What do you think I'm trying to do, fly down? "Move Up!" I hit random buttons, hoping to at least fire a cannon and blow something up. "Move up immediately!" There's madness in the engine's scream now, madness that explodes. A countdown appears on the screen — 10, 9, 8 … Pressure like this I don't need! I take my foot off the brake and at last I rise, I rise!

"Turn right!"

I jerk the joystick to the right, the orange landscape goes perpendicular, and then blows up with sounds of crashing and a tinkle of glass. I've wrecked my copter. Game over. The instant replay (an unexpected courtesy) shows how things looked from the control tower. Me just sitting there burning up my engine, and sitting there, and sitting there, and finally lifting off and flying sideways into the ground about 30 Air Inferno feet away. Real dumb.

And fairly expensive: about a dollar a minute for the incompetent. For those aces on the high score list — PDQ, TAT, POOP — punks who can fly this bird through training sessions and fire-fight missions, all the way to the level of congressional boondoggles, staying aloft to face ever greater digital annoyances, ever heavier electro-imaginary responsibilities — for them the game may be more cost efficient. But then they are dwellers in the Air Inferno.

Like that kid over there by the round Barrel of Fun entrance, the little Galaga junky sulking by the token machine. His latchkey sister is banging gators with a rubber sledge, but the young Goodman himself is up chit creek without a token. When I feed a bill into the machine he watches me with keen greedy eyes, then makes his pitch, hand out, grinning with that alleged charm of the very young, his small square teeth widely spaced like those of a tiny killer whale: "Can I have one?"

"No way," I say. Punk. Homunculus. Manikin. Larva. "Oh, all right. Here."

His little paw closes over the token and off he trots — no please or thank you — back to the whiz-bang din of the game room where photons and phasers and laser cannons zoom; small arms crackle; race cars rage; blows thud and big men in green underpants offer up orgiastic grunts. It's the wee id of male childhood canned for vending and the little ones soak it up with their big eyes and supple fingertips, slapping the dispenser buttons like bewitched lab rats as long as their money lasts. We shouldn't be surprised. All boys want the Bomb. They are born too close to the bone and blood of nature to be naturally good or innocent. Pac-Man said it all: life is no better than nor distinguishable from that electronic blip that eats another blip. Virtue must be learned. Innocence must be earned! That won't happen here in the Barrel of Fun.

But never mind. Think instead of the male destructiveness deferred, no small boon for the caregiver. Look at that pair of whelps giggling over the Simpsons' machine, crown-headed Bart whacking away with his skateboard — whackety-whackety-whack! And look at that older fellow, that strapping lad, how he zaps that intergalactic tapeworm wiggling down the screen. This guy is good! He's chewing that worm to bits. But there's always more worm! They're in a kind of stasis here, boy and worm, satisfaction and frustration wearing the same Janus mask. When the real worms come I want this kid as my door-gunner. Meanwhile, I better learn to fly that bird.

When I was small I had a tiny tin moose. It was brown. Animal brown. Wild brown. Except where someone in Taiwan had hastily dipped it into black enamel up to the fetlocks in front and to the rump in the rear. The limbs were not posable, but I unwisely posed them a few times, as if to make my moose paw at the loose sphagnum of the tundra, in anticipation of the trumpeting rut, perhaps, or after whirling, as I'd read it must, to face the pack of timber wolves that had singled it out for age or infirmity, or because of their own desperation, and one limb broke off in my grubby little fingers.

The tiny tin moose never stood on its own again, unless it leaned against its companion, a little plastic dog that could be made to puff little paper cigarettes (this was in the days when dogs stilled smoked). I kept the tiny tin moose with me in a matchbox, bedded down on cotton. My sweet sister offered an aspirin, which rattled hollowly in the box in my pocket with the tiny three-legged tin moose. I became known as Moose ("the kid with the moose. Moose") among the three boys who constituted my society, until we moved, and I lost those boys, and that name, and that miniature moose as well.

Love of the miniature, so natural to the child, nourishing our tender personal devotion to the huge, to the cosmic, the infinite that miniaturizes all of us — I went in quest to Toys R Us for the little, the littler, the littlest of all.

Take for instance the horse, the real-life horse, stomping, farting, making large caca, the heavy horse of coarse mane, strong square teeth, conking hooves of horn, exuding its aura of hay and heat; and trace its descent in the child's imagination from the stick-horse (a stick-moose here, too) — a forward looking horse, all head and wish and child's pounding sneakers — to the $100 rocking horse, the $80 rocking horse, down to the fuzzy $40 rocking horse with child-seat; down to the scale model of the breeds; down to My Little Pony; down, down to The Adorable Li'l Pretty Perfume Pony, a mere thumbnail nub of a horse.

I like to think of the gulf between the real and its most pathetic imaging, and how the child's mind, surging with gigantic, oceanic forces, bridges that gulf in a bold leap worthy of a steeplechase.

Take the warrior, too, the boys' tool and fool. Of the men in bags: large green molded army men, titans among tykes, three to a bag, with faces like a favorite uncle; and the faceless cannon-fodder in bags of two dozen; and the traditional antagonists, the red and yellow cowboys and Indians, bowlegged, with mounts. Action figures, fist-sized, with posable limbs, have especially proliferated, and been given the power of speech — a risk, and a mistake.

Listen to the Warriors of M P.A.C.T.: "Destroy it!"; "Hit the switch!"; and, eerily, "Lock 'em up!" G.I. Joe, the fashion-plate fighter, says, "Let's party!" and "Eat lead!" and makes battle sounds: "Blast!" " Boom!" "Zeeeooom!" But what will become of the boys' art of battle blather ("I'm hit!") and sound effects, the long-practiced and finally perfected near-miss ricochet: "Beeerunngh!"

It seems anything can be drafted into battle these days: the Turtles, of course, and the co-mutant, eco-conscious Toxic Warriors, and Bucky O'Hare of the Toad Wars, the Noid, Kevin Costner, Hulk Hogan, Jack Nicholson, Beetlejuice and even Julia Roberts. Police Academy, Swamp Thing, the X-Men, He-Men, the Rocketeers and the Food Fighters — Fat Frenchy the bag of fries, Meenie Weiner, Lieutenant Legg the egg, Bad Bacon, and his earlier avatar Hamfat Lardo, the bazooka-wielding pig of Barnyard Commandos, victim/assailants of the universal draft.

The Dino Warriors have strapped what looks like a convenience store onto a brontosaurus, an inevitable wedding of prehistory and Pentagon spending. Weirdest are the Squirt Heads: Hulk Hogan, again; and Kevin Costner, again; the Squirt Head Killer Tomatoes.

One aisle over in Little Girl World and it's all pink nurturance in diminuendo: from the uncanny realism of baby-sized La Baby, down to Cherry Merry, Muffin, Tummy Luv, Li'l Softskin, the infestation of The Quints, Cutie Fruity Cupcakes; down, down to the sinister Tiny Teens, Toodles, Snookees, Baby Beans, and ending with the wee wee Kidgettes, perfumed babicules. All of this, I'm afraid, prepares girls all too well for the intentions of the Squirt Heads.

For an alternative to motherhood, girls still get Barbie and the other high-maintenance Material Churls (available with Ferrari-Testarossa): single, age twenty-nine, on perpetual tiptoes to look over your head at a party for someone with more power.

I went looking for the small at Toys R Us, for the miniature, the pocket-sized, for everything that has been taken from me by time, that big bully. I was looking for my tiny tin moose, too, lost somewhere between Atlanta and Miami, between age six and the half-life of tin, and time's nosedive into eternity. Irretrievably lost, as everything will be until dreamed again.

Elemental moose! I see you bursting from the big red toy box of oblivion and raging in miniature up from the molten center of the earth, blasting out of that trap at the end of the world, flung into space in moose particles still pursued by the gray wolves of form, turning at last to face them in triumph, pawing suns, whole constellations hanging from your antlers like huckleberries, you bellowing your challenge to the cosmos. Well done, tiny tin moose! Oh, well done indeed!

High School Football

When I was in high school and we went to the football games, me and my entourage and my entourage's entourage—me—us, the guys, the gang of us, we stuck close together. Like Chinese dancers in a dragon suit—head, legs, legs, legs, legs, tail—we stuck very close together, snaking through the crowd. I couldn't see much through the scales of that costume, and I was only looking for one thing: Abigail O'Shea.

She was up there somewhere among the glitter-lettered posters of the spirit section, in her autumn sweater, with an autumn flush on her cheeks and the wild light of Friday night in her eyes, which were the bright and happy eyes of a fine upstanding citizen of our high school's society. In pointless rebellion, I was down there somewhere among the knees and feet and paper rubbish swept against the chain-link fence, mere legs following a cooler head, the collective consciousness of the gang. And the gang was very hard to steer toward Abby.

In my thoughts, though, I was like a mole in the soil of self-conscious egomania. I nosed blindly ahead in spurts through an emotional medium so thick it hardly needed seeing. It was all emotion—the random hoof beats of the game, the cadence of cheers, horn blats, the stalag lights atop the concrete seats. Ever alert for my natural enemies—Bradley Woodall and Quinnie McClendon—and my unnatural enemies—anybody with a critical opinion of me—I moled to my goal in an underground of complex self-referential root systems, navigating allegiances, nibbling the tasty grubs of grudges. When I popped up beside her waving my sensitive sensory instruments in the open air, I would look down at the field and still see nothing but Abby O'Shea. I always went to the games and missed the games anyway.

Recently I went back to a high school football game to see what I could see. Parents, for one thing. I could see parents now, and the things they do to make the game happen. They grill franks and flip burgers, pop popcorn and dispense candy bars and brew gallons of coffee and boil water for hot chocolate. And they do these things badly. And for no money. It's touching, really. They are good people, obviously, and I was sorry for the eggs I used to throw at their houses.

That Friday night a 40-knot nor'wester bulled through the stadium, freezing the parents as they tried and failed to buy or sell hot hot chocolate. They shivered in the cardigans and parkas, while with mittened hands tried, and probably failed, to camcord the feats of their teens. The teenagers weren't cold. Teenagers, I remember, have very little weather. They just don't have it. It's either sexy with frost coming from your head or sexy with perspiration dewing your upper lip. Little kids are in for it, though. The little brothers and little sisters were swaddled in blankets fighting hypothermia. Children have weather and whine for their parents to do something about it. Try getting a hot hot chocolate out of those parents. I mean, kids, get some perspective.

By half-time I had a serious case of cold concrete butt. Still, I saw my first high school football game half-time show. And I was entertained. I was thinking, this is probably as close as I'll get to seeing 18th Century warfare. The long lines of redcoats came marching at us most impressively, high-stepping, blowing aggressive horns, rendering "Also Sprach Zarathrustra," and in general doing whatever they could to draw our fire. The parents stood and opened up with their camcorders. There was a lot of competence and hard work on display out there. I was entertained, like I say, and touched, and sorry for all the eggs I used to throw at them.

As for the game itself — Leon vs. Rickards — it was pretty one-sided and thus a little depressing, from a Marxist point of view. You could see that money — well, you know what money does. Anyway, powerful Leon had a hero, this kid Vandover, who was, as the sportswriters say, a Houyhnhnm among men, just trampling everybody. He'll be a star. Then he'll be a parent. The weather will be lousy and he won't be able to do anything about it. He won't even be able to get a cup of hot hot chocolate.

What I saw most clearly, though, seeing the game for the first time, was that somebody got dinged on just about every play. I'm not opposed to it; I just wouldn't do it myself now, which would, in distant retrospect, really please my mother, who used to be fanatically opposed to tackle football, so much so that I always had to lie about the grass stains and bloody knees of sandlot tackle. She was so down on it that I wondered if she's been tackled herself, I mean really blind-sided or clothes-lined one time on her way to work for nothing in the concession stand. Mom, I see your point. And sorry about that egg.

Nothing is more comforting to me than the sight of an empty tennis court. I drove out to Forest Meadows one blazing hot afternoon to look at a few of them, my racket and togs on the passenger seat just in case. Kids were in school, adults at work, or daunted by the 90-plus heat. There they lay, the unoccupied, untormented courts, carved out of a low piney wood, 16-plus courts with a glaze of Fata Morgana shimmering above them, so knowable in their geometry, so predictable in their symmetry, so open with opportunity. A safe haven for one, say, serving a basket of balls; but a utopia only for none.

I closed my eyes there in the shade of a metal umbrella and thought I could just hear phantom sounds of tennis coming from the empty courts.

"Thwock! ... Thwock!" — the tense trampoline of the tennis shot, the "Chock! ... Chock!" that hallows hollowness, such a pretty expression of that property of matter we call "Give." With stroke and touch and fuzz and gut, the players pass back and forth something like a perceptual tiger, so bounding and dashing and swift can their shots be. Ideally!

I heard them, ghostly players in the noonday sun, the tumult of a large desperate mammal scrabbling on grit, the hard-court squeaks of protesting rubber, like 180 pounds of tofu trying and failing to clamber out of a hot frying pan.

When I opened my eyes a single player had arrived, introducing an element of anxiety, an air of threat. As he unpacked his gear he began to sweat. Limbering up with some windmilling toe-touches, he inventoried his sports injuries. Rehearsed his excuses. Examined his planets in his pocket horoscope. Looked at his watch. Let three new balls come hissing out their can. Then sat down to wait. The jerk.

I knew him, Horatio. The peace of this court was ruined. Here was the static element of the tennis match — the unlikeableness of the opponent. Mark me! Either he would serve too hard for one's return game, or he would serve too oddly for the preservation of one's own dignity.

He would hit the ball deep so that you had no time to react; or else hit it so short you practically broke your neck getting to it. Either way it was to spite you. He would jerk you around with his unorthodox strokes, or grind you down with expensively tutored precision. He was killing your feet besides, crippling your knees, you were wearing away like an eraser. You had a headache anyway before you started, a bug or something, a touch of flu. You were not yourself; it was not your game he was beating. Because you never hit shots like that, you very, very rarely sucked *that* much. At least you never lost to him. And he knew it. The jerk.

And say for once things were going your way, you were playing your game, hitting your shots, playing the way you think you should play, the way you've paid the dues to play, and how you always imagine you'll play when you contemplate that empty court. You knew what this opponent would do. You'd be jerking him from side to side like a puppet and he'd start to affect a limp. He'd net a shot and roar like a galled bull: "I can't believe it!"

But he ought damn well believe it! He'd been netting them left and right. Nothing commoner than an error from this cad. He'd double fault and stand their mugging for the balcony seats while you waited through the curtain call. When he finally got a serve in you'd nail an untouchable return and he'd just shrug and laugh bitterly.

Yes, before you could savor the pleasure of defeating him, he'd be well into the process of disassociating himself from himself, as if he were just the butler or valet of his tennis game, not the gentleman himself. The game is pointless anyway, he'd discover, and look bravely into the horror of the void. Backpedaling listlessly after another of your perfect lobs, he'd tumble to the ground, and finding himself suddenly transformed into an enormous insect, he'd be unable to continue. A sharp breeze could scoot him from the court, his wasted carapace as hollow as your victory — or so he'd hope.

In truth it was great fun beating him, and so I stepped forth and offered myself as his opponent. Then he beat me, which was really weird because he never beats me. And he knows it. The jerk.

Canyoneering

You really don't want to spend a lot of time contemplating a huge rappel, but I could see by the luminous dial of my watch that thirty minutes of steadily raining, rapidly draining daylight had ticked by since I'd tied in to the anchor. What the hell was keeping Clint? Presumably he was just a little ways back up the canyon with the rest of the rope. I knew he was a little hard of hearing ("too many rock concerts in the '70s"), so shouting didn't seem helpful. I also knew he was sick with a horrible head cold, so that he could've conceivably collapsed, semi-comatose, in a tangle of rope. Perhaps my heroic rescue of both of us, our epic retreat up and out of Secret Canyon in the dark, should've begun some minutes ago. Actually, anything remotely survivable had come to seem slightly preferable to the awful rappel that faced me.

Four hours of grappling over boulders, sliding down chutes, and swimming freezing pools had climaxed with this little room, a troglodyte's box-seat in the nose bleed section of a vast stone amphitheater. The scant slick rock floor sloped dangerously downwards, becoming concave at its terminus where it bulged out over the cliff face like a gargoyle's tongue — the wickedly slippery, algae-green spout of a sometimes waterfall that overhung a drop of two hundred feet. It looked like two thousand. Down in the wide, scree-strewn basin below, one full grown cottonwood tree looked like a tumbleweed.

At last, I heard an enormous splash. I couldn't entirely suppress a semi-hysterical laugh. Clint had arrived at the pool just above me. The water was deep, and there was no avoiding a total dunking as you rappelled down into it, and it was preposterously cold, never seeing sunshine in that dungeon-like passageway. The rain, the cold, the drop — it was just a wonderfully miserable situation.

Water surged, boots beat on rock, and moments later Clint was clipped in next to me at the anchor, coughing and wheezing and dripping buckets from his beard. Unpacking the big rope and tying it to the anchor, he cradled the coil in his arms, rocking it back and forth. One, two, three! — he flung the rope out over the spout. It made a seriously eerie whirring sound as it fell — woomp! woomp! woomp! — like a boomerang in a kung-fu movie. "A good sound," Clint said, the sound of a lot of rope falling a long ways, hopefully all the way to the bottom of the cliff, though we wouldn't know for sure until I went over the lip. He fastened the rope to my rappel device like a man who faces one last difficult task before two days' bed rest with plenty of fluids, but he looked up from the knot grinning. "You ready for this?" he rasped.

Ready? Hey, the way I figured, we're all born canyoneers, tied on at the navel. It's a poor explorer indeed who doesn't quicken to the call of the crevasse. In the past I'd been enticed into numberless natural grooves, whether tropical stream beds, Georgia gorges or mountain ravines. But whenever the going got stupid, I always hearkened to certain caveats: Don't crack your skull, old son, and walk out with fibias and tibias intact. In contrast to that sort of dilettantish dabbling, the sport of canyoneering proposes that, with the right gear, especially enough rope, no canyon, however wet, however precipitous, need turn back the intrepid. Swim that river, climb that rock, rappel that abyss — a horizontal hoot, much more dramatic than hiking, not so relentlessly exposed as rock climbing.

So I'd jumped in with both water-proof boots when the opportunity came to do a few established routes in Arizona with some experienced canyoneering guides. Thanks to the uniquely diverse geology just a few hours east of Phoenix, we could hit three very different canyons in three days, each carved from a different type of stone, but all of them "wet canyons" — wet canyoneering being the cutting edge of this young sport. The influential Euros particularly favor das wasser, borrowing techniques — and peculiar challenges — from the frequently sodden precincts of spelunking. Water beats rock for falling onto, was what I was thinking, so long as the water didn't come in the form of a flash flood.

For an Intro to Canyoneering, Clint Graham, a 53-year-old Phoenix-based American Canyoneering Association-certified guide, had picked Salome, a pretty little pink granite slot at the base of a massive butte in the high desert around Lake Roosevelt. Graham, a former 100 mile endurance racer and current rock climbing instructor, is long and lean with a grizzled beard and the deeply etched smile lines of a happy outdoorsman. On the two mile hike down to Salome, he confessed to feeling less than 100 per cent, though once we stopped to suit up in neoprene from head to toe and stash our street clothes among the cactus and sage brush, he said he felt the adrenaline rising: "No matter how many times I've done a canyon, it's always a thrill."

Clint's Salome route begins with a little jump of about ten feet from a natural stone platform into a blackwater pool. It's a waker-upper. I watched the 6 foot 3 inch guide smack the surface and disappear. He came up gasping from the cold. I was soon briskly dog-paddling to join Clint on the far side of the pothole where he stood trailing strands of green algae and sluicing water from his suit and boots and rope-laden pack. Here at the start Salome was wide and shallow and completely benign, with patches of mud and green bulrushes, the sun beaming down pleasantly on our steaming neoprene. The smooth pink boulders reminded me of a giant Gila monster's tail, with the rest of the monster curled up somewhere ahead. We worked our way down a chaotic stairway of scoops and potholes and pour-overs until we all but deadended at a tight S-curve chute of glistening slick rock, a 70-degree slope of about thirty feet. Thanks to the friction of our excellent canyoneering boots and the neoprene suits, we were able to scooch surprisingly far down before surrendering to gravity and ottering into the drink. "Boulder on the right," Clint advised, wincing in the waist deep water. Gotcha.

Every good canyon route, I was finding out, is a true picaresque of episode upon episode, each new passage of water or stone a literal cliff-hanger raising the tension until the penny dreadful pitch of the crux. Salome's arrived where we side-climbed along a ledge and tied-in to a pre-set anchor of canvas webbing bolted to the granite. At that point the canyon was little more than an arm's span wide, the walls soaring vertically high above, below a mere fissure a falling body might wedge into, or else slip through to dark points unknown. And directly ahead was the first drop that would kill us — though in an introductory sort of way, I supposed, this being a canyon for beginners, after all.

"There is a strong human instinct against leaning out over a cliff," Clint allowed. In order to rappel, obviously, this first of all must be overcome. He checked the snugness of my harness — "In case you invert" — and then I clipped on a figure-eight device and observed, with pointless skepticism, Clint's cold-reddened, rock-battered hands as he threaded the rope through. It seemed to be like tying someone else's necktie, so that the process had to be started over, reversed in the guide's mind, as if he maybe didn't know exactly what he was doing. Well, of course he did.

"Soon as you see how easy it is you're gonna look up at me with a big, shit-eating grin on your face," he said. I found instead that not only do you have to lean out over a cliff — "I'm leaning out here! Why am I not rappelling?" — there's so much friction in the figure-eight that you must actually thrust downwards like you mean it: "Argh! Die, fear of death, die!" Or was I strangling the rope with my anchor hand? I let a little out. Jerked downward. Let a little out. Swung sideways a bit, but didn't "barn-door," or face-plant. My funky self was getting down.

"You did all right," Clint said. "But I never saw that shit-eating grin." We were hiking back up to his truck, the Salome route a done deed. I told him I was saving it. After all, Salome was the easy canyon, right, the place Clint took pallid indoors people, corporate groups? Tomorrow was Secret Canyon, a whole other magnitude of difficulty, a place the guide said he hardly ever took anybody.

Salome had been desert and sunshine; Secret Canyon, a couple hours further north in the Coconino National Forest, was pine trees and a soaking rain. After suiting up in our still-wet wetsuits, we got back into Clint's truck and blasted the heat. I tried one last time to dissuade him — it was November, it was raining, he was not a well man — but his work ethic was too strong. So we skidded and monkey-gymned down through the trees, bottoming out among giant moss-topped boulders, the way ahead barricaded by trunks of fallen trees. Packs snagging and helmets rattling against branches, we plunged on. The scale of the place was both enormous and intimate, a tremendous, craggy, tree-topped vee of red-rock, where we were constrained in the squeezy part to perform a series of slippery down-climbs into flooded troughs, damnably cold. Having started late, we had to move fast, which was great, exertion and adrenaline making for the best heating fuel.

The night before, over chicken-fried steaks at the Kountry Kitchen in the town of Globe, Clint had sketched out the Secret Canyon crux on his place mat. The tricky part was swimming that last pool on rappel, letting out line from your pack while frog-kicking. At the far side of the pool, you mantled up onto the rim, then resumed rappelling another twenty feet to the little room and the final anchor. The big rappel was pretty straightforward, except that it was overhanging, and BIG.

"It will definitely get your attention," Clint had promised. And indeed, despite my mind's rat-like search for another way out, my body felt electrified to the core, subtly vibrating with acrophobiaphilia — the love of being terrified by heights. The worst bit of course was getting over the lip, of bidding farewell to the rock with your boots, without saying howdy to it with your head. Once well adangle, you could just say fuck it, and enjoy. It was a long, long, long way down, though, and at about three-quarters of the way I started to twirl. This worsened, till it was like a Cirque du Soleil act. I was going like a dervish when I finally touched down, laughing and cursing a happy blue streak, shit-eating grin and all.

Clint soon zipped down in one continuous, expert glissade, with nary a twist. "I see you got all the kinks out of the rope for me," he said.

Before he took to his sick-bed, Clint's parting advice me to was, "Whatever you do, don't give up." He was talking about waiting for Greg Henry, the Apache guide who was to take me into Cibicue Canyon. "The guy is chronically late." But I'd only waited an hour or so when Greg and his uncle, Lorin Henry, pulled into the general store parking lot at Salt River. They seemed immensely pleased with the guiding gig — these days access to Cibicue, on Fort Apache Indian Reservation, requires an Apache guide — mainly because it meant missing a number of important tribal meetings that day. Life on the rez, as they related it over the course of an increasingly wild ride through their family grazing land, sounded like a cross between a communist state and a college fraternity. "We do a lot of community service," Greg said. "Yeah, working for free," said Lorin, who is community president of the White Mountain Tribe.

Greg, the first Apache to become an ASA-certified guide, explained that because of yesterday's rain we couldn't do Cibicue the usual way — upstream as far as you like, and then back — but had to circle around the canyon and come downstream, a total of eleven miles of canyoneering. "Pick us up at four," he told his uncle as we unloaded gear from the truck. "Four-thirty, say?" said Lorin, grinning. It was close to noon by then. They seemed to be sharing some private joke.

Greg Henry set a fast pace from the start, but whenever I caught up he tossed out bits of lore — traditional uses of various plants, the names of certain rock formations. One was called E.T., another Freddy Kreuger. Growing up, his hero had been Mighty Mouse, who he somewhat resembled in physique, having a big, muscular torso and little bowed legs. He'd been a bull riding champion, after which all other work must've seemed easy, the risk of canyoneering negligible to the point of non-existence. And did I mention he was fast?

I can't say that the experience passed in a blur of motion, because in canyoneering you have to consciously place every footstep, but in memory it has taken on a truly dreamlike quality. Cibicue Canyon is a massive wedding cake structure of basalt and quartzite; from down in it you can never see all of it, or even much of it — it just rises in mighty stacks all around you. There were several rappels, one a hundred foot beauty down a filigree fall. Numerous tricky down-climbs and side-climbs. Thousands of boulders to go around or over. We waded acrosss the Salt River rapids at least thirty times, Greg toughing it out in just a tee-shirt and surfer shorts. From time to time he would give a progress report: "Once we're down the Third Waterfall, it's six miles to the take-out spot." We negotiated the last few miles by starlight. At one point I pulled up short at a precipice. "How'd you get across that?" I called out. "Walked," the guide said. "It's shallow." In fact, my "precipice" was just a big puddle. I was hallucinating.

At last Greg Henry raised his arms and shrieked a war cry, which was answered by someone ahead in the dark. "A couple of more crossings and we're there," he said. We came out of the river at the base of a cliff where several Apaches had a campfire blazing. Lorin Henry greeted me, and I apologized for keeping him waiting so long. It was seven o'clock. "I knew when you'd get here," he said. "I have visions, you know. I see the future." He introduced me around the campfire. Everybody seemed to be a chief. One grasped my hand in a soul shake and said, "Dude, canyoneering in the dark? I'm impressed. You are welcome on Apache lands any time."

Fwoomp! Zoom! Splat!

It's like the opening scene of "An American Werewolf in Utah." After a white-knuckle drive across the high desert in a blizzard, I finally see a glowing Vacancy sign ahead and pull into the motel next to a big yellow school bus which, though driver-less, seems to be idling. It's not. It's full of shaggy wolf-like dogs standing on the seats and barking their heads off at me. As I scurry to the motel office, hunched against the cold, the beasts hurtle themselves against the windows so hard the bus rocks. I casually mention the Iditarod team to the kindly inn-keeper. "Oh, the dogs, yeah, they're just living in the bus for awhile until the owners move to their new ranch."

Not a problem. I've got a nuisance barker of my own so it'll be just like not sleeping at home. I slide across the icy street into the Home Plate, a mom-and-pop diner. Before I order my bacon and eggs, the guy in the next booth lowers his newspaper — wildly tousled hair, haunted eyes, biblical beard disappearing into a bulky Yule-themed sweater — and says, "I don't know about you, my friend, but I'm quite concerned about the course of the present administration." By my second cup he's run the gamut of conspiracy theories from the Zapruder film to the Knights Templar; he's calling me Grasshopper and giving me Internet research assignments.

"Find out why the Bushes named their youngest son Neil," he coaxes with a wink, "Then you'll know whether to take the red pill or the blue."

As I'm peeling my peppermint, preparing to escape further duties, the café savant sizes up my socio-economic signifiers and says: "You must be here for that kite thing."

Indeed I am. Of course I am. These days strangers don't much wander into tiny Fairview, half way between Price and Manti, unless they have a hankering to attach themselves to a giant kite and go hurtling across the backcountry on skis or those new-fangled snowboards. It's the sport of anywhere and everywhere windy and cold — though in fact Fairview, the closest village to Skyline Ridge, a wind-consistent and spectacular patch of the Wasatch Plateau, may just be the best anywhere anywhere.

Skyline Ridge in mid-winter is a vast backcountry playground of blue declivities and gleaming white domes the size of sports arenas. The sheer scale of the place would be hard to grasp except for a scattering of distant snowkiters, their parachute-shaped foils flitting along a sea of whipped cream like brightly colored gnats. When one of them launches a big air on Bosco's Hill, you can see the rider's shadow suddenly detach and give chase across the snowpack for what seems a very long distance.

Every time I see that I want to kick myself for sucking — why can't *I* do that? — and I'm more determined than ever to get over the first steep hump in the learning curve. No question about it, a snowkite is the single coolest piece of sporting gear I've ever hooked up with, like a super-light-weight prosthetic wing sprouting from my navel. And while I may not be up to any big airs for awhile, surely by now I ought to skittering across the snow and carving turns under kite power. But for all that wealth of technology and terrain, my patient instructor, Brian Shank, and I have been confined most of the day to a few hundred square feet of powder, now pocked by the impact craters of my many crashes.

It's been the same thing every time — pilot error — and though I've been doing it for three days now, pilot erring, I mean, and wrecking repeatedly, albeit harmlessly and often hilariously, I think I'm finally on the verge of a breakthrough. For instance, I'm becoming competent at the reclining re-launch.

This is the drill: I'm once again sprawled on my back, my kite crumpled in a heap where it crashed some seventy-five feet away at the end of its lines. With my left hand grasping the control bar — an ingenious device that functions both as throttle and steering mechanism — I reach forward with my right and pull the front lines, lifting the kite's leading edge to the wind. Brian calls it "fishing" — as in, fishing for a low-flying gust. Jiggy-jiggy. Jiggy-jiggy. Come on, kite: Get your limp, flappy ass up out of the snow.

Sooner or later, this will happen: The kite will fill up and flare out dramatically to its full 8-square-meter flying form. Yet, hampered by the inevitable twist in the lines acquired during the recent crash, it will fly wounded, about four feet off the snow, yawing treacherously, awaiting intelligent instruction from the control bar. I'll ease out the bar, cautiously, causing the kite to rise, just high enough to steer it into a brief loop to remove the twist. Then — holy shit! — up she'll rise like a breaching Moby Dick, yanking me out of my crater and onto my skis.

And so it comes to pass. *Fwoomp. Loop. Yow. Zoom.* I'm snowkiting, blistering across the pack. I hear Brian shouting, "Punch it! Punch it!" *Wha ... ? Whoops. Watch out! Splat!*

Brian slides up to my new impact crater on skis and poles, beaming encouragement. "Nice re-launch!" he says.

See what I'm saying.

"Snowkiting is about 80 percent kite flying and only 20 per cent boarding or skiing," Brian lectured on my first day. Long-haired and lanky, the Salt Lake City-based instructor had loped into my motel room like an amiably upbeat arms dealer carrying a sample flying machine in a lightweight bag. Its silky billows soon occupied half the room while Brian explained the riggings.

"Punch-pull. And be aggressive," he said, control bar at chest height, demonstrating the karate-like technique of snapping a turn. This made partial sense to me. I'd come to snowkiting by way of windsurfing, and all the parts were roughly analogous: the lines were the mast, the control bar a miniature version of the boom. Mechanically, the advantage seemed to be on the side of the kite. Because it was up there where the wind was, the kite was a lot more powerful than a sail. I have a recurring dream in which I launch my windsurfer off a lake and sail above trees and houses, eventually towards some power lines. But the kite, close cousin of the paraglider, was the real thing, made for flight and soft landings. I was psyched.

That afternoon, with the storm abating, Brian, his wife, Heather, and I piled into their van and headed up serpentine Skyline Drive through stands of icicle-clad aspens, eventually topping out at Mile Marker 14. Back in the spring of 2002, Brian and Heather had discovered this spot for snowkiting driving back from a climbing trip in Moab. In fact, rock climbing was how it all started for Brian, who got into paragliding as an adrenaline-boosting way to get down from the crags. From paragliding to kiting was a natural transition. And since he was also a back-country snowboarder, he soon discovered he could kite to the top of a peak, pack the kite, and free-ride down.

We scrambled up from the road, hauling gear onto snow pack, where Brian plunged a fifteen-foot flag-pole through the crust. A tangerine-colored Mylar flag unfurled, claiming this spot as his temporary headquarters — and a world-class three-dimensional extreme sport playground. Class was in session. Lesson One was pure kite flying, no boards or skis yet.

We began by launching a little three-meter trainer kite — the Imp — which rose briskly straight up to the end of its simple dual-line tether. It hung there obediently at the zenith. But a "punch-left, pull-right" on the bar sent it whirring into a clockwise loop. I flew the sucker straight down into the snow — bam! — but only that first time. Soon I was looping the Imp either way, doing figure-eights that had me shadow-boxing with the control bar. When I tried the same techniques with a kite twice as big, the turns were both slower and more dynamic, and I could really feel the oomph of the wind's power zone, trying to dig in my heels but staggering after the kite — *whoa!*

By then I figured I knew something about kite-flying, which was this: Any idiot can fly a kite, but nobody can fly a full-sized kite without being dragged all over the landscape. It was time to strap on a board.

Though equally mediocre on skis or snowboard, I'd chosen the board for its slope creds — a decision I regretted at once. With feet confined to six inches of plank it was a challenge just to stand up on the trampled crust. I was rag-dolled, Punch-and-Judy-ed, hoisted up and flung down, a hapless marionette at the hands of a cruel puppetmaster kite. A couple of exhausting hours later I asked Brian what he thought about my giving skis a try.

"Oh yeah, man," he said, "I think you should!"

Day Two was a sunny, breezy Saturday, made to order for snowkiting in the backcountry. Wind direction called for a different site, a little lower down on the ridge. A lot of Brian's Salt Lake kiting buddies turned up for the day, along with a cadre of semi-celebrity riders from Northern Cal — the noted big wave surfer Jeff Kafka and two of his amigos, the team that had recently attempted the first kitesurfing trip around the Farallon Islands and back. It was a happening scene.

I continued to suck, but with skis I had a chance to adjust my stance and find my balance at take-off. Immediately I was making forays out onto the pack, feeling the rush as I steered the kite down into the power zone, leaned back into the harness and let her rip. Which led to every different sort of high-speed wipeout. But I was putting in my time, gaining muscle memory, the kind of unconscious reaction-time you need to anticipate when the kite/ski relationship is about to run amok.

And so, late in the afternoon of day three, back up at Mile Marker 12, under the brow of Bosco's Hill, I finally begin to snowkite. I park that bad boy in the power zone and set my edges for a screaming reach. I hit a bump but keep my eyes on the kite. It veers off in a gust and I punch-pull it back. I even take a hand off the control bar to shake a shaka — the first primitive step towards freestyle showboating. Drawing closer to the road and the unexplored territory of crashing into parked cars, I swoosh to a stop with the kite high in the neutral zone, crank around and zip back to where I started.

"All right!" Brain cheers me on. "You're doing it! Just don't go into the bowl."

Yeah, sure, the bowl. It lurks off to the right of Bosco's Hill, its topological antithesis, where an unfortunate dude named Derek once got himself lost during a white-out and had to be rescued by search party. Every downwind run brings me closer to it until the whole world seems to be tilting bowl-ward. About an hour after Brian's warning I finally have to admit to myself that I am going into the bowl. I feel myself leave the earth and, looking up at my kite, wonder for an instant what the proper steering correction would be, the punch-pull combo that would softly land me pointed out of the bowl. Then time speeds up: I'm suddenly on my back, plowing at high-speed head-first down into the bowl, the kite still fully powered. I reach for the release cord and pull it. Everything goes still.

"Well, now at least you know it works," Brian says. He's skied down to meet me at the bottom and we're thinking how we're going to get out. He puts on my harness, launches the kite in the light temperamental wind down in the bowl, and with an awesome display of technique, looping and looping the rig, tows me back up the rim.

It takes a long while, though. It's time to pack it in. But on our way back down to Fairview, Brian sees Jeff Kafka & Co. high on the main ridge, getting in a few last rides before the sun disappears behind the Wasatch peaks. We park and watch, bringing out our cameras. It's the golden hour, after all, when the snow takes on a fiery tint and everything looks fantastic. The kiters know it, too. When they see our cameras, they converge on us like seagulls swooping down for stale bread. Most on snowboards, a few on skis, they come skittering at us across the crusted snow, kites bent like scimitars biting into the wind, and then with a jaunty tip of the steering bar they boost themselves twenty feet above the snow, right over our lenses. You want rail-grabs? Helicopter spins? Their kite lines, taut as piano wires, make a weird zooming sound like Poe's Pendulum when they pass.

These guys, these pros, operate in a sci-fi world where anything is possible. But it's fine to see, and good to know somebody's doing it, using these wonderful toys at something near the limit of their performance.

Kayaking Waterfalls

Once I'd said yes — yeah, sure, I would love to paddle the waterfalls of Rio Micos, why not? — time seemed to flow with inexorably increasing momentum, kind of like, well, a rushing waterfall. First there was plenty of time between me and that dimly imagined Mexican river, a big placid pool of weeks in which to train, rent a kayak here at home, learn the Eskimo roll. But time was moving faster than I thought, and before I could do any of those things — whammo! — I was right on the event-horizon, shouldering a boat (and a burden of steadily increasing anxiety) and picking my way down a hundred concrete steps to the roaring river.

The put-in spot, under a massive hydroelectric plant, was like a plumber's nightmare: waterfalls firehosing out of the forested mountainside seemingly from all directions. We had to traverse a complex staircase of falls, boats on one shoulder, the cascade pounding the other, a bone-cracking fall awaiting any misstep. It wouldn't even have been possible except that the pounded limestone was like sandpaper underfoot. Still, I crept across so cautiously my boat half filled with water and I had to drag it the last little way out of the falls to where I could dump it.

Our group of five paddled out into a wide blue pool, everybody looking around in awe at the Huasteca Potosini landscape. Canyon walls soared above us, carpeted with giant, moss-draped trees where herons perched and parrots shrieked. Upstream, the powerful El Toro falls, sixty feet tall and about as wide, gleamed bone-white in the morning sunshine, its thuggish proximity and booming cannonade a constant adrenaline boost. Where El Toro's foam-line faded, the pool resumed its gorgeous turquoise hue, the curious effect of dissolved travertine rock. Downstream, the Micos simply ended in a kind of what's-wrong-with-this-picture perspective, a near-perfect straight-edge sprouting intermittent tufts of foliage beyond which arose a suspicious-looking smoking mist.

Loosening up, guide Grant Amaral sunk the bow of his boat and began to cartwheel across the pool — bow to stern to bow to stern — like a demented orca. A former whitewater rodeo champ, and an explorer with a dozen first descents, from Canada to Chile, to his credit, Amaral still retains his extreme sports chops at 44. In imitation, Sheldon Litwin, wearing a football-style kayak hockey helmet, attempted a cartwheel of his own. He ended up upside-down, but deftly rolled up streaming water. Litwin, a cardiologist, travels frequently to far flung rivers with longtime pal and fellow M.D. Scott McKee, who was still staring up at the sky. A new dad, he was blissed out from his first good night's sleep in ages. Finally, there was David Solis, alias Polo, an agile young Mexican guide, Grant's protégé, charged specifically with the survival of the only novice in the group — me.

Then Grant beckoned us all to follow him to the edge of the first falls. I hung back a little, not trusting my ability to brake. "Come closer!" All right, dammit. He was watching me like a hawk, a creature he resembles — big wingspan, piercing stare. Amazingly, the water at the top of the falls was so shallow we could get out of our boats and scout the twenty-foot drop, our feet crunching bits of crenellated limestone. I asked where was the "chicken route," the easiest way down, and Grant said I was looking at it.

"Like dropping into a big wave?" I suggested.

"Yeah, that's a good way of putting it," Grant agreed. "It'd be a pretty big wave, though."

Scott was the first to go over, then Sheldon, followed by Polo. Grant reversed his boat, waggled good-bye with his fingers on his paddle staff, and went over backwards — the badass. They all just disappeared, like medieval mariners sailing off the end of the earth. And then there was one. I scrunched my naked toes on the foam of my foot-pegs, and pressed my knees outward against the sides of the boat, sort of the way you'd grip a horse that was about to jump, only from the inside — and then I stroked for the edge. Huck it, as they say. It was a good day to die.

"Every kayaker dreams of launching himself off a waterfall," Grant Amaral told me. Of course, dreams are relative, and consequences measurable, in feet per second per second. "But anything higher than about twenty-five feet can really hurt. You start seeing a lot of bloody noses, broken ankles."

When Amaral was poking around down here in the precipitous canyons of San Luis Potosi State back in the late '80s, he found plenty of world class whitewater rivers — the Gallinas, the Tampaon, the El Salto, and the Santa Maria — and some superbly suicidal falls. Where the

Gallinas, the Tampaon and the Santa Maria meet is the 300-foot-plus Tamul Falls. Better bring a parachute. And the El Salto climaxes with an in-your-face 180-foot spouter called El Mueco — "The Ejaculation." No gracias.

In '89, in the aftermath of a tropical storm, with the water higher than he's seen it since, Amaral pioneered the Cascadas Micos run (at least the hombres at the power plant said they'd never seen anyone do it before then), and knew he'd found the river that would answer perfectly those Everyman dreams of survivable flight. In its first couple of thumping kilometers, the Micos staircase boasts six major air-ops for the boufmeister; best of all, these falls are all about the right height so that there isn't time for the boat to go off line during free-fall, the guide explained. Hence, disastrously bad landings are rare on the Micos, as are injuries. Add warm water, big pools where paddlers can regroup, and a park-like setting, and what's not to like: play-time for the expert (cartwheels, anyone?), and a safe challenge for the intermediate paddler. Basically, for all its hydrological drama, the Micos is Class III: not a serious risk to life or limb. Hell, even a novice, a flat-water sea-kayaker, a freaking rafter-cum-rubber-duckie wussy without an Eskimo roll in his repertoire could have a blast running these falls.

Amaral was so impressed by the adventure travel potential of Micos he bought a two-acre parcel at the bucolic take-out spot, where the last little rapids burble, and built his camp there. Since then, along with the usual clientele of intermediates and experts (the week-long itinerary includes the Class IV Tampaon and the Class V Santa Maria Rivers), Amaral has guided a number of novices down the Micos falls — I was the eighth, to be exact. "You'll be scared well within your limits," was the way he'd put it the day before when he was giving me a crash course in the basics. We'd paddled out into the pool right in front of the guest cabanas, a fine spot for beginners' lessons.

Lesson One: you don't sit in a kayak so much as you wear one, like a big plastic mono-slipper for a merman. And once you've snugged the spray skirt onto the cockpit, sealing yourself in, it's best for all concerned if you don't break that waterproof seal and swim, though your instincts may tell you otherwise. That was Lesson Two: stay in the boat. To that end I practiced the "hands of God" rescue, a mere matter of holding your breath until someone (God would work) reaches down and rights your boat. More proactive was the "bow rescue," in which you stretch your arms up out of the water and wave them frantically until you encounter the bow of a rescuer's boat. Grab on, hip snap as you haul yourself up:

KAYAKING WATERFALLS

nothing to it. In addition to trying out various strokes, I also attempted to learn the Eskimo roll, the mainstay of whitewater self-reliance, but failed, damn it. I would've loved having the roll as backup. Finally, plenty water-logged, I flipped intentionally one more time, popped the skirt (to see what that was like) and swam the flooded boat to shore. It weighed a ton and was time-consuming to drain. Point taken: it was a pain in the ass. I would stay in the boat.

"Unless you really think you're on the brink of drowning," Grant said. "Then you should get out of the boat."

So that was what I was thinking — if you could call it thinking — as the bow passed the point of no return and began to dip: Stay in the boat! Get out of the boat! But also this: keep your eyes open, and look! Stay in the moment, Zen boy, cause it's gonna be a weird one. And it was, it truly was. I went vertical, standing on the foot-pegs, paddle held just so, and fell with the water — *with* the water, droplets glistening all around me, falling — one Mississippi, two … I penciled in smoothly, softly penetrating the pillowy super-aereated impact zone. The river went dark a moment, and then I porpoised up into sunlight. Yo bravo! High fives all around from my waiting compadres, and so on to the next falls.

We didn't exactly "bomb down" the run as the boyos would've done without me. I had to be exactingly guided through the more complex falls where one line was heaven and one would be hell. At the "Bean Tree Falls" Scott and Sheldon took the eponymous route to the left, under the overhanging bean tree branch where rapids crisscrossed, confusing the line to the safe landing zone. Grant and Polo coached me down the chicken route, a zig-zag course down to where my boat bottomed out at a ledge. I had to "wheel-chair" — that is, push off from the rock with my arms — over the brink, a nice little eight-foot plop. My favorite falls, though, was "The Tobaggon," a long sluice through a bizarre mid-river meadow of flowering cress-like plants. It was so narrow you could hear the hiss of the stiff leaves bending to the boat, and then it opened up to a real gusher with a ten foot vert at the finish.

All credit to my boat, a lender Wave Sport Y, known as "the Invincibility Bubble" for its superb stability. But I *was* six for six on my landings. Never tipped. Never swam — not that first run, anyway. All in all, what with the fear overcome, the friendships fostered, it was one of the most fun things I've ever done. We took out at a riverside cantina, a couple of kilometers upstream from camp, where Grant's driver, Pedro, was waiting to take us on to another river, a new adventure.

Up the Grand: An Epic Backyard Climb

The Grand Teton, at 13,770 feet the grandest peak in the whole Grand Teton National Park, is so damn grand it's practically a brand, an icon of the wildly picturesque mountain West. Early French trappers, looking up awestruck from their beavers, bestowed upon it lovelorn man's highest praise, naming it "the big tit." Climbers call it "the American Matterhorn," our most famous, most perfectly pyramidal peak. Lording over the park, gilded by the morning sun, the Grand appears gloriously daunting — and taunting: It's *right there*, in plain view of millions of motorists driving south from Yellowstone to the playgrounds of Jackson Hole, many of them wondering, as I have, what it would take to get to the top, and fantasizing about actually doing it.

I've been wanting to climb the Grand for decades, ever since I read a chilling account of a climber frozen in fear on the notorious Friction Pitch in one of my father's magazines. I've read plenty more since, the lightning-plagued epics, the daring rescues of battered amateurs caught by sudden summer snow storms. On the other hand, the venerable Exum Mountain Guides lead about a thousand climbers to the summit each summer, so how hard can it be? "It is never easy," writes veteran Exum guide Jack Turner in his excellent "Teewinot" (named for one of the Teton cathedral peaks). "For some people it is the hardest thing they'll ever do."

It's not really all that close to the road, either, as my hiking partners and I are finding out, tramping along the Garnet Canyon Trail. We can't even see the peak any more, though we've left behind the mild summer weather and wild flowers of Lupine Meadow and have climbed into the high alpine country of waterfalls and stunted pines. But the Grand is remarkably accessible in another way. Anyone in moderately good condition with a hankering for heights can sign up for a two-day training class and on day three test the limits of their acrophobia and endurance in a shot at the summit. Which is why I'm nervous. Before sunrise tomorrow, one of my new friends on the trail, Michael or his daughter Angela, will be dangling from my rope and vice versa.

Michael, a retired airline pilot, is an avid hiker, whippet thin but approaching the upper age range at sixty-one. Angela, in her mid-twenties, is an outdoorsy chip off the old block with some climbing experience but also a rebellious streak. (During training, she took exception to the Exum style of seated hip belay and is still arguing about it.) As for me, I haven't exactly impressed our guide, Tom Bennett, with my cardio fitness, my blistered feet, or my borrowed down jacket, which is steadily leaking feathers. I just might be the weakest link in a pretty weak team, I'm thinking during a rest stop, butterflies in full flutter.

Five hours later, we hobble up onto the Lower Saddle at 12,000 feet, where we'll over-night before starting the actual climb. We've hiked eight miles, gained 5,000 feet in elevation, and a whole new perspective on the peak, which cants away from us, seemingly into infinity, like a medieval painting of the Tower of Babel. And the wind — the wind is just blowing like stink.

Up here on the Saddle, everything that isn't mountain, or a piece of mountain, or bolted to the mountain by steel cables has been scoured away. It's like we've walked to Mars. We stagger into the Exum Mountain Guides' hut and find everyone already there: the Exum guides, catching up on far-flung exploits as they bustle about the gas stove boiling water for their clients' cups-o-soup; and a peak summer season population of climbers, packed like pilchards in the back of the hut, some already burrowing into their bags for sleep. We slump to the plywood floor, happy just to be out of the wind in the companionable fug of bodies and musty sleeping pads — until we learn we're the "overflow," assigned to an extraordinarily well-pegged tent.

All night long the wind blasts and batters that little tent. We're beat; we have to have at least a *little* sleep. But the wind is impossible to ignore. It slyly seems to relent, only to pounce again with redoubled fury, go completely bonkers and, howling maniacally, flatten the fabric tube nearly on top of us. At 3 a.m. we're wide awake in a state of fretful awe when Tom gives us a wake-up shout, his light bobbing outside in the hurricane.

We fumble for our headlamps, look at each other, and burst out laughing.

Wow. In our six hour silent meditation we've each reached the conclusion — oh, many, many times — that the climb is off. Climb in this wind? No way, Jose. In *this* wind. You've gotta be joking. But apparently the climb is not off. We'll be starting in the dark — and the gale — in order to get up and down before the notorious afternoon thunderstorms can strike.

We belly out into the blow where Tom is already pulling ropes and harnesses from the big lock box in front of the hut. All the other teams are gearing up, huddling with their guides. Michael and Angela and I, bonded by our night in extremis, grin idiotically at each other under our helmets. How cool is this: the star-filled night sky, and the mighty tooth of the Grand just a few hundred yards to the north of us taking a great big bite out of it.

On the hike, we voted to tackle the Exum Ridge Route, the more exposed and difficult of the routes on the upper mountain (the Owen-Spaulding is the other), and we're going for it, Tom tells us, gathering us into a tight scrum to be heard above the wind — at least as far as the last safe turn-around point.

"But if we get up there and it's still blowing too hard, we're coming back," he warns us. "And if we get up there and I don't like the looks of the way you're acting — if you're stumbling around and looking scared — then we're coming down."

We nod like siblings who've evoked the dreaded paternal "I'm turning this car around" threat. Fair enough. Already teams are wending their way upwards, a lamp-lit procession of pilgrims staggered at various heights against the jet black backdrop of the Grand — one of the prettiest sights I've ever seen. We fall in behind them.

What with the sleepless night, the thin air at height, I hit a wall of fatigue almost at once. From the Saddle to the south buttress is still about a half hour's scramble, sketchily illumined by headlamp and starlight, and I'm sucking air with every step. But when we rope up for the first slab, adrenaline kicks in with a burst of second wind. I can tell I'm gonna need a third and a fourth wind when we arrive at Wall Street, the famous ledge where the difficulties of the 13-pitch Exum Ridge Route commence. Where we've intersected it, Wall Street is about as broad as a country blacktop, but it steadily narrows as we pick our way eastward, becoming the classic pinched catwalk of every B movie involving plummeting native porters. It abruptly dead-ends in a spooky little alcove above a sheer drop roughly the height of the Empire State Building. Here, should you wish to turn back, you are all well and truly screwed.

There's a team ahead of us so we wait, backs against the wall (lesson number one: never turn your back on a drop), sweating it for some minutes. We're out of the wind now, at least, a huge relief. I study my spot-lit boots and try to decide which of the accounts I've read to take to heart: the article about Exum guides, in which the pro climber "flitted" across the gap and up, or the longer version in Jack Turner's "Teewinot," which makes the Wall Street move seem more like a solo game of Twister.

When it's our turn at last, Tom re-checks our harnesses and knots, then fastens an anchor, screwing a cam device into a crack. "We call this 'civility pro'," he tells us, grinning. "In case I fall I won't pull you all off the mountain with me." He steps off the ledge and onto the ridge under a bottomless chimney, turning a corner as he goes up, and quickly disappearing. He pretty much flitted. Minutes later we hear him cry out "On belay!" and Michael bellows back, "Climbing!"

I try to study Michael's move but the bend in the wall blocks out just about everything. He makes it though, the rope spooling out of my stack. A lot slower than Tom, of course. More sweaty palms time. Then it's my turn to get off the ledge, brave the big drop. I reach up as far as I can with my right hand to an unsatisfactory down-sloping hold, and step out onto an equally unsatisfactory down-sloping stance. Now what did Turner say you do next? I streeeeeeetch and grab, kick and smear and scooch, snake-bellying up to better holds. Whew! That was pretty bad.

But to get it so wrong and still make it is a real confidence booster. Soon I'm high-fiving Michael and bringing Angela up to the ledge. And so we go a-caterpillaring up the Grand. By the time we reach the fifth pitch, the Golden Staircase, the sun is fully risen, warming the granite, and you couldn't imagine more congenial climbing, all cups and flakes and "chickenheads" — knobs of rock that seem designed for the human hand. It's serious fun at this point, an endless staircase, a Jack's Beanstalk of rock angling up into the ether. Even the Friction Pitch, the crux of the climb, a near-blank stretch of wall where the steepness relents just enough so that you don't really need holds (you just think you do) seems relatively benign, though I can't see how you'd do it at all in snow or rime ice, or an unnerving gale. In "Teewinot," Jack Turner describes being so freaked by the wind on Friction that he bit a nubbin with his teeth to keep from being blown off. But this morning the sun-warmed stone is tacky enough that the A-cup bulges and shoe rubber smears are all we need. All the same, I don't look twice at the 2,500-foot drop.

We regroup at a big ledge, scramble a bit with our ropes in coils, and then spread out again. The thing about the Grand is that it just keeps coming at you with exposure and variety — overhead cracks to jam your hands into, a narrow ledge to mantle with your elbows, a chimney to body-wedge up, and then something else again. Now when I climb up to Michael his grin is strained, and I know how he's feeling. Angela has developed altitude sickness symptoms — nausea and a splitting headache. We're gritting it out.

"Just a couple of more pitches," Tom tells us.

"Good God!" I say. "I hope you're kidding." Fortunately, he is. The summit is just up ahead.

Traditionally, the top is an anti-climax. It does have a somewhat unfinished look to it. You'd expect something a little more from America's most picturesque mountain, something raked and finned, say, like a 50s Plymouth, but it's just a blunt rock pile. Some view, though, in this morning's bright sunshine: a hundred miles in every direction. If we waited long enough we might see Old Faithful blow fifty miles to the north.

We linger just long enough for a snack and a gawk. Here at the summit we're in the wind again; it's 32-degrees, wind-chill probably closer to zero — and that's the good news. The weather could change at any moment. One time while Tom was at the summit a sudden thunder storm moved in. "We heard this high-pitched whining sound," he tells us. "Our hair was standing straight up from all the static electricity in the air. We got down in a hurry." That sounds like a good plan to me.

"Half-way home," Tom says as we sling on our packs. Guide humor.

We down-climb in shadow and wind, a quicker but creepier route, with one gnarly over-hanging rappel in one of the windiest spots on earth. "I've seen a guide throw a heavy 300-foot rope and it blew straight back up over his head," Tom says. It's not quite that bad today.

At the bottom of the rappel, we're on the Owen-Spaulding Route, just a long scramble back to the hut. We can see it — a speck on the Saddle — and spend the next several hours reeling it in, rock by rock. A break for lunch, and then the zombie death march on aching dogs. At the end, I collapse face first. Fortunately, this being Jackson Hole, it's onto a massage table at the Four Seasons resort.

"Where does it hurt?" my masseuse asks.

"Everywhere."

In the Land of Shitty Bill: Sea-kayaking the Big Bend Saltwater Paddling Trail

A powerful cold front had swept away the dregs of summer (along with the biting insects), and left behind a fresh-scrubbed morning that was flash-bulb bright but briskly chilly — and a wind blowing so hard that we stumbled among bundles of gear, our pant legs and shirt sleeves snapping, bent double to keep our hats on. Just as we finished strapping the last bags onto our sea kayaks, a concerned citizen came trotting out of a nearby bait-and-tackle shop clutching a sheet of paper. "I think ya'll should see this," she said. It was the NOAA daily report, declaring a small-craft advisory for the Gulf of Mexico.

"Advisory, not prohibition," I clarified for the team. And then, as the more experienced kayaker, I launched my friend Dan, and H.B., my trusting spouse, from the beach, following mother-duck fashion close behind.

Moments later Dan dropped his paddle, his face contorting with pain. "Foot cramp," he gasped, salaaming forward over his deck. H.B., meanwhile, had paddled bravely across the Steinhatchee River where, despite her best efforts battling the wind and tide, was actually being pushed backwards, upriver. Twenty minutes later we staggered out of our boats onto the same scrap of beach where our shuttle driver had dropped us, our boats, and the great quantities of stuff essential for a three-day camping trip. A good belly laugh often calls for a certain amount of build up, and our several days of preparation to achieve this start had us all helplessly quaking.

"I'm thinking about hitch-hiking back to Suwannee and getting my truck," Dan said. "It wouldn't be a problem. People always stop for me. It's the beard, I think."

"What're you talking about?" I said, mastering the last convulsions of mirth. "This wind is going to die down in a couple of hours. We've got all day."

"Yeah, all day," he chuckled ruefully, massaging a cold blue foot. "That's what I'm worried about."

"I dunno, maybe we should get a motel room," H.B. suggested.

Was this mutiny? Already?

In the end it wasn't really that hard to rally the troops. All we had to do, after all, was turn that corner at the mouth of the river and we'd have the wind at our backs and some 30 miles of pristine wilderness coast in front of us — possibly the most scenic portion of the newly opened 105-mile Big Bend Saltwater Paddling Trail. The whole of the trail, from the Aucilla River, south of Tallahassee, to the mouth of the Suwannee, traces one of the longest — and wildest — continuous stretches of wetlands in the U.S. Once we were silently cruising above vast sea grass meadows, we might glimpse gators, manatees, manta rays, schools of cavorting porpoises — who knew what? Even the weather, once the wind settled, should be fortuitous, with lows in the 40s and highs in the 70s, exactly how you'd set the perfect camping thermostat.

"You'll see," I promised. "The Gulf's gonna roll over for us like a puppy."

To their everlasting credit, my novice crew got back in their boats and we started for the channel again, this time maintaining close formation. We negotiated the dicey cross-chop from holiday boat traffic, making full-steam for the southern spit of the river-mouth and the silver-spangled, white-cap tormented Gulf beyond.

There things quickly fell apart again. The wind wasn't exactly at our backs but side-on, and the dry-bags strapped to our decks acted as sails, making the kayaks extremely difficult to steer in the 30-knot gusts. I sounded the retreat. We hauled our boats up the beach on Lazy Island, not our scheduled, officially permitted campsite, but a port in the storm, and pretty cozy as it turned out. We hung a tarp between a couple of gnarled evergreens to block the wind, gathered downed timber and got a fire going, brewed coffee and just took it easy the rest of the blustery day. Dusk was spectacular. A full moon rose above the pine forest just as the setting sun ballooned and eased into the sea. And shortly after dark the well-armed citizens of Steinhatchee (a town notorious in the 1980s as a drug smuggling port, now catching on as a fishing and hunting resort) opened fire on the stars, giving thanks for ample ammunition. Distant strains of Allman Brothers' tunes and the howls of hunting dogs serenaded us to sleep.

In the morning we set out in a light chop for the Sink Creek campsite, still some ten miles distant. After our trial by tempest we were confident enough not to hug the shore, but cut boldly across broad bays.

There were diving pelicans to admire, and soaring ospreys, and wading herons stalking their dinners. By noon the wind had died to a whisper, and the Gulf turned smooth and glassy. Looking down, you could see the shallow bottom go by, the occasional silver flash of a fish, a tawny horseshoe crab, a sculling sea turtle. The peace of the pellucid Gulf invited contemplation, though if you became too contemplative, we found, you stopped paddling and just day-dreamed. Time to re-awaken the inner cockswain: Stroke! Stroke! Stroke!

Under ideal conditions like these, sea kayaking is a lot like Zen, with its twin bugbears of the restless mind and the aching back. And despite the wondrous efficiency of the narrow-beamed boats, and their propensity to glide, nobody said it wasn't exercise.

Mainly, we just didn't know what ten miles meant in loaded boats. But thanks to H.B.'s diligence with the GPS (she loves maps), we usually knew exactly where we were, which was often strangely satisfying, lining up guidebook map, hand-held device, and the authentic report of our senses. "Sink Creek" said all our sources, and there indeed was a creek, and channel marker. Even with stops to stretch where the marsh grass relented to higher ground, we had made it to camp by mid-afternoon and, by chance, on the high tide, as the guidebook recommended.

Half a mile up twisting black water, the site was admirably isolated, smack in the middle of black bear and bald eagle habitat, wilderness which, as the guidebook notes, was far more populated 50 years ago than today. Once upon a time, this part of the Big Bend had been the refuge of pirates, Civil War deserters, outlaws of all stripes — people unfit for North Florida society, however low the frontier standards. It had been logged for cedars and hardwoods at the turn of the old century, a heroic effort by man and mule, but never much occupied — grace of the brutally long hot summer, the gators and snakes and skeeters — except by eccentrics like Shitty Bill, whom I'd met a few weeks earlier while scouting for the trip.

Bill — I couldn't bring myself to use his full name — is a bald-headed fireplug of a man, like a robust Uncle Fester, who lives in a handmade, one-room house on stilts on an oxbow creek with a million dollar view of the Gulf. Inside were all the rustic comforts and ready-to-hand tackle of the fishing-obsessed bachelor, plus an outstanding collection of antique and not-so-antique firearms, hunting bows, deer antlers, turkey wattles, and a six-foot string of Eastern Diamondback rattles. With a good truck and better dog, he seemed materially well satisfied — though admitted, with a chuckle, to owning another house in "town," his wife's domain.

"Shitty Bill's Fish Camp," as the sign outside designated this residence, was a place where he was "free to be an asshole." A country genius, in short, and probably rich into the bargain.

Taking my cue from Bill, I grabbed my fishing pole and set off alone up Sink Creek, casting for a big redfish for the skillet. Of course, the more packed food we ate the less we had to haul, so I wasn't too terribly disappointed to get skunked. In the last of the daylight we explored the coontie palm scrub and the salt barrens, where the hardpan was a veritable cuneiform tablet of animal tracks, patrolled by armies of scuttling fiddler crabs. Back at camp H.B. whipped up a gourmet meal of onions, taters and canned chicken, while Dan broke out his whiskey flask. Under the naked constellations we sipped from dented camp cups and murdered the songs of our people, "The Eastern world, it is explodin' ... "

We awoke to a dilemma: no water. Drinking water we had, but paddling water we seemed to lack. Sink Creek had sunk to a trickle. We didn't think we could wait for the tide to rise, so we dragged our boats down to the stream and optimistically poled towards the Gulf. Soon we were leaping and thrusting inside our kayaks like seated mystics trying to levitate — which was exhausting as well as ridiculous.

We climbed out of our boats to take stock of our situation. The air was dead calm, the sky blending seamlessly with the sea, which created strange optical illusions. Looking towards the horizon, we couldn't tell if things were large and far away, or small and quite close. We saw what looked like the bright white sails of tall ships.

"Is that the Steinhatchee fishing fleet?" Dan wondered.

"I think those are seagulls," I said. "The question is, are they floating or standing?"

We were going to have to drag our kayaks by their bowlines at least that far. But when we got close, they rose en masse and flew further out to sea, where they settled again, as far away at least as when we had started. No problem: I liked the feeling of the crunchy algal substrate giving way to cold oozy mud between bare toes — and I think Dan liked it, too. He's always been an armchair fan of polar exploration with its sled dragging. This was similar but a lot more temperate, and entailed no paddling, which allowed our upper bodies a good rest. "Just to the birds," I promised H.B., who liked it least.

It was tricky going, the mud sometimes sucking up to the knees, and we all eventually fell, provoking hilarity among the still standing. It was seabird paradise, though, and we stalked among rising and falling clouds of them, their capital being the Pepperfish Keys, a protected rookery.

Beyond the island, we found navigable water again, and caught our first glimpse of the Horseshoe Beach townscape, a eye-teasing speck of color from red-tiled roofs. But headed towards us from the same direction was an ominous purple sky. With the window of ideal weather about to slam shut, our leisurely puttering became a race against the storm. Lightning struck, once, with a whomp, illuminating the scene, including a single suicidal fisherman who stood up in his aluminum boat like Charon himself. We really put our backs into it after that.

The boat ramp at Horseshoe Beach was bustling with holiday boaters retreating from the weather, and like the Ancient Mariner we stopped one in three to recite our sorry tale: the ill wind, botched plans, our trucks still an hour's drive away in the town of Suwannee. The locals seemed especially sympathetic, offering us leads, if not rides: "My son-in-law might, if he's at home ..." Two hours later, walking listlessly in a drizzle back towards the boat ramp along the village's one residential street, we saw a gentleman relaxing with a beer on his front porch swing. H.B. pitched our woe, and tossed in fifty bucks to sweeten the deal.

He stood up tall — ruddy face, flannel shirt, blue jeans, work boots — and regarded us with the mild wisdom of an Atticus Finch.

"I don't want your money, but I reckon you can take my truck."

"Really?!" we all said. "That's so generous!" *Are you crazy!* we didn't say.

We offered to leave him wallets, credit cards, gestures of citified accountability and mistrust which he waved off. It didn't occur to us until later, as we drove towards Suwannee, that he hadn't even asked us our names.

It's Saturday night, the climactic night of the weekend-long Ski Like You Drive, the biggest ski bash in the whole Midwest, and up on the stage the contestants — two inebriated couples in vaguely Polynesian attire — await their instructions from the soft-spoken, flannel-shirted, charisma-challenged emcee. A nice guy, no doubt, but utterly lacking the brash obnoxiousness of a good strip show barker. Still, he has gamely given each of the guys a voodoo doll — in keeping with tonight's "Voodoo Luau" theme.

"Whatever you make the dolls do, the ladies have to do," he tells the willing, grinning men. Dolls are manipulated, vaguely obscenely, but, alas, not much imitated. Boos soon ensue from the beery crowd. A rather lengthy off-mike discussion follows, punctuated by giggles from the blushing babes.

Those of us mashed against the stage front enduring this entre-act while the bands switch out have grasped the gist of the entertainment, and can see the problem: the dolls aren't wearing tops, and so getting the ladies to flash their tits is going to require some pretty advanced voodoo signing. Visibly sweating now, Adam's apple nervously bobbing, his act in bomb trajectory, the emcee interposes: "You do what the dolls do!" he tells the girls again. Geez! What's so complicated? Finally, a beefy, bare-chested guy in a grass skirt speaks out for the crowd. "Why don't you just take off your clothes and fuck each other so we can move on!" he yells.

Exactly! I think. That's the very question I'd been asking since about five in the morning, in the bleary aftermath of yesterday's festivities. My head buried under hotel pillows, I'd just drifted into a fitful doze — despite the bovine pounding of footsteps in the hall, the staccato slamming of doors, the basso vibrato of boom boxes rattling the walls, one harridan's non-stop laughter, like a dental drill — when some moron set off the fire alarm. "BRRAAAT!!! BRRAAAT!! BRAATT!!" That, for about twenty interminable minutes until, I supposed (hoped) the authorities came. There went my simple plan for "Ski Like You Drive," which was to get some minimal rest and actually ski for chrissakes!

True, this was Wisconsin, land of cheese and cows, not steeps and powder. The skiing would suck, but I meant to get on it, all 500 vertical feet of Devil's Head Resort, itself a Stalin-esque hulk of echoing stairways and underground passages, its threadbare carpets unshampooed since its early-6os heyday. But with the rosy nose of dawn about to poke up over the corn-stubble hills of Merrimac, I had resigned myself to all-nighter number one. I was finding out that the SOP for SLYD — which offers room, food, lift-ticket and all the beer you can drink for a bargain price — is to drink all night, and then drink all day and all the next night, too.

Which raised certain questions. Would anybody be in any kind of shape to snow-plow down the bunny slopes? And, more philosophically, how much partying is conducive to a good ski party? For that matter, how much partying is actually conducive to "partying"? If this Heartland ski weekend was essentially intended as a raunchy form of foreplay between faux ski bums and ersatz ski bunnies, then, as my grass-skirted compadre so boldly articulated it, WHY DON'T YOU JUST GET IT ON YOU FREAKING MANIACS SO I CAN GET SOME SLEEP?!

Okay, okay. So I'm some years past prime kegger age. I don't even much like beer (give me wine for social lubrication, whiskey for the odd visit to the Twilight Zone). I'd been forewarned, too, by a promotional video of past Ski Like You Drive events, which aspired to the "Girls Gone Wild" genre of expose, but was instead more like what you'd imagine — could you imagine — the special features sections of the DVD would be — interviews with the guy delivering the kegs and so forth. Still the assignment had two things going for it: A) it was a job; and B) I needed a job. The assigning editor from a Colorado-based ski magazine had set me a formidable task. I was to be mordantly witty, yet not condescending (yeah, right); fulsome, yet brief. This above all — hitting his sententious stride — to thine own self be true, and it must follow as the night the day thou canst not be false to any man. So I would go and enjoy the Twister, the Chuck E. Cheese inflatables, the Moon Walk and Fat Suit wrestling — Kindergarten with alcohol, as one wit from the video put it. And I would ski, too, like I drive, which, frankly, these days, is with caution and respect for the consequences.

Panic, however, crept in from the start as I stood in the registration line (alphabetical, by last name) in the Devil's Head lobby with about a hundred other guys. Instead of "Girls Gone Wild" it looked more like "When Men Work Out, and Women Don't Show Up." These were not your typical skiers, but rather your typical genetically selected pro-time beer drinkers: big, barrel-chested, thick-necked menschs, for the most part. I mean, who can drink two hundred bucks worth of keg beer in a weekend anyway? These brawny motherfuckers, that's who. It was like a casting call for "The Sopranos." Worse still, I *knew* these guys from my years of teaching freshman Lit. at State U. Tardy, hungover, but still with a smirking cockiness, they couldn't trace the theme of soul-crushing materialism in John Updike's "A&P" if their lives depended on it.

But hey, that was just me being misanthropic and feeling insubstantial at a mere 185 pounds. I waited my turn and got my yellow wrist band and goody bag (Mardi Gras beads, aromatically synthetic grass skirt, custom whiskey flask — tool-kit for the high life). Behind the registration table, organizing and facilitating at a furious pace, was Stephen O'Connor, the creator of Ski Like You Drive. A Chicago ad-man by profession, Steve-O (as he's known in SLYD circles) is a whip-thin tow-head who seemed to vibrate with nervous energy. I'd expected the generalissimo of brew-ha-ha to be more like the Brando of "Apocalypse Now," mopping his bald dome and lisping: "Are you an athathin? Or just a party pooper?"

In an earlier phone interview, Steve-O (Stevie-O to friends) gave me the SLYD back-story, how 15 years ago he and some buds at Chicago's prestigious Ogilby and Mather ad-firm made their first road-trip to Devil's Head, the best slopes within a three hour's drive of the Windy City. Bantering at a bar apres-ski, a friend who's a notoriously bad driver said to O'Connor, "You ski like I drive," and something immediately clicked in the ad-man's mind. "We advertisers like to brand things, and Ski Like You Drive seemed perfect," O'Connor told me. It proved to be a brand with legs, growing steadily each year by word of mouth, and later word of web. The last couple of years attendance has neared two thousand, the count of kegs consumed almost 200. In SLYD parlance, veterans of past parties are known as "veterans," first-timers as "virgins." "I'm a virgin," newbies say. "Well, you won't be by the end of the weekend," say the vets. Wink wink.

Since Steve-O admitted that some years his "labor of love" loses money, I couldn't figure what motivated him to turn a private party into a public one, unless it's the same motives behind most things men do: power and women. I'd heard rumors of an after-after-party party up in the sixth floor "Summit Room," and imagined Steve-O in that Devil's Head penthouse sipping Courvosier and nervously fondling SLYD groupies. And if not that, what then?

I planned to top off my SLYD experience scoping out the Summit Room action; Friday night I meant to retire early, say, about 3 a.m., which meant I had six hours of partying ahead of me. That first night I popped into the Devil's Den, the resorts's main bar, but soon backed out, choking. These Midwesterners smoke like Eastern Europeans. You'd need a full fire-fighter's suit to spend much time in there, or at least your own pack of Marlboro Lights. But then a lot of SLYD troopers are in their mid-twenties and have a few grace years of puffing ahead of them. Party on, I say, but I needed the more spacious environs of the Cliffhaus, where the first band was starting to set up. Through the picture windows I could see horizontal snow flurries gust past. Cold out there. But not cold enough for the snow to stick in this unsettled warm front. It would be slushy skiing, and yet I'll admit I looked forward to dominating on the Double Black Diamonds of nearly level Devil's Head.

About ten o'clock the chick rockers "Catfight" hit the boards and began fiercely deconstructing Pat Benatar. The second band, "Hairbanger's Ball," a quartet of big-haired, Spandex-panted, Paul Bunyans wielded their guitars like chain saws and promised to "Rock 'n' roll all day, and party ev-er-y night!" It was synchronize your heartbeat with the bass or drop like a felled steer. Meanwhile the crowd of about 700 remained fairly subdued. There was steady drinking, but no dancing — no orgiastic bacchanal at all.

Concerned, I discussed this matter with SLYD's official videographer, and he theorized that the numbers were off this year — both total attendance and the male/female ratio. It wasn't quite so bad as the yard of a maximum security prison, no, but parallels could be drawn. The chicks collectively could sense the tidal swell of testosterone and were low key out of basic survival instinct. But wait until tomorrow night! Everybody said that. They were saving themselves for the big Saturday night blow out.

With that in mind I nipped down to my room and watched a pretty good movie about these white sharks that become super-intelligent? Have you seen it? It's not bad. Then back to the Cliffhaus where it seemed nobody had moved except in the peristalsis surrounding the kegs. One change for the better was the sudden apparition of a silicone-enhanced goddess about as tall (hair included) as Yao Ming, in hot red leather pants and straining halter top. She was with the band, naturally, but that didn't stop one shirtless Hercules from dropping to his knees and worshipfully kissing her hand. Mother of all bimbos!

If you ski out of bounds off the top of Devil's Head you'll find yourself slaloming through a cornfield — which is comforting, and not just for the future of America's farms. Rest assured, if you can drive a tractor on top of the mountain, then you probably won't break your neck skiing down it no matter how drunk you are. But there were very few of us yellow-wrist-banded daredevils taking that chance. During a break from the half-pipe (where there should've been a video camera encouraging lemming-esque leaps off the edge) I met Tim and Jonas, who were not skiing but were saving their strength to consume their money's worth of beer. I asked if they'd heard the fire alarm last night. Dude, they knew guy who pulled it. He was in jail in Madison. Worse, nobody was sober enough to go bail him out, nor would they be until Sunday. Harsh! Fucking-A.

Meanwhile, the big event of the day was unfolding: a foot race half way up the mountain. At stake, a chance to win back your $290. It was good fun watching the body builders fade at the three-quarter mark where the ectomorphs surged to the fore. The winner was a young commodities trader, who I would later watch drink a phenomenal amount of beer during a four-plus-hour co-ed game of flipping cups. The girls, he told me in a whispered aside, were all lesbian nurses — which I didn't entirely believe. What I did believe, based on the relentless grinding of molars, was that the whole cup-flipping bunch was high as the Himalayas on coke — not that there's anything wrong with that. But no wonder nobody was sleeping!

By then it was midnight and the party was rocketing towards escape velocity. You had Sumo wrestling in fat suits in the inflatables room; you had Too White Crew rapping on the stage. The biggest of the brawny boys were all outfitted in the plastic grass skirts, and accessorized with massive sock-puppet genitalia. Out in the hallway I encountered King Voodoo, who wore a skull mask, beer belly, grass skirt, and a wicked plastic dildo. He carried a seven-foot beer bong, lovingly decorated, Hawaiian style, with different colored pinto beans, standing in for cowry shells. After explaining the workings of the big bong (an ounce per inch), King V told me the score, which was that if I wasn't getting laid tonight then I just wasn't trying.

"I'll bet you five bucks," he said, "that if go you up to that chick and just pull up her skirt and start humping her she won't even look over her shoulder to see who you are." My jaw dropped. I'd seen such behavior in "Quest for Fire," but those were early hominids. And I believe she *did* look.

Seriously, he said, the girls were taking on the guys two and three at a time. Well, they'd have to, wouldn't they. "All you have to do is ask." Yes, my friend, but it's all in the way you ask. The way you ask. Such directness calls for rock star charisma, or maybe just a grass skirt and a dildo. Anyway, I was glad to hear that love was all around. Periodically, Stevie-O would take the stage and give a keg count — 120, 125! — and promise that the suds would flow all night. Oh shit! At least the dance floor was finally rocking, the outdoor hot tubs were frothing. But no doubt the real parties were in the rooms, and who knew what was going down in the barracks. I can only say what happened in my room, which was a lot of tossing and turning. I had imagined a final interview with Stevie-O, in the Summit Room, ensconced on a primitive throne: "What do you think of my ski-party?" "I don't ... see ... *any* ... ski party."

Instead, the flesh too weak, I crashed around 4 a.m. and listened in unwillingly on the death throes of party-hearty in the hallway. It commenced with the gallumphing of many footsteps, and an insensible bellowing. "Hey, man, don't shout! There might be people trying to sleep," said the voice of reason. "Fuck that!," rejoined the voice of John Barleycorn. "What kind of asshole would come here and sleep?"

Touche, SLYD.

Later Sunday morning I snuck up to the Summit Room anyway, just to satisfy my curiosity. It was a shambles, every stick of furniture overturned, the expected blizzard of empty plastic cups, about a thousand cigarettes stomped out on the carpet. One window was open to the cruel Wisconsin wind. At some point in the course of nearly unimaginable hedonistic frenzy — or just plain stuporous boredom — somebody had stuck his bohunkus out that window and attempted to take a flying dump on the shrubbery below — and missed. The evidence was lumped on the windowsill. He — we may suppose it was a he — had then put out his cigarette in it. Frankly, I was impressed. As a pure statement of "This is how freakin high I am, deal with it," the butt-stubbed twist of poo was quite eloquent. Could I go there? Brother, I have been there, or nearly. Thankfully, there is no way back.

I exited Devil's Head through the shattered plate glass front doors and drove away faster, surely, than I have ever skied.

It's night. Tallahassee. I'm walking uphill toward the English-department building on the campus of Florida State University. Ahead, beyond a parking lot where a few cars gleam out of the shadows and across a street lined with tall oaks, rises the redbrick building where I'm due, where I'm late. Like a ghost I've returned to haunt the joint, attracted by the minor-league trauma of grad school and teaching freshman comp. Oh, it's the old academic anxiety dream shaping up, all right. And what I expect will be what I get: labyrinthine halls, missing grade books, rioting students.

I'm not particularly anxious, though — which is strange — just a-travelin' along the top of a brick wall that's getting narrower as it rises higher. Maybe I should've gotten down earlier, as I should've done many things earlier. If I'm not careful I'll fall.

No sooner feared than found — whoops, look out! — I'm going down. Grab something! There's a tree. A branch? Got it. It's just a twig, though, a green stem. It couldn't possibly hold my weight, except that I'm suddenly weightless. Why? Because in this particular nothing, it seems, there is nothing that is not-I. Fall where? Fall how? Impossible, for the moment. I hover on the border of two worlds, trembling perpendicular in an electric breeze of wonder like an explorer's flag. From that other hemisphere of sham, with its impossible reading assignments and phantom classes that never convene, never conclude, nothing protrudes but the twig with its spray of leaves that I still clutch against a slight but increasing suction.

And now I remember. I fucking remember!

It's not night. It can't be Tallahassee. What I remember is that the one who floats, suspended in an aspic of pure mentation, is Dream Me, a functional model, if you like, a mock-up of the self, while the so-called Real Me lies on his back, mostly paralyzed by the motor inhibition of REM sleep, in a single bed on the Big Island of Hawaii about four thousand miles from Tallahassee and a decade removed from his last school bell.

I'm in two places at once. And I think I like it!

To be aware that I'm dreaming while I'm dreaming — to impose some control and invest some wisdom in the third of my life I spend asleep, compulsively rehashing the past and rehearsing the future — that's the gist of lucid dreaming. And lucid dreaming is what I'm here in Hawaii to learn, along with a dozen or so other oneironauts, aged sixteen to eighty-six, from Sweden, Germany, Canada, and the U.S. We're all participants in "Dreaming and Awakening," a seminar taught by sleep scientists and lucid-dreaming expert Stephen LaBerge.

Why, in our insomniacal age, tinker with the balm of oblivion? In *Exploring the World of Lucid Dreaming*, our text for the seminar, LaBerge has laid out a laundry list of enticing reasons — dream flight, dream sex, hassle-free travel, free psychotherapy, nightmare reduction, witting access to the unconscious, and glorious adventures in transcendence, to name just a few.

And you think I'm going back to that other school?

Not if I can steer this dirigible self, this feather-light homunculus I've become, elsewhere toward other, better adventures.

* * *

Though accounts of lucid dreaming date back to at least as far as Aristotle, and LaBerge's book wasn't the first publication on the subject — predecessors include nineteenth-century French Orientalist Hervy de Saint-Denys's *Dreams and How to Guide Them* and Frederik van Eeden's "A Study of Dreams" (1913) — LaBerge, a Stanford Ph.D. in psycho-physiology, is the guy who first did the science. In his landmark experiments at Stanford's sleep lab in the late seventies, LaBerge asked self-proclaimed lucid dreamers to carry out distinctive patterns of eye movements when they realized they were dreaming. These prearranged signals appeared on the polygraph records during REM, proving that the lab dreamers had indeed been lucid while unambiguously asleep. In subsequent experiments, LaBerge compared perceived dream time with actual clock time (a very close match), found that dream movements result in corresponding patterns of muscle twitching, and discovered that dream sex results in physiological responses very similar to those that accompany actual sexual activity. No wonder we frequently mistake dreams for reality, LaBerge argued: To the brain's perceptual systems, dreaming of doing something and actually doing it are closely equivalent. Along the way, he took on the bugbear of anxiety dreams — Can't find your keys? Won't make that meeting? Hello! There are no keys. There is no meeting. You're dreaming! Go do something fun or useful — reducing his frequency of dream unpleasantness from 60 percent (about average, according to dream content studies) to 1 percent. In peak lucid dream experiences, LaBerge accepted his Shadow (in Jungian terms), a seven-foot barbarian who held him in a death-grip, then transformed into a rainbow and disappeared into his heart; he met God, or a version thereof, in deep outer space, singing joyous hosannas; and he reconciled with death.

And it shows, indeed it shows. LaBerge seemed extraordinarily collected and contented and still as excited about the potentials of lucid dreaming as when he was a kid having serial lucid dreams about being an undersea pirate. As he paced and discoursed on the subjective nature of all consciousness, the dynamic Dream Doc cut an impish figure in Hawaiian shirt and shorts, with his shock of gray hair, hypnotic blue eyes, and burgeoning Buddha belly, owing to a lactose-extreme diet. Possessed of a sly wit (when I asked at mealtime why so much milk, he answered simply, "Mu!" — a famous Zen koan to the importunate monk), he's given to referring to the human race as "beach monkeys." But thanks to his solid grounding in evolutionary psychology, he never let us wander too far into the mists of new-ageism. When someone asked, for instance, "Can characters in your lucid dream also become lucid?" LaBerge attentively nodded along and then, rephrasing the question, gently steered the questioner back toward planet earth, like a Mr. Rogers for pyschonauts. Though his own scientific understanding of the brain and the dream was always "a little more complicated" than the summaries we finally settled for, in the end he made lucid dreaming sound both obvious and easy. Possible, certainly. Ten years from now, he predicted, everyone's going to be saying they knew about it all along.

Dream sex, dream flight, creative control — we novices wanted some of that. But either nobody was talking or we weren't getting any. Not much. Not yet. The key for us — as Stephen LaBerge discovered as a young Ph.D. candidate at Stanford's sleep lab, under the gun and needing to lucid dream on demand — would be memory. Simple, mysterious memory, the brain's ability to remember to remember to do something. And memory training, along with the science of sleep and consciousness, has been the main thrust of the seminar. We've made lists of dream signs — bits of recurrent bizarreness — to try to remember to recognize and thus use to trigger lucidity. I once owned a horse, for example, that shows up regularly in my dreams, still angling for the crippling kick; I've been on the lookout all week for that brute. And all week we've been playing a game in which every time someone in the group hands you something, you must wink or tap your brow — I remember! — or else get a flower sticker on your name tag. We've made countless "state checks" during the day, asking ourselves, "Am I dreaming?" trying really to examine the nature of waking awareness, making little hops to see if gravity is operational, so that the question will become habitual and the likelihood that we will remember to ask "Am I dreaming?" while dreaming goes way up. And then we'd try to fly. For in the dream, to ask is to know, sometimes; but to fly is to dream, nearly always.

In short, we've cultivated at our leisure an absurd obsession. And I remember it was starting to work.

The previous night — the eighth night of the seminar — I'd had an epic, stupid, non lucid dream set in a Central American banana republic. It featured drug-dealing, gun-running, kung-fu-fighting thugs, flying cars towed by helicopters, yachts the size of the *Queen Mary*, LaBerge himself and his sweet assistant Keelin, and, finally, three comely brides of Dracula who, as we tumbled into bed in a seedy hotel and I extracted my right hand from the jaws of a savage dark midget, suddenly became quite palpably real even as their illusory nature became clear. There was a subtle shift in distance and a stark uprise in Is-ness, like a sharp whack from an invisible interior Zen master: was blind but now could see, or, rather, *think*.

Now there was a knower who knew (Real Me), as well as a doer who did (Dream Me), and what I intended to do and savor with the tang of full awareness was quite pithily summed up by a leering blond as she crawled toward me across the mattress. "You'd like to do us all, wouldn't you?" she said. And all bets being off, all things being equal, and nothing being real, I supposed indeed I would. But just as I gained control I began to lose reception, and the blond to fade like the Cheshire cat. LaBerge had instructed us how to maintain lucidity by spinning ourselves — our dream bodies — to reactivate the visuo-motor neurons, or by rubbing our dream hands to refocus sensation. But pinned under a sensual pileup, before I could free my arms I was back in Hawaii. Damn!

But really I wasn't in it for the dream sex. Rather it was that extraordinary moment, which I'd savored in its evanescence maybe a dozen times in my life, when you pull back the curtain on OZ and see the magician laboring at the switches and levers, and the set pieces come crashing down, revealing ... well, that's what I wanted to know, what I wanted to see for myself.

I remember how, following that partial success, I'd been high all day and gone to bed that night full of anticipation and optimism, only to plunge into yet another non lucid, anxiety-driven dream. When my eyes popped open and I glanced over at the clock on the nightstand, it was 5 a.m. Perfect. A little miracle of intentionality. I was participating, you see, in a side experiment for LaBerge's Lucidity Institute (lucidity.com), the protocol of which included a half hour's sleep interruption to clear my head and reset my intention, my intention being to become aware that I'm dreaming the next time I'm dreaming.

And I remember, all right, how, stealthily, so as not to disturb my snoozing roommate, I gathered up notebook, pen, the clock and a baggie marked 52-B containing an enormous green capsule. I slipped out of the dark bedroom and tiptoed to the screened common room. In the quiet of the kitchen I got a mug of water from the faucet and swallowed the pill, doing my part (as subject 52) in a double-blind, placebo-controlled trial of an herbal acetylcholine enhancer code-named Nohaibanda. (David Lynch fans will recall the line, "No hay banda," from *Mulholland Drive*.) I was hoping last night's dose, capsule A, had been the placebo, and that this was the real thing. According to the activation-synthesis theory proposed by Harvard sleep experts Robert McCarley and J. Allen Hobson, the aminergic neuromodulators — dopamine, serotonin, and norepinephrine — run the show during waking consciousness. Their exhaustion is what we feel as sleepiness, sleep their downtime. While the amines rest and replenish, the cholinergic neuromodulator acetylcholine takes over, using different neural pathways to run a very different show, one with striking physiological similarities to LSD trips.

Will capsule B make the difference? If indeed last night's pill was the placebo, my moment of lucidity showed I didn't really need it. Certainly LaBerge's experience and that of thousands of other lucid dreamers has shown as much. Still, as an impatient beginner, I wasn't averse to a chemical assist, especially one as (hopefully) benign as an herbal extract. So I'd volunteered for the experiment, as did most of my fellow dream campers, in the interest of science. LaBerge's theory was that since lucid dreams occur most frequently during brain states of high activation, the acetylcholine booster, taken at an opportune time, would produce a superdream, a big REM episode rife with lucid possibilities. The sleep interruption was LaBerge's theory, too. Since it's well established that the longest and strongest REM periods come at the end of the sleep cycle, in the early morning hours you could enhance your chances of lucidity by getting out of bed, obsessing a little more on your goal, and then hopping back in the sack clearly focused for the exciting conclusion of the circadian cycle. I expected my next dream to be a whopper.

Meanwhile, still in the predawn quiet of the kitchen, I began to scribble in my dream journal. For the past two months, following instructions in LaBerge's book, I'd been recording dreams, sharpening my dream recall, giving them clever mnemonic titles while lying in bed. The one that woke me up at five I called *Tsunami: That Dumb Big Wave Dream Again*. As a surfer who's spent some time in Hawaii and other dangerous places, I've seen big waves coming at me, and dreamed of preposterously bigger. By now, giant surf should be an obvious dream sign to recognize and use to become lucid. Instead I just scrambled madly to get out of the way and ended up, sans transition, in the penthouse restaurant of a high-rise hotel in the middle of the Pacific. As the first wave smashed into the building and crockery crashed, women screamed, and the lights went out, I just held on like everybody else, hoping the quaking tower wouldn't fall. Big waves? Well, it is Hawaii. Look out!

Thus musing on my dream gullibility, I gathered my effects and tiptoed back to my room, where I checked the time — 5:36 — and fumbled in the nightstand drawer for a couple of silicone earplugs to block out my roommate's snores. Then, lying on my back, relaxing in the balmy Hawaiian night, I began a counting meditation: *One, I'm dreaming; two, I'm dreaming ...*

With careful attention, you can sometimes sense the chemical changing of the guard in the brain that signals sleep onset. The amines, having toiled all day in concert with the senses to construct a three-dimensional, purposive world out of whatever the fuck is really out there — and in here — begin to subside. To fizz. To sputter. You may feel an electrical tingling, little bolts of lightning from the command centers in the brain stem as the neural pathways switch. High-end frontal-cortex-dominated thinking disappears — ah! — often pleasantly, even as random hypnagogic images and voices begin to percolate up from the preconscious in a sort of mental jazz improvisation. The Beatles got the hypnagogic mood just right with snatches of *King Lear* and that ominous "Number nine!

Number nine!"

Even then, in the borderland between wake and sleep, it was still Real Me, barely but recognizably, still in Hawaii and still counting: *Fourteen, I'm dreaming ...* oops! Only supposed to go to nine and start over ... *One, I'm dreaming; two ...*

It's night. It's Tallahassee. Then it isn't. It's nowhere I've ever been before.

And then I remember. I fucking-A remember!

The relief alone is terrific, followed by a wave of triumph. I've broken into the fun house, and this time at the beginning of REM! Wonders await the psychonaut. Forward ho in all directions at once. All I have to do is let go. And remember.

Still feeling the suction from the other side, I release the leafy green stem and fly, feet first, backward into blackness. Great hope, a little terror — is this the nightmare? No? Good — an excited tattoo of racing heartbeats, a disembodied oceanic expansion, a contraction to pure feeling ... and I land back on earth, about a block further south, headed for the Williams Building on the campus of Florida State. I'm like the goddamn Terminator.

It's night again. Tallahassee, again. Still, I'm elated that I've done it — had a lucid dream and apparently woken up at night in Tallahassee, fully dressed and on the march. I can't wait to tell Stephen LaBerge. I can see him clearly, somehow, in his Hawaiian shirt, drinking from a gallon of milk, presiding over a dormitory of sleeping dreamers on the fourth floor of the English-department building. I see an old friend, Geren Goldstein, seated on a bench, reading. "Man, I've just had the coolest experience," I tell him. "I'm salivating with curiosity," he says, not sarcastically, and sticks out his tongue to illustrate. It's purple, as if he's been eating a Popsicle. Soon as I get back, I say. I've got to hurry, meet Stephen LaBerge.

LaBerge emphasizes the role of schemata in the brain's modeling of dream locales. Earth, night, a college campus — round up the usual suspects: the ground, the sky, a horizon for perspective, functional structures of some formal dignity. Activate a few memory neurons and it's a snap. Inside these buildings I can expect, and so will find, school things: offices, classrooms, blackboards, chalk ... Yet while the anxiety dream's physical schema is intact, the anxiety itself has been transformed. I'm only anxious to show off, to present myself in triumph, if I can find my way through the labyrinthine halls.

The Williams Building can be a confusing edifice, especially if you enter through the basement aquatic center, where women in bathing suits are performing a Busby Berkeley-style water ballet and waiters in tuxedos carry trays from an elaborate buffet. Now wait a minute. Come on. There's never been a basement aquatic center in the Williams Building. Aha! The force of compulsive automaticity — the feeling of no choice, no respite — abruptly halts. The blinders of credulous belief are off again while the scene still whirls all around me. Now, wonder of wonders, I'm conscious of being in a dream again, of being in an illusory body surrounded by other bodies that are also illusory, though they seem real enough, as I do. The rising steam from the pool, the sound of splashing, the pungency of chlorine, that banquet table laden with turkeys and sliced hams and little pastries — so richly detailed, so gratuitous. I step in front of a waiter. His eyes bug slightly as he tries to go around. "Pardon me," he says. I pat his back as he goes by. Pardon me! Believe me, friend, all are pardoned here. I appreciate the work you're doing for me. A woman in a black one-piece is headed for the pool. I embrace her, kiss her neck, her cheek, her lips. She is neither surprised nor resistant. I pull the straps of her suit down over her shoulders. Her breasts are beautiful, and Christ! — I'm about to come just holding her. And while I can't exactly see how this furthers the study of consciousness, the work is irresistibly attractive. I'm a kissing bandit, a bee with a brain and a hard-on zooming from flower to flower, and yet there's a nagging notion that to climax would launch me out of the dream world. And besides, I'm due upstairs in the English-department office.

Transition? None. New schema: the office. Walls and smaller spaces, file cabinets, desks with tchotchkes and family pics, and two middle-aged women in conservative pantsuits giving me a deer-in-headlights look. They are, apparently, the administrators of my academic anxiety dream. Were I a lucid dreamer of some sophistication I might ask what I have to sign to get out of this institution permanently. But no, sadly no, I only want to have sex with them also. They are understanding — they can see my problem — and cooperative, as I sweep the little snow globes and the daily *Far Side* calendar off one of the desks. I grasp the nearest of the two, but under her pastel blouse I encounter only a sort of burlap material. The other stands nearby, wavering like a column of flame, cycling rapidly through a variety of matronly identities, each more elderly than the last. Better get out of here!

In one of the loopier "Dreaming and Awakening" discussions, we hashed over the pros and cons of passing through dream walls. It is said to be impossible. It is said to be a cinch. LaBerge once had a claustrophobic client who repeatedly dreamed of walls closing in on him. LaBerge counseled that, with a degree of lucidity, the dreamer could remember to imagine a door, or fly up through the ceiling. "But since I never heard back from him," LaBerge said, "I can only assume he was cured. Or crushed." Remembering this, I decide to give it a try in the English office. The wall is an oddly mottled collard-green color, sickly organic in appearance. My arm, as I extend it toward the wall, doesn't look so good either — all chitinous and glimmering, reddened and singed. Numerous grub-like fingers sprout from my fist — more the longer and more closely I look. Habituation, LaBerge cautioned. The longer you look at anything, the stranger it becomes. Which is true in waking consciousness, true to the nth degree in dreams. And so it is a normal-enough-looking hand I put forth — action restoring the model — to insert into the movie-monster flesh of the wall. My arm slides in to the shoulder — very Cronenbergesque — and I follow with eyes closed …

… and find myself struggling on my back under the blue plastic bottom of an above-ground pool. It becomes a thin latex membrane that I'm at last able to burst through, though I have blue plastic goop all over my hands. Fortunately, here's an outdoor spigot under which to rinse. All that has taken place so far has been in a sort of buzzing nocturne of unnatural light. At last I'm outdoors in daylight and feeling calmer. Excited, astonished, but acclimating to the rhythm of lucid dreaming, the start and stop of belief and disbelief that provides the traction for events to unfold.

LaBerge explains: "Especially at the onset of lucid dreams, there is the danger that too much thinking about what's going on will withdraw attention from the dream and cause a premature awakening. On the other hand, too little reflection and you lose lucidity. The key is a balance between participation and detachment."

Just so with this tree in the sunlit garden. Clearly it is little more than a hedge, and spiny, not good for climbing. Never mind. A little ways up, the branches are stouter, well-spaced, so easy to climb, in fact, that I'm at the top. Now all of a sudden it's the Tree — the great forked apotheosis of all things upthrusting, a towering hardwood a thousand feet high. So high indeed that I'm hanging on in the crook amidst a thunderstorm, inside swirling clouds that flicker volcanically as sheets of hot rain pour down. When the storm subsides, I can see a patchwork tropical landscape far below. The rain-slick trunk bulges out about twenty feet beneath me, offering a natural launching pad should I care to bump and jump.

Now, strangely, though I often dream of semi-extreme sports and of performing them with none of my usual cowardice, I'm reluctant to tree dive. I know I can't be hurt by the fall, but I'm less sure about that launch, the slight juke needed to avoid a pair of barky knobs. I could bust my butt! But summoning some real courage, hands at my sides, toes pointed, I let go and slide down the slippery trunk, and nail the launch perfectly (did you expect less?), entering free fall facedown, back arched like a practiced parachutist. The wind roars in my ears, rips at my clothes. Terminal velocity, it seems, is just what the unconscious ordered, for with the steadily rising ground as its canvas it lets loose with a torrent of mesmerizing imagery: scenes of global devastation followed by delicate, intricate line drawing that are at once cartoons of the world geopolitical situation and comments on the aesthetic compensation of complexity, however disastrous. Someone's a genius in here, and it ain't the flying beach monkey who, before dream-smashing to the dream-earth, intuitively levels off and begins to cruise — in face-prowed, wonder-powered flight — through a suburban neighborhood, more determined than ever to find beach monkeys of the opposite sex.

Other episodes ensue — a comically ineffectual encounter with a girls' softball team in the crowded dressing room of a discount sporting goods store; a stupendously banal bit in which a thug offers cocaine as a pretext for flicking my nose — and other anomalies, too, blips of bizarreness impossible to categorize, before I seem to surrender flight at sunset, splashing down in the shallow end of a rather swank hotel pool. Nice landing. And how can she resist her hero from the sky, the water nymph who awaits? She's found the coziest spot in a nook away from the resort's tiki-torch lights, where I come swanning up, naked as she is. "Who am I to you?" she says, holding me at arm's length, smiling playfully, thank God, though whether this is a rebuke for the anonymous monkey sex I've tried to indulge in or the witty repartee of an amorous Anima, I can't summon the cranial voltage to decide. She lets me in to her embrace and I gratefully subside there, cheek on breast at the warm waterline. I know I'm going, we're going, dematerializing. Whatever subtle Kegel exercise of the prefrontal lobes has kept the illusion alive, I'm letting go.

And wake up. Check the clock: 6:39. Nearly an hour of lucid REM. I feel as giddy as Scrooge on Christmas morning. Wonderful dream! And though, in immediate retrospect, I seem to have fucked it up in the same little ways I fuck up my waking life — except for the Tree; that was a hell of a Tree and a good jump — I can't wait to tell Stephen LaBerge and Keelin and the rest of the dream campers. My first full-blown lucid dream. I hadn't really believed, and wouldn't still if I hadn't seen it with my own dream-eyes, that such a surpassingly strange brain state could be accessed and sustained.

There's one more day and night of dream camp. I cadge another acetylcholine booster Stephen LaBerge — "The first one's free," he jokes — and follow the sleep interruption protocol exactly as before, and dream, non lucidly, that I'm traveling with my wife and our families to a tourist destination, a quaint little backwoods community founded by lucid dreamers who are bearded farm folk, sort of Amish. "Did you get the name of that town?" my wife asks. I have my pen and notebook handy, but, no, I can't read the sign, the name of the town, which is written in shape-shifting hieroglyphics — the quintessential dream sign.

Now it's been several hectic weeks, but I still recall the elation that lasted days afterward. My lucid dream was psychedelic, obliquely psychotherapeutic, and, oddly enough, more restful and restorative than the usual non lucid muddle. On the whole, a damn good nap. As soon as I can clear my desk and take a day or two to revive the obsession, I'm going back in.

FROM AN ILLUSTRATED
DREAM JOURNAL

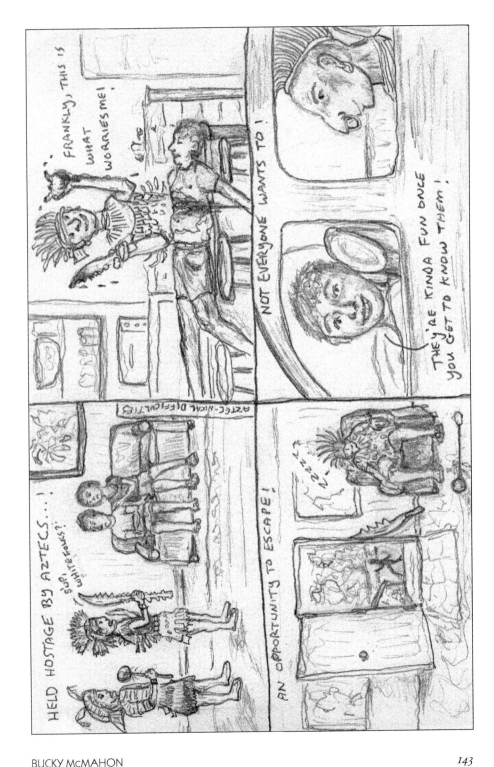

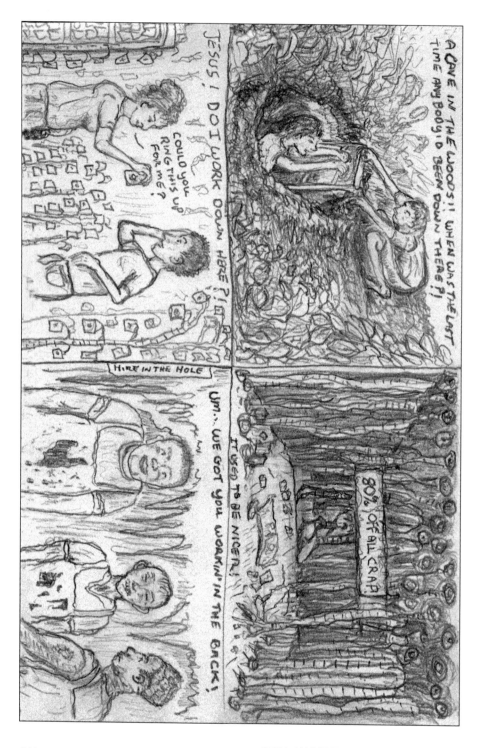

FROM AN ILLUSTRATED DREAM JOURNAL

FROM AN ILLUSTRATED DREAM JOURNAL

FROM AN ILLUSTRATED DREAM JOURNAL

FROM AN ILLUSTRATED DREAM JOURNAL

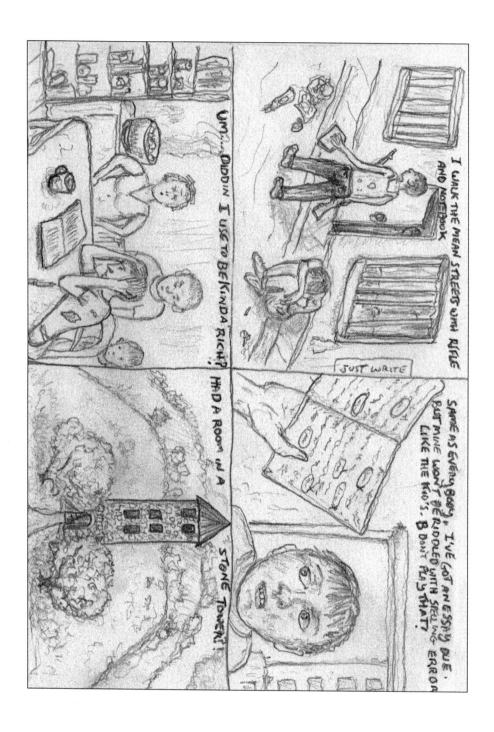

FROM AN ILLUSTRATED DREAM JOURNAL

FROM AN ILLUSTRATED DREAM JOURNAL

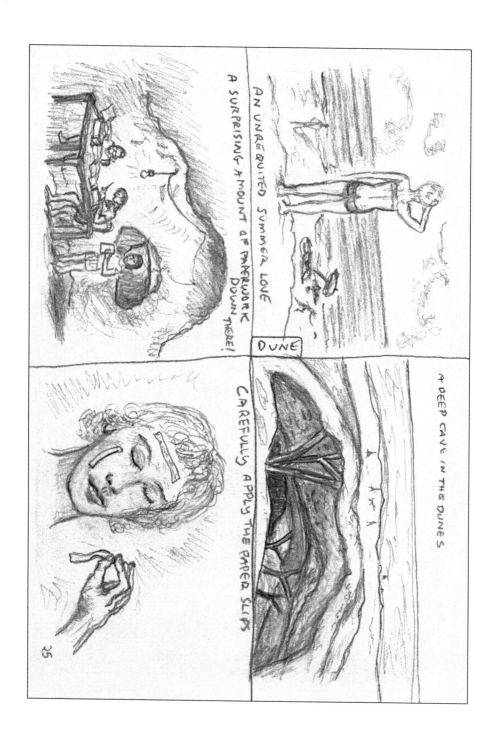

FROM AN ILLUSTRATED DREAM JOURNAL

FROM AN ILLUSTRATED DREAM JOURNAL

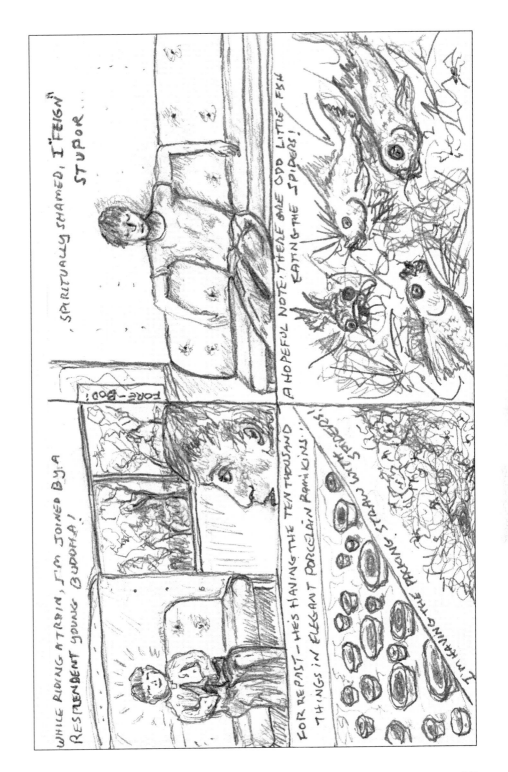

Searching for Madonna
at the Mahakumbh

New Delhi: The biggest stars of showbiz are expected to visit the Ma-hakumbh in Allahabad later this month. The premium guest list includes Madonna, Sharon Stone, Pierce Brosnan, Demi Moore, and Richard Gere. British tour operator Cox & Kings confirmed the visit of Hollywood stars but refused to reveal names on security grounds. "We are bringing in more than six hundred premium guests to the Kumbh from around the world,"— Indranil Pramanik in the development department of Cox & Kings told the Times of India.

The man who died for a living had dragged himself, or had been dumped by some assistant, near one of the pontoon bridges crossing the sand flats on the wide, pre-monsoon shores of the Ganges, and there he had set up shop on a wretched scrap of blanket. That meant that hundreds of thousands of pilgrims passed him on their way to the river to perform their ritual bathing to cleanse their souls. Yet no one seemed to notice him. True, a few rupee coins had been tossed onto the blanket, maybe fifty cents' worth. The look I gave him was brief, the sort granted to those apparitions that float up out of dyspeptic insomnia and jolt you awake. The man who died for a living had a bloody hole in his face where his nose should've been. A bluish foam bubbled from his purple lips. He looked all-over scorched, with patchy hair and peeling skin. Blind and leprous, he'd propped himself up on one elbow in the classic pose of prostration, his other arm raised, petitioning the heavens. Amid the greatest crowd of people ever assembled in the history of humankind — local officials put the number at seventy million over the six-week course of the Mahakumbhmela; others estimated more — the man who died for a living was dying alone.

I hurried past. In my pockets I had one last hundred-rupee bill left over after paying the sadhus, the Hindu holy men, for various performances. One jolly, bald-headed Baba, a grinning Telly Savalas, danced with a lemon balanced on his head. His companions in blue silk robes carried pikes. "Money," one of them had finally said, when merely standing subtly in my way with his weapon at port arms hadn't worked. Next, after Mike had made inquiries, we watched a young *naga* ("naked") sadhu, his skin dusted blue with ashes, dreadlocks piled in a beehive atop his head, casually stretch his penis back between his legs and knot it around his Bronze Age trident, symbolic of Shiva. Then another naga nimbly hopped onto his back, bare feet on the weapon's shaft, radically elongating the first naga's unit until it stretched down to his knees — Ta da!

Whatever the performance was worth, my American friends, Mike and Micki, and I had apparently underpaid. "The headman is very angry; he says you must leave at once," a volunteer interpreter informed us. So we beat a hasty retreat from the camp, which Mike and Micki called Naga Town, and rejoined the thousands drifting toward the river.

Just beyond the man who died for a living, I was ambushed by twin boys — I think they were twins — about four or five years old, who held up tin beggars' cups. Curly heads, smudged faces. Cute kids. Trick or treat. I stopped, made eye-contact with the boys (bloody amateur), and reached into my pocket. A man selling flutes quickly angled over to make a pitch; a postcard vendor drifted in. I knew that the slightest attention towards these two would release a torrent of enthusiastic persuasion. A small crowd began to gather round me — a Westerner in cash-dispensing posture. I dropped my last hundred-rupee note into one boy's cup and signed that the two were to share. "Fifty each," I said. Generous. Extravagant, really. But the tot with the hundred rupees began to slip away. I pointed after the fleeing kid, as if to say to the other, "Hey, he's getting away with your money!" and the little curly-haired mendicant with the smudged face gave chase. I saw him catch his partner and be roughly elbowed away. He came trotting back to me, cup raised, wondering aloud, in rapid-fire Hindi, where was his one hundred rupees. I thought he had an excellent case against me. Behind us I heard the man who died for a living wailing like a dog being burned alive. Time for me to be moving on.

Up ahead, Mike was bulling through the Kumbh crowd with his heavy cameras slung over his shoulders. At six feet six, Mike towered over the Hindu faithful who surged all around us in brightly colored dhotis and diapers and saris or just plain starkers, all hurrying along on skinny bird legs. Mike and his wife Micki, fiftyish early retirees from Orlando, had invested well and were just cruising the world photographing and videotaping everything. I'd met them that morning at breakfast, attracted by Micki's friendly aura and Mike's forthright Americanness.

He asked if I'd just come from the world and if I had any news about the stock market. I didn't, but wondered just how important the stock market could be to him, that his only question was about its rise or fall.

"Let me tell you," Mike said. "By way of a little story." On the way to the Cox & Kings camp on the Allahabad highway, their driver had turned down a little side road to show them a very old temple. It wasn't so impressive from the outside — but it was what was going on inside that was amazing: the sheer religious fervor! He said it had been like a rugby scrum, the congregation crawling all over one another to get to the idol. "That's kind of how we feel about the stock market," Mike said. "We've been very lucky," Micki stage-whispered to me.

Now I saw the big guy working his way back toward me, shrugging: there was apparently nothing ahead of particular photographic interest. He saw the beggar boy tugging at my elbow and observed, "He must detect some weakness in you." Mike had told me about being pursued at the Taj Mahal by a cripple on a handcart, a slow-motion chase that lasted an hour, resulting in Mike finally giving the guy five American, in reluctant admiration of his sheer doggedness.

"Have you seen Micki?" Mike asked.

"I'm right here," Micki said, and then she gasped and grabbed my arm. "Oh, God! That man just *died*!"

The Mahakumbhmela, the great Hindu festival of river bathing, dates back millennia, beyond the Vedas and the Upanishads, probably back to the original riverine culture at the dawn of awareness and language. Water! someone finally said. *Love it*! Pure, fresh from the Himalayas. Sky and river were married by osmosis; sensuous Saraswati, goddess of wisdom, lived in the blue Yamuna River, and Shiva, with his perpetual hard-on, gargantuan in power, filling the sky, came down into the muddy brown Ganges. People multiplied under the union, for the sky and river were good together. *Amrit*, the nectar of immortality, was in the water thus fructified, it was said. And in A.D. 2001, great crowds of millions mobbed the river banks and got in the water to praise and absorb it.

On particularly auspicious days, dawn processions of thousands of sadhus in great juggernaut carts drawn by tractors (until recently, by elephants, thus does the world decline) led millions of Hindu pilgrims from all over the Indian subcontinent to the temple steps at the river. Some of the sadhus, down from the Himalayan caves, hadn't slept in years. Some had held an arm overhead till it withered. Or two. Their fingernails grew in wild spirals on gnarled fence-post limbs. Some traveled very far, advancing by throwing themselves down, rising, then throwing themselves down again. Some did tricks with their dicks. Why these austerities and contrarieties? To show contempt for the body and for "reality," to stoke the faith, the inner fire, for this event. To kick-start the gods. At their appointed time, they charged the river, shaking their weaponry and roaring, letting the gods hear it. Three dunks and they were out of there, for here came everybody else, the tidal surge of aroused believers. In the ensuing rush to the river, people were trampled to death or drowned or separated from their families forever (sometimes on purpose; there was much "granny dumping" going on according to the newspapers) — but never too many, the losses acceptable, and all who bathed were blessed.

Mahakumbhmelas happen only once every 144 years, and so this was the first Kumbh where Western photographers shot pomo photos of sadhus posed in front of studio backgrounds hugging big briar bushes to their naked flesh. It was the first with Internet buzz, celebrity rumors, auguries of world significance. Thousands of Western tourists were expected. Many might come to bathe, and a percentage of those would actually go through with it after seeing the condition of the Ganges. Mike and Micki weren't bathers.

Carey and Claudia Turnbull of Long Island were, potentially. They had met thirty years ago at a small, hip private college. Claudia studied organic farming. Carey taught TM for years, then became a very successful energy broker. He wore the wire-rimmed glasses of the perennially youthful student, had bright blue eyes, shocking white hair, and the untroubled pink brow of a devoted meditator. Since moving to the Hamptons, Claudia's interests had expanded to include the equestrian art of dressage. The sweetness of the former flower child still shone through sophistication, though, along with the maternal steel of a mother of teenagers. Both were devotees of Indian philosophy, and this was their first trip to India. They were definitely thinking about bathing.

The Turnbulls and I had been on the same flight from Delhi and convoyed in two cars from Varanasi to Allahabad, and we'd shared culture shock. Our drivers were stoic middle-aged road warriors who might've driven calmly had it been their karma to be driving elsewhere. But the law of the road here was, *Pass every obstacle as soon as possible, with one hand on the wheel and one hand on the horn.* And there was never an end to the obstructions. The whole history of transportation was on the move to the Kumbh. A Mardi Gras of pedestrians. A China of bikes and rickshaws. Camels and oxcarts and failed futuristic Eastern-bloc cars, all vying for the two narrow lanes, with an endless stream of heavy trucks trumping all. Twenty centuries of *T. rex* couldn't have terrorized the countryside more thoroughly than those trucks, manufactured by the firm Tata, blasting past, their grilles gaudily painted to resemble Hindu gods, horns blazing — *Taa! Taa!* — stirring the dust of the exhausted soil and soaking it with fumes.

The great Gangetic plain at dusk was Halloween colors, miles upon miles of rows and rows of little shops selling swigs of tea and tiny plastic forehead decorations costing less money than we could conceive of. In the patches between towns, six-foot-tall bee-hive-shaped mounds of dung dominated the desiccated landscape, as if at any moment you might hear a high-pitched shrilling and see a giant ant waving its antennae above the huts. But sci-fi wasn't needed here to announce something new to this earth, namely everything all at once — the industrial age atop the cow-dung age, all five thousand years of history and every blow showing.

The Turnbulls and I were both clients of Cox & Kings, the venerable outfitters based in London, and had similarly been sheltered in Delhi by that company's thorough attentiveness. It was fucking great, don't get me wrong. I wasn't merely assisted at every turn but cheered on, rooted for. All the Third World hassles smoothed away, India for Idiots. And I was rooting for them, too, for the clever and able guides like Bharat, my guide in Delhi, who showed me the beautiful stone carvings at Qutab Minar, an ancient temple site, and explained that all the Hindu statues were missing their noses because the Mogul conquerors had finally been too exhausted by the sheer volume of devotional statuary to break every-thing. Here, even Bharat's personal favorite deity, Ganesha, the elephant-headed god, was proboscis-less. "The long trunk is wisdom," Bharat said, stroking the broken stone.

In Delhi at red lights, beggar women worked the traffic. I'd been advised by my travel brochure not to support public begging but to con-tribute to a reputable charity and to carry simple toys and puzzles for children. I was reaching into my pocket for a rubber ball when the light changed and the woman who had been making hand motions at the mouth of the infant on her hip had to dodge the onrushing cars to make it back to the median.

"The ball won't help," Bharat had said. "Educate the child. See that it has a career. By this means only may karma be improved."

Now at the outskirts of Allahabad, the Turnbulls and I struck a bot-tleneck, soldiers in military vehicles weaving through a caravan of cam-els and pilgrims on foot. A half-hour later our cars were cleared to prod through the crowded cobbled streets of town, down to the river, where we turned south onto the main Kumbh road. The pilgrims on that newly ploughed temporary thoroughfare parted reluctantly at bumper point, many turning to glare, or gape, or send some haunting message through the mental telepathy of pathos: We're alive. It's India. Bearded brother, mother, grandfather, great-great-great grandmother walking bent in half, and the driver shifting her with his horn. Here was everybody who had ever lived. It was like being caught in Armageddon with the resurrected dead, in the last two cars on earth, honking through a gauntlet of hard times and lean, malnourished limbs, breaking through at last to the Cox & Kings' camp, gasping: "Ah, thank God! It's the rich again!"

There, in the compound, on good high ground, territory a shrewd commander would've seized, you were safe. You could think; you had space to contemplate. You could pick a promontory and look out over the Kumbh, both banks of the Ganges lit up to the horizon. A battlefield haze of dung and sandalwood smoke hung over everything. Neon swastikas flashed on and off, and pinwheels whirled above the canvas cities and the countless Stone Age campsites. Fervent prayers sputtered from hundreds of competing PA systems, and underlying it all was the constant din of a million muttered mantras, shouted imprecations, laughter and lamentations dunning the naked sky, wringing the teats of eternity, begging for amrit, the nectar of immortality. I wondered if Madonna was here already.

A week earlier, the sadhus has staged a sit-in against the so-called luxury camp. Formidable opposition, you'd think, considering the sadhus' ability to sit. But the holy men had been mollified by a VIP tour, a little show of respect. See: Cox & Kings had erected a little open-sided temple with its Shiva lingam, the smooth, upright phallic stone that set a pious tone. True, there were flush toilets and showers in the tents for the Westerners — no big deal, not the saloon the mystics had perhaps been fearing. Alcohol and meat were strictly forbidden. It was just a nice camp, all right? With a couple of armed guards at the entrance, like what you'd expect on an expensive African safari. It offered the upper-class faithful, well-heeled seekers, trust-fund hippies, the idle, moneyed curious a ringside seat at the ancient bout between the credulity of men and the nullity of the gods, as well as a fighting chance against airborne infectious diseases.

Could tea be had by a weary traveler at that chill hour, past suppertime? It could. I followed a raked gravel path lit with candles in little clay pots — a pretty touch — to the dining tent for refreshments and to look for famous people.

None of 'em had showed yet.

Turning in, I wore just about everything I'd brought and pulled the down cover on the camp bed over my head and was awakened anyway by the cold at around 4 a.m., that auspicious moment when a mad hair-splitter would say that night had just begun to ease its obscuring ass off mankind, that very first slim crack of dawn. Already the mantra-fying was intensifying, as if the whole Kumbh were trying to lift off: *Gimme amrit, gimme gimme amri, gimme gimme gimme amrit, gimme the shit, dammit, gimme amrit!* I staggered through the tent flaps and stood kicking the cold turf around a guttering campfire until real light.

At indubitable dawn, a French couple came out and stood nearby, wrapped romantically in cloaks, gazing down at the expanse of smoldering Kumbh-scape. I sidled up and asked what was good. What had they liked so far?

"Now is good," the Frenchman said. "When everyone is just up is interesting time, though maybe it is a bit too incredible, the reality."

The sleepy guards were wrapped in shawls like shepherds, with heavy shotguns for staffs. Metal junkyard walls made a narrow alleyway down to the Kumbh main street, already busy with troops of robed monks marching by, each with his metal meal bucket. They were members of a sect that did everything in unison. Brigades of them swept down the main street, swinging wide around obstacles like the segments of a saffron-colored caterpillar. I took the first dirt road that led down toward the river. The place was on the scale of Spartacus's army. A hundred thousand campers were waking up, going through their ablutions as best they could in the cold wet dirt — coughing, hawking, spitting, blowing their noses — the Hindu obsession with cleanliness tested under impossible conditions. It had been a hard, cold night for camping, and everyone in this poor sector looked perfectly miserable.

The road turned sandy and churned. There, a hundred yards distant across a beach, was the Ganges, silver in the mist, and the beautiful Sangam steps at Allahabad and the Muslim fort hard by. Admiring the view from the beach were thousands of pilgrims squatting. Oh, excuse me. I looked down at my feet. There was a little twist a yard away. Another just beyond it. I was standing in a pointillist landscape of poop! Holy shit!

Back at camp, I saw the Turnbulls at breakfast in the dining tent. The noise wasn't helping Claudia with her jet lag. She, too, had been awakened by the din at 4 a.m. "I woke up in this panic, wondering what the hell I'd gotten myself into," she said.

The Turnbulls were debating bathing in the Ganges but stayed at the camp and rested most of the first day, while I accompanied Mike and Micki in a hired jeep to Naga Town and saw a bit of the epic ten-hour Ramayana sung by a turbaned tenor, costumed dancers accompanying him onstage. Holy men, some as young as two years old, sat on thrones in ornate pavilions and gave out ritual blessings to coin-paying throngs. I met a young Hindu in Western casual attire who said, "I think the reason you are here is for the nudity, to put it on the Internet." Got it in one, I congratulated him. But, overcoming his prejudices, he became our interpreter with the nagas, the "Cock Babas," as Mike called them, who were puffing cigarettes like Irish priests, red-eyed from the chillums they stoked with tobacco and hashish. They wanted money to buy a cooking log for their campfire, our interpreter told us. We could see it was sputtering out. We settled down on rugs with them, and they served us tea, and shortly after they got angry and threw us out., for reasons I couldn't guess but didn't doubt were reasonable.

Next day, the Turnbulls had the idea to take a river trip, and perhaps to bathe. Yes, a river trip would be delightful. Carey hired Manoj, a dapper and amiable freelance guide who spoke some English and could smooth our way. Manoj found a boat at the riverside and negotiated for two boatmen to row and haul us canal-style upcurrent in their heavy twenty-foot boat. They held umbrellas to shield us from the sun. First we crossed the wide Ganges and visited some friends of the Turnbulls who were living in an ashram outside Allahabad, right in the midst of the Kumbh. The friends came out to the gate, all four old pals, positive, energetic American men in robes. They had bathed in the Ganges earlier in the day and had been approached by TV people. "We were more interested in doing our thing than in talking to the press," one said. "But if I were telling the story, I wouldn't focus on sensible phenomena — what you see, or smell. Because a lot of what you see isn't pretty. And a lot of it stinks. No, I'd focus on how it feels, how it *feels* to be in India."

It was a perfectly beautiful afternoon to be on the Ganges, back in the boat, the oarsman straining with his still-youthful arms, his partner on the dune up ahead, the rope taut over his shoulder. Carey, I could tell, was going in. He had the look of someone on a high dive doing all the right things mentally to jump. Claudia and I saw a corpse bobbing against a buoy, tangled in the ropes. We decided not to mention it to Carey.

Where the Yanuma meets the Ganges, a flotilla of boats had clustered on the V-shaped shoals. Here the mood was festive, families having their ritual bath with flowers and prayers and anointing of the body with blessed unguents, marking the foreheads of the just-bathed with sandalwood and burnt umber. Even the gaily colored crowd on the Sangam steps, and for miles along the river's edge, looked, from this distance, blessed and safe, saved.

Manoj said he had secured permission to cross the deck of the boat next to us, and Carey, stripped to his skivvies, climbed over and into knee-deep water. "Very cold," he announced, hugging himself and slogging out to join a dozen other bathers in deeper water. He held his nose. "Here goes!"

Claudia wasn't going in. Nope, nope. She'd decided. She was meeting her daughter here and would be in India for a month. She couldn't get sick. Carey at least would be back in New York where he could see his doctor.

"How about you?" Claudia asked me.

"Me?" I said. "No, I don't really believe in any of this."

In fact, since she asked, I'd never felt more dismayed by the religious urge of mankind. What I felt like doing was rushing home and pressure-washing my house. Then maybe finding some small soluble local problem and bitching till it was fixed. Because it looked to me like we were all in terrible trouble. I know it's tough in other places, too, but here — a billion people, religious conflict, environmental degradation, the nuke.

"I believe the planet could crack open right here," I said. "I mean, it looks as if it's going to."

"You think so?" Claudia said.

"Oh, I really don't know," I said. Because I really didn't know anything, less than ever, if that were possible. I was too newly arrived in India, too whiplashed, to be at all objective, or even to guess how India would *feel* from one moment to the next. And I was right about that, at least. Because the next day Claudia did bathe, to considerable fanfare, a Western woman overcoming her fear. And because the man who died for a living, after he had collapsed on his blanket, his chest heaving once and then sinking with an enormous groan, a real death rattle, after he lay still — it seemed like several minutes — all eyes on him, Mike's, Micki's, mine, the flute salesman's, the postcard vendor's, all except those of the beggar boy, young Smudge, whose were fixed to mine while he continued to plead with or curse at me, tugging my sleeve, after all that, the man who died for a living sat up. He reached out and patted the coins on the blanket and drew himself upright with sudden dignity and grace, like an athlete, a gymnast of disaster, and carried on.

Newt New

Call him Newt New, onomatopoeia for two quick toots of the horn, startling you — Newt New! — as he pulls up in the Flambeau parking lot across the street from the Late Night Library, and because there's something salamandrine about him, rubbery like the newborn, and in his posture something grappling, as if every gesture were a climbing forth onto a new rock.

There! — the way he grapples out of his new red Mazda surprised and eager as if it were an egg. He takes three sudden steps toward the road as if chasing his own head, his body weaving under it as he scoots across the street in a zigzag rolling motion to the gaping Late Night front door. Let's follow him in.

Scared? Come on. It's dark like a spookhouse. And loud, with a beat that vibrates the bones, and lots of people standing cheek by jowl and shouting to be heard, faces slashed with strobe light, high-tech war paint.

There goes Newt, moussed embryo in whiteboy zootsuit — ultrabig trou, loose swashbuckler blouse — down into the dance pit, wriggling towards the heat of the middle swarm. It's after hours; if we're going to follow we'll have to check our beer or bottle and mixers with an attendant who'll assign us a storage niche and a bucket to throw up in; that and the public-park restroom plywood interior lend the Libe an inappropriate subterranean gymnasium quality, like a nightmare set in a high school locker room — post-apocalyptic sixth-period gym chic.

That's the mood, too, anxious, hyper-expectant, the peak of the week, the last scrap of Saturday night to snatch. There's an esprit de corps in the crowd of several hundred undergrads, the shock troops of John Barleycorn, the elite party corps doing what it does best — being there and not being square. In the contest between John Dewey and Dionysius that is the student psyche, the old pedant has been knocked down onto his chalk-dusted duff. Enough with the delayed gratification, the long-term promises of education. Whatcha got right now?

Drums. Fire. Dance dance dance. '92 skidoo and go Rimbaud! The pit is a furious boil of bodies, white flashes of perfect teeth; at the pit's edge a fringe of bopping half dancers waiting to hop in. Time's almost up. Don't wait too long.

All at once, music off, lights up. Furious squinting. A hushed near-silence, almost shame. Sudden shocking tableaus: six young men on a scruffy patch of brown dirt wincing like rats in a flashlight's beam as they look up from examining a pool of vomit for sports prognostication purposes. Hideous surroundings, really. This building, site of skuzzy bars since biblical times, may house an unclean spirit. Highly religious Swedes with heart conditions beware!

But there goes Newt New, scooting through the exiting crowd — slippery bugger. Newt New! Where to, Newt New? Party at the Timbers, you say. Where at the Timbers? Big place the Timbers. You'll know when you see it. Follow that Mazda!

We pull into the Timbers, 3 a.m., a caravan of us circling through the dark complex. Yeah, this is the wrong place, and you've led a dozen of us here, damn it, New. Where to now? Newt New, point guard of pandemonium, grapples out of the Mazda, takes his quick rolling steps around the parking lot, tongue flickering out to taste the air, gestures briskly with a little forearm — "Come on!" — wriggles back into the Mazda and vrooms away.

We follow, the dozen lost cars weaving through the Timbers, then we're there. Couldn't miss it. Bam bam bam of slamming car doors; magnetic march towards the music, the same Late Night crowd reconvened like a swarm of bees, the honey-making business never done. There goes Newt, slipping in the townhouse door.

After you?

Same throbbing beat. Wall to wall bodies in a stranger's living room — stranger to us, that is. In the center of things, couples, the queens and kings in a tight vertical dance, the rest of us in slow peristalsis around them to get to the person behind the person in front of us. My god, it is very late now indeed. Newt New is on the move again, out the sliding glass doors. But let's concede. Let 'em go. Just rest, hang in the quick-flowing stream like a battered salmon, the time-blown fry of generation jostling shouting, shoving. Such hubbub!

Note to self: This energy should be harnessed since it can't well be educated. Suggest we haul out the engines from *our* aircraft carriers and set these youths to rowing them about the Mediterranean. Just what I needed at that age: to be taken in hand by some far-sighted fascist. Eternal gratitude, that kind of thing.

ENC 1102: Writing About Death

I was fuming when I left my late-afternoon, first-year Writing About Death class, a special-topics course I had proposed specifically to attract nosferatu, somnambulists, and automata, the life-like subjects I required for my post-doc research in Ennui. Still, there's a difference between the slavish obedience I expected and the mulish irresponsiveness I was getting, and they damn well knew it. Those callow youths, I whined to myself, gimping across the campus green, my hump smarting, they were incapable of focusing their attention for more than five minutes on the subject of death.

We had been discussing this hypothetical situation: "How would Michael Jackson feel if he awoke from cryogenic suspension in the distant future to discover the simultaneous regeneration of the giant saurians?" That would be a Thriller, eh? I'd snorted. Beat that, eh Jacko, what? Despite my promptings the discussion had not gone well.

I shifted tack immediately. "True, I am far more moribund than yourselves, and have furthermore glimpsed certain neurological horrors owing to a post-adolescent attempt at non-mechanical flight from the third-story balcony of the Daytona Beach Sheraton, and yet I ask you to share with me, from your immature perspective (you to whom life still seems endless as a child's summer, yet it is brief; class longa, vita breva, as the saying goes, my chickens). I solicit your opinion on this essential matter: what is your favorite thing about death?"

"Anyone? Anyone? No one? All right then, take out a piece of paper!"

I gave them a pop quiz — one diabolical question — and after snappishly collecting the papers, I tapped my chalk three times on the blackboard and brought them out of their trances. "On the count of three you will awaken, it will be the end of the semester, you will remember nothing that has transpired here."

And then I stomped theatrically from the room flourishing my cape.

Luckily, the Mecca was nearby, under new ownership, and serving beer. The place has been revamped since the days they called us all "doc."

Seminole-iana dominates the décor — retired jerseys, photos of Renegade, Bubba B., Burt, a young Hugh Durham (a man who was born looking thirty; I'd love to do a lost-wax cast of that head). Candy-striped tablecloths clash gaily with the linoleum checkerboard floor: very preppy, very collegiate in a crew-cut, go-out-for-long-one-Biff sort of way.

Nice. But not to my taste, I who prefer things massive, dim, Gothic. "The Rocky Horror Picture Show" played upon the opposition of the Gothic and American pop nostalgia, though no better than I did myself, sulking over my quizzes in that bright soda stand, half listening to a volley of Bobbie Segar and Steve Miller. I ordered skinny fries and a Bud Light draft and wondered if 2,000 years from now someone would be sitting on this same stool, some millennial dolt named Zoldar or Quareg, his blue jeans in a slightly different cut, listening to Steve Miller complain about being called a "space cowboy." I fucking hoped so.

I ordered a second draft and flipped through the quizzes. I scribbled "Not!" across the top of one, sniggering at my ironic usage. It was a nice crowd, multi-ethnic, multi-clique, some neo-hippies, some ball-capped Kappa Alphas, but mostly preppy recessionauts, one eye on fashion, one eye on the bottom line.

Could I get snottier? No, not and continue to drink. I was mellowing. I decided not to count the quiz after all. The question had been: "Why does bread go stale?" Some had answered how it loses its pliability, employing chemical symbols to illustrate the loss of moisture. But what was that but description, albeit sophisticated, a mere model of the thing that in no way addressed the essential question of *why*. No one had grasped that I meant bread as a metaphor for life. Why do we grow old? Why is there time? Why?

I was musing on that question as I headed for the door, when the bartender politely called me back. Oh. *Pay* for the beer. Right. I shuffled shamefacedly back, reaching for my wallet with, let us call it, a practiced gesture.

Hangovers

Somebody sing the praise of hangovers. Only quietly, OK? Please?

That was some game last Saturday, huh? We gave them hell, though personally, what with my knees, and lower back, my sciatica, I probably wouldn't survive a single collision on the field. I spent the entire game in a bar destroying God's property and hiding from those big SUVs flying little garnet and gold pennants.

Predictably, the Strip around midnight rollicked with the frenzied, bell-ringing joy one might hallucinate while being rescued from a shipwreck. By then the god of wine was using my Nikes to trample toes on some of the Strip's best dance floors; he was spending my money as if he were trying to impress me; and by last call he seemed to be in some god-awful hurry, as if there were some train to catch to another dimension — where the atoms are happier, who knows? — as if he were an angel missing his flight, taking little leaps at the moon (poor thing, like a frog in a jar), then bent double, finally apotheosizing all over our sneakers.

Sunday morning I had a little hangover. Not a bad hangover. Nothing, really, anybody who, in addition to being afraid and irresolute, used to living on the brink of broke, of personal, existential annihilation, encouraged by society and programmed by heredity to drink and who actually *likes* to drink would call memorable. It was observable. It wasn't the sort of condition you'd have to be mad and deaf like Goya to look at, the very nether face of the Dark Side. Never again I said after *that* time, and so far so good.

This Sunday morning I was up with my hangover before the sun could heave across the meridian and call me a bum. I splashed hot coffee on my stunned brain cells and cornered my attention in a wedge of newspaper. When I'm hung over the limited interest I normally bring to the world's daily crisis becomes qualified by a fatuous sort of infantile regret that if I didn't have this headache I might bestir myself and set some of this to rights, as if as soon as I feel strong enough I'm going to get up and go to the bathroom and throw up, and then look out world!

I lingered over the paper. Much later, after many pathetic paw scrapes at the door, I said Oh, all right! And we got up and walked the dogs, my hangover and I.

It wasn't bad company, this hangover. It wasn't threatening me with death, for instance. I wasn't even sorry I had it. Still, in the world of heat and light outside, it seemed I had finally ruined something delicate, some mechanism that performed a vital function you'd never miss till it was broke, like controlling the volume of the music of the spheres. The world now had a phantom electric hum to it like a clock radio with the alarm left on for a week. But I wasn't complaining. I could eat. I could smoke. I could walk. I could curse. If anything my cursing was improved.

You know what I like to do on a Sunday morning when I'm a little hung over? I like to go for a spin. Take it on the road, show it the sights. Nothing too taxing — just a little Sunday drive in the country. Since the brain with its big ideas lost its vote last night, a perfect destination is some place of nearly neutral attraction, a movie you wouldn't see if you were healthy, or a culinary quest for a foodstuff the sulking body designates as desirable — never you mind, brain.

Go get a Nutty-Buddy, maybe? A Klondike Bar? Some flan? How bout some hot boiled peanuts and a beer? My hangover began jumping up and down, rolling its eyes and squealing like an idiot child at the suggestion. Then boiled peanuts it would be, my lad. This is, you must know, a great town for boiled peanuts.

Our first stop was a transitory shred of blue tarpaulin casting a kerchief-sized bit of shade over a sawed-off beer barrel and the ball-capped warlock who stirred the roiling goobers within. He had the kind of nose I'm going to deserve, lipped an unfiltered ciggie in a blistered slash of mouth, hair by Injun Joe, fashions by Pap Finn. "You look like hell," he said to me. "Rough night?"

I bought a dollar dipper of his "Hot Boiled P-Nuts."

My hangover liked them fine. It greedily processed them into our mouth while I drove. We swung north counter-clockwise up Capital Circle Southeast, looking for more and still more hot boiled peanuts. A hangover can be as imperious as a sultan; in its grip the mind cowers and quails like a dove that wishes only to fly toward some chaste future. Better to fly no farther than the next peanut stand. While we fed on the goobers in hand, the mind sought fitting metaphors, as it must. The celebrated circus elephant Jumbo came lumbering to mind — Jumbo, who turned upon and killed his cruel trainer. Therein lay a fable of drinking: the poor, shackled body, civilized, socialized, conditioned, covered up, bullied, goaded, made to balance atop beach balls before children, finally breaking free on a trumpeting rampage, laying waste all around until, having run its course of havoc, it comes to rest miles away in a field of daisies, a bit a amazed, a bit sorry, maybe, to find that cruel trainer of a superego still impaled upon its bloody tusks.

Thus ruminating, we snuffled our trunk in the bag for another nut.

Ochlocknee, Dionysus, Pine Sol

I believe if the doors of perception were cleansed everything would appear to man as it is: in need of a good Pine Sol scrubbing. Last Saturday morning, in an attempt to keep my mind off of certain events of the previous Friday night, I set about a total prolonged derangement of all my furniture. I have a little beige recliner from Goodwill that manages to convey the heartbreaking pathos of genteel poverty striving for respectability but failing and sinking back into drunken despair—a regular Barrymore, that one. I frisked it for change, then set it out in a sunny place in the yard where it could emote to its heart's content.

The Tibetans have a word, "Bardo" — literally, between-two-existences — which they use to describe the hellish space between the refrigerator and the wall. Nothing, however, a little Pine Sol and elbow grease, a roll of paper towels and a scraping tool wouldn't take care of. Or not. I stumbled to the nearest window and decided to set upon it with a toothbrush and Ajax, for I believe if the windows of perception were cleansed everything would appear to man as it truly is: covered with teeny-weeny little parts of dead insects.

Pine Sol fumes and gnat-wing inhalation drove me into a Dionysian frenzy right around sundown and I had to be thrown into the back of a pickup truck in a shipping box and driven, scratching and frothing, to the Ochlockonee Banks Restaurant and Bar for some Saturday night stomping. But I wasn't by any means the only animal in the back of a truck. One animal-lover had left the radio in his monster truck tuned to WTNT Country to console his boxed Dobie, who was howling inconsolably anyway.

A good Dionysian frenzy will put you in touch with the vegetative regenerative powers of the unconscious, with the crazy wisdom of the body as animal expression of universal mind. Yet even in my frenzy I thought the $3 cover a tad steep. They were packing them in, though. The only space in the place was on the dance floor, which suited me and my bacchante just fine. We were soon slow slam dancing to a cover of

"Magnolia" — "you sweet thang" — and cheering on an intrepid cockroach as it tried to run the dance floor gantlet between the Scylla and Charybdis of innumerable scraping cowboy boots. It didn't make it.

Dionysian frenzies can be messy, expensive, and dangerous. Also known as "the dentist's best friend" for the boost they give to the half-plate business, they'll frighten your pets, alienate your friends, turn strangers into hostile litigants or make them come upside your head, mothah-fuckah! Our prisons are full of people whose only recollection of their crimes is a mixture of ideas taken half-baked from Sir James Frazier's "The Golden Bough," and, say, a quart of hard liquor. Still, it often feels too good to stop, and if you employ a little common sense, a designated driver, and a Hannibal Lecter-style face-mask, there's no reason why you should have to.

My bacchante and I sure didn't. We headed on to Roosters, where there's never a cover and the ballroom-size dance floor always jams with some of the strangest birds in the whole Big Bend. Saturday night the Hutch and Brand Band belted out dead-on covers of Rod Stewart anthems to the delight of spandex-clad Britt Eklund-ites. I wanted very much to lie on the parquet while they "threshed" me corn-god style with the spiked heels of their boots. Instead, I was hauled away, protesting vehemently, if incoherently, to Kahunas to ride the upsidedown Margarita barber chair — "twirl till you hurl" — and then hit the disco dance floor, where I indicated the ceiling repeatedly with a divinely directed forefinger. But you know your frenzy has about run its course when you begin to calculate the dance. You glance into the wall mirror and see your ego, like an errant parakeet, fluttering above you, looking for a way back in. It alights upon your head and, alas, you look ridiculous.

That's what *she* said. Me, I believe if the doors of perception were cleansed, everything would appear to man as it truly is: inifinite, or at least big enough for a little interpretive dancing.

Armadillophobia

They come in the night, up from their burrows, out of pre-history, little sinister dinosaurs from South America. Andale, andale! — they've come galumphing, across Mexican arroyo and Louisiana swamp, out of the woods and into our backyard, where they dig divots in the lawn, scuffing, snuffling, poking, as if looking for lost change. Genetic freaks — all identical quadruplets, and highly susceptible to leprosy — they give my wife, H.B., the creeps. They look half insect, half humanoid — body of a pill-bug, head of one of those poor kids who age too fast. Our four loud dogs despise them.

For me it's more personal. I identify. Back in my single days I was "Barmadillo," my bar-reviewer's by-line appearing under a cartoon rendering of an inebriated armadillo. A legacy of Christmas present trinkets links me to the brutes. Now I'm just a totem assassin. A typical armadillo whack goes like this: I'm in my P.J.s and rubber boots, down on my hands and knees sweating among the spiders and toads in the dirt under our deck. My right arm is thrust to the shoulder into a freshly dug burrow. I have an armadillo by the tail.

It chirrups and grunts — "Nyuck nyuck, nyuck nyuck" — ratcheting itself deeper into the earth. It's flexible boney carapace seems to copulate down into the dirt, like a rayfish burying itself in sand. The plated, bristly tail is cold as the grave. In its earthy element, the primitive insectivore is immensely strong, like a little roto-tiller run amok, headed for China.

"Golf club!" I say to H.B. standing by with flashlight and varmint tools. In my voice I hear a little of the arrogance of neuro-surgeon barking to assisting nurse. What I've got going for me is experience. I've been here before — damn plenty of times. And it always ends badly. H.B. raps the nose of our Irish setter, normally a sweet aging coquette, now a Madame LaForgue whining for bloody heads — then reaches me the handle of a two-iron.

I shove the club blade underneath the 'dillo, then twist and pull. Out it comes all at once like a bad tooth.

H.B. shrieks, "Ewwwww!"

And it is hideous, writhing in the flashlight beam, a chthonic gnome with pallid, wizened face, a poor Piglet far gone into leather and S&M. It scrabbles at my arm with its claws — the horror! — and I let go. You would, too.

Above all it must not dig again! I stab for it with an aluminum-handled fishing net. Breaking cover, it corners the house at a gallop, then cowers under H.B.'s car in the gravel drive. H.B. fetches her keys, starts the car and begins to back up. Alas for Dasypus novemcinctus, the nine-banded armadillo, its tendency to leap straight up when startled makes it synonymous with roadkill. There's a clunk and a crunch, and the stricken 'dillo makes one last dash, trailing viscera.

Suddenly the setter swoops in and snatches it up in a great mouthful and lopes off into the woods. Silence at last — and then the terrible scraping of tooth on nubby bone carapace. In the morning, cranky with lack of sleep, we find the armadillo half-buried atop a heaped-up ziggurat of dirt under the deck stairs like a "Lord of the Flies" idol, the dogs arrayed in attitudes of worship. Jesus. It didn't have to go down like that. Or did it?

For armadillos or Barmadillos, one day it does.

Horse Walking

One day on a whim I bought a horse. I was living on some land with a pasture and fences. My landlord said he didn't mind. And the horse was so cheap: a hundred bucks for a pinto! Who could say no? Everybody whose advice I asked told me, "Don't buy a young horse. You'll never be able to do anything with it." They were partly right. I did plenty with my brown and white spotted colt, most of it dangerous to myself. But in general I just raised Kidd like a dog, and like my other four dogs, made a spoiled pet of him.

Eventually Kidd consented to be ridden — reluctantly, indignantly. I didn't ride the other dogs, did I? He would come to a whistle, but always with an air of grievance, more a like a human teenager than a proper dog. It was easy to see why; herd animal that he was, the dogs and I were poor company for him, and though horses cannot weep or acquire piercings or wreck your car for you like a teenager, the Kidd could sulk with the best of them. If other horses and riders passed by on the dirt road in front of his pasture, it was Academy Award time. Such pathos, such heartbreak, such poignant equine shrieking. So I bought my horse a horse, and not just any horse but a mustang — a part of American history, or so the ad in the paper said. And then I was really in over my head.

For the horses it was love at first sight. They were Heathcliff and Cathy. Them against the world. I never rode the colt again in any direction but towards his paramour. Any other suggestion of mine led to wild bucking. To make matters worse, the mustang, Argentina, was a fence jumper, and Kidd, a 1,000 pound brute by then, would push down any barrier to get back to her side. When I'd return from work, my wife would meet me at the gate with the news: The horses had escaped again into the Apalachicola National Forest, which began where our pasture ended.

With a couple of leads looped over my shoulder, I'd set out to find them, the delighted dogs all along for the outing. It was easy to track the horses on the sandy logging roads. I became a veritable Sherlock Holmes at reading their gaits: the neat parentheses of a walk, the deeper commas of a canter, the gouged exclamation points of a gallop. If they left the roads, though, the mystery deepened. Then I'd have to depend on subtle impressions in the leafy duff, a snag of tail-hair on a briar. A mile, five miles, or ten miles later, I'd always find them, just hanging out, ripping at the landscape with their great square teeth. Then I usually wouldn't even need the lead ropes; they'd docilely follow me home. After all, it was feeding time.

Eventually, many dollars later, I horse-proofed the fences. But that just brought new troubles. The horses had had a taste of the open road and pleaded constantly for more with mournful whinnies and agitated trotting along the barriers, like a pair of Benjis from "The Sound and the Fury." I was too soft-hearted to walk the dogs and leave the horses behind. It wasn't fair! Boo hoo hoo. So I began to walk my horses.

With Kidd on a lead, and Argentina pressed close to his flanks, remora-style, and the dogs bounding ahead, we'd set out for the deep forest, where I could let them loose. I'd bring a book for the long dull passages of grazing, but sooner or later some electrical current would pass between the two horses; they'd clash together, nipping, rearing up, and off they'd go. They'd set out at a canter, and then, their own commotion exciting them, stretch out into a gallop, hoof-beats pounding thunderclaps, fading away into silence. The Questing Beast was loose — the hunt afoot.

I never walked farther, or for a clearer purpose, than when I was a walker of horses. It brought out the best in all of us. The dogs loved the mayhem and the gratuitous extra miles that increased my endurance — not to mention patience. There was never a dull moment with those two idiots along. The horses invented dramas in the barren scrub forest: They still believed in tigers, in the bottomlessness of a puddle, in the menace of a discarded appliance. Following horses, I learned that a walk would last as long as it took. They were large living embodiments of the Serenity Prayer. Above all I felt the joy of helping something big and habitually hindered — by fences and halters and bits — realize great gulps of freedom.

Of course, such chaotic fun probably couldn't be legal. It was certainly unsafe. To this day I have disturbing dreams of horses running loose in suburbs and cities, suddenly rearing up in the headlights of innocent speeding motorists. I met with a real horseman, an ex-rodeo champion, who was interested in purchasing Kidd. I hemmed and

HORSE WALKING

hawed, conflicted. He frowned and spit tobacco juice. "You can't make a horse into a kinda damn dog," he said. "A horse gotta be a horse." He offered me $400 for Kidd, $300 total to take the both of them off my hands. I accepted.

I still have photos, shot mostly from the rear, of my wild horses running free, and still feel the powerful pull of their appeal: Follow me.

Suwannee River

Though the old songwriter never saw it for himself, somehow Stephen Foster guessed right about the Suwannee River. It's a bathetic heart-breaker, the Blanche DuBois of waterways. Sometimes when I drive across and glance down at the tannin-dark river, I think of an old maiden aunt who lives in genteel squalor with her bourbon and bonbons and a dozen obese dachshunds. Or I remember my Intro to Cave Diving course, which took me a thousand yards under the limestone bed of the Suwannee and culminated with a lights-out, buddy-breathing emergency exit drill. That was like being mugged in a coffin. And sometimes I'll think of both — the Old South expiring in an alcoholic haze and that cave dive — and I scare myself.

Truth be told, though, I can't stay away. I remember those gothic banks, the gnarled mossy oaks bending solicitously over the river like a chorus of Elephant Man gentlemen callers, and know I must see her again, privately, in the back room. At every turn — and she's all curves — the Suwannee seduces with the promise of intimacy and silence, of shade and sloth and cool compliance. A cane pole, a catfish, a hibachi; a jug of wine and that girl of mine — now that's easy recreation!

Just the other day, in fact, I drove down. As usual, the Suwannee country was utterly undefended by traffic. I made the one red light in Perry, and then I was looking at 60 miles of blacktop and trees, a straightaway so vast I might have been in Brazil. I passed only one theme park where, through a ten-foot wire fence in the jungle, I glimpsed a pair of over-heated "Trophy Wild Boar" up to their beards in a wallow. Locals, I suppose, drive by this hunting camp with their rifle racks loaded and dream of being able to afford to shoot what's inside.

Down narrow leafy canyons shrieking with bugs I chased a puddle on the blacktop that I could never catch, and then slowed at last behind a battered pick-up truck that I couldn't pass. A good old boy waggled his toes out the passenger window while a woman drove; in back was the tow-headed brood, unwrapping candy and making themselves comfy on top of inner tubes. In downtown Mayo, under the staid old stone court-house, they turned north, bound for the Suwannee at Peacock Springs, while I crept east down Main Street then goosed the gas and raced back into the trees.

At Branford I crossed the iron-girdered bridge, passed the sign that read HISTORIC SUWANNEE RIVER and another that bore the lyrics of the first verse of Foster's song, and I thought, I'll show you "way down"! Just beyond the river, at the Steamboat Dive Inn, I parked and went inside to price some cave-diving gear.

I stood gaping at a rig of twin steel Scubapro 95s yoked with polished chrome dual-manifold valves, not cheap. Then Dustin Clesi, proprietor, came out from the back of the shop. We talked, and after a few minutes he pulled a roll of bills from his jeans pocket and tossed it onto the concrete floor. "A cave is a deep dark hole you throw money into," he warned. "Think about it."

All the lonely green way back to Mayo, I did think about it. I brooded on Suwannee River fun — the cheap fun that is floating on rafts and fishing with cane poles, and the costly fun that is shooting pigs and cave diving. Then I took that northbound turn at the courthouse and headed for Peacock Springs. I heard the screams and splashes of children, the scrunch of rubber rafts. I saw the beat-up truck and the family picnick-ing in the shade near the water and, coming out of the water, elaborately laden cavers, a community of the downward-drawn elect. I plunged into the spring in my shorts and hovered in the cold azure, which deepened to black at the cave's entrance. Sink or swim? I could feel it in my genes, the Suwannee's call to come on down. I was thinking sink.

Lake Ella

I am walking with my fellow citizens counter-clockwise around Lake Ella. Counter-clockwise seems to be the prevailing direction and I feel its rightness myself, first time around. The light is soft and gray and fading; fall's first cold front, passing through town heading southeast, piddles a light mist in brief bursts. Umbrellas bloom on the benches. Pigeons agitate in the surf of sound from the cars going home on Monroe Street. We walkers keep walking in the light rain.

We admire the reflection of the steeple in the lake, and the lake that makes the image, stippled with lily pads where minnows hide from fishes and fishes hide from ducks and ducks come waddling up like the uncoolest kids in the class, so forthright and questing, tilted forward into honest desire. Admirable ducks. A five-fingered fountain flares from the center of the lake, representing, when it's working, perpetual civic competence. Or maybe merely illustrating the physical laws it obeys, and costing what it costs to fling water at the sky — not that I'm complaining. North-northeast a Boy Scout troop intones the nagging tropes of the Pledge of Allegiance as if they'd been planning a coup or something, and then been talked into giving it up. We walkers walking round it think the scene — lake, steeple, Boy Scouts, clever, cozy park-side homes — would make a decent 1,000-piece puzzle.

Just off the puzzle proper, transients under the picnic shelters pass bottles and raucous bluster behind our staid murmurs. We all look employed, we murmuring walkers, some of us in soft silky training togs, some of us pumping our elbows and setting a pace to lose enough weight to justify a trip to the nearby Mill Restaurant for cheesecake. It's a meditative walk for those of us who aren't doing even that. We stroll in the failing light — three laps, four laps — and the furred indefiniteness of the far shore circling with us around the black radiance of the lake evokes the contemplative trance. We are sated with satisfying sensations, or most nearly, slowly revolving around the orb, as if it were a sort of prayer wheel of the ordinary. Yet in our quiet minds the odd thought may yet approach like a piebald duck.

The same Puzzle-maker — or not — who made the planets move in their rounds, makes us yearn to move, and moving, yearn, in perpetual corner-turning expectation. I know the shape of this desire, I remember it, an enchanted dogleg left down into a forest valley, around another bend to a series of falls, then up, up, up, to a gusting fountain in a meadow of flowers. Maybe aliens took me there; maybe I died for a moment in the dentist's chair; I maybe I just saw the picture in a supermarket tabloid — "Original Site of Heaven Discovered Near Massachusetts Golf Course" — when I was a toddler riding in the cart. Maybe it's just the groping reach of objectless desire, or the periscoping bend of the eye trying to see around itself. Maybe if we strollers troll slowly enough, as if we've all but given up, whatever we've been chasing will come up to us, our own bashful questing beasts, and nuzzle us.

But mostly I think it's the new season moving through us like a colossal dreamer stirring in sleep that asks us to say something sweet about the eternal: the enormity sweeping in the from the northeast, the impermanence — lake, ducks, us — over which it sweeps. It calls for a thought shaped around the quickenings of fall, a phrase turned just so, almost into resignation, yet on the verge of opening absolutely to hope.

Ahead, seated on a bench, is a family of three feeding the pigeons and ducks. The father tosses out a steady shower of popcorn. The birds make a purposeful commotion like the floor of a stock exchange, waving the bits of corn in their bills as if they were bids for more corn, and more. The baby girl, striving forward from her mother's lap, shrieks again and again at the drama of the ducks, wanting more and more ducks, and the ducks, flamboyantly feathered, fanning their wings in haste, are coming from all directions towards the hubbub now, so that we walkers keep walking past the new arrivals, the mothers and their ducklings, down to the least little ducklings hurrying past us in ellipses. ...

Wakulla, Mother of All Springs

Sunday afternoon at Wakulla Springs there are so many young mothers sunning among their many children at play that I can't help thinking of my own mother grown old and exhausted from loving, shivering in a hospital bed in July, wearing a sweater with the heater running, an inner cold upon her. I watch the warm madonnas at the spring and remember mother-love and all that she gave.

Here under a giant cypress tree, a skinny boy child squawks from the edge of the icy spring water. "Mamma! Bring me a towel, Mamma! I'm c-c-c-cold!"

Mamma glances over her mystery novel but she just can't budge on that fool's mission, despite the winsome smile, the imploring hand helplessly outstretched. The child is at the age of selective helplessness, of volunteer babyism. It's two steps from the water to the family picnic on a Peanuts blanket — coolers, jugs, chip bags, assorted water toys, towels — but he just stands there hoping: "Puh-leeze, Mamma!"

"Baloney," Mamma says. The baby-act collapses, and agile as a goat, he springs across the strip of beach and plucks up a towel his own self. Shivering, purple-lipped, robed like a prince by the reclining shrine of Mother, he pouts a moment for his lost babyhood. Then he bounds back into the water saying, "Mamma, watch!"

Two towels down is a real bald Buddha of a baby bundled in powdered donut rolls of pale plump flesh. From his throne astride his mother's belly, he has just flung down his foaming apple-juice baba and is making a two-fisted grab for both her breasts. Mother parries the thrust with a pair of thumbs. An auntie attempts mystification with an inner tube. Inner tube! Yes! He latches on to that bit of buoyancy with his powerful little hands and grips, squeezes, tweaks till it squeaks. He grins. The beautiful, squeezable, bitable inner tube.

And yes, the inner tube is beautiful in the naïve, sensational style of the child's summer — bright clear plastic with yellow fishes and green turtles and blue wavy water lines, the ABCs of the beach, vowels of vacation wonder. A pointy triangle means a fang; two Os spells snout; green means gator: here's a little tyke who loves his gator water-wings, here's a little girl who clings with such serious sentiment to her wet stuffed dog. Up the hill from the spring, in the Wakulla Lodge gift shop, there are trinkets in the bent-spoon shape of Florida, Wakulla mugs, wildlife erasers, segmented rubber snakes: art treasures of the six-year-old's world. Mementos of immortality.

For what it gives, Wakulla Springs is a miraculous place. The waters render our worst summer heat benign. A few minutes' swim invigorates for hours. On the dock after a dip, your flesh seems to rise off the bone toward the heat of the sun, a simple demonstration of the illusion of disconnectedness — goose bumps zipper you to the sky. Lately, with the heavy rains, you can't ride the glass-bottom boats and look far down into the mystery, but it's enough to know it's there, to contemplate the sheer drop down hundreds of feet, and that incidental mastodon whose teeth are in the Lodge under glass, still chattering from the cold like big blue bricks — and the flow itself, 10,000 gallons per second of bone cold water.

Here the earth heaves and opens and gives: it is generation herself. She opens to the imagination with torrential obviousness, a steady silent shout of affirmation that the earth is willing to give even beyond our greed. We could hardly ask for this; we haven't got the words. We're like the birds and the reptiles and the fish who are drawn to the mouth of the spring, who swim down and hang, finning in the cathedral hollow of the flow — and it is good, it is good, it is good.

Alaska Under Water

The raven pecks at the eye of the dying salmon, then cocks its head and looks at us. "Srcaaa-awkk!!" it says.

"What!? Scuba diving in Alaska!? Great idea!"

The bird hops closer, across the sun-warmed boulders beside the salmon stream, as if speculatively interested in this latest manifestation of human folly. To the Tanana and the Tlingit Indians, Raven was an important god; he created the world, and later, for his amusement, that poor forked creature, man. They called him Chulyen, and painted no pretty picture of him. Like this bird dining on the dying here in a quiet cove near Juneau, Raven persistently pecked at everybody's weaknesses, his steadfast purpose to eat their tasty soft parts. A cruel theology but an immanent one, and a right fitting god for Alaska.

"Any bears here?" I ask as I cinch my weight belt. Whatever may have been said before, in Alaska that question is never a non-sequitur.

"Oh, yeah!" says John Lechelt, owner of Juneau's Channel Dive Shop, who's teaching me to dry suit dive. "What do you think? This is a bear fast-food restaurant."

Suited up, I surface swim toward the sanctuary of deeper, bear-free waters. This dive site is called The Shrine, for the rustic, hand-built wooden church that perches atop a rocky spit. The stone is sliced like a staggered loaf with glacial striations that disappear into the deep trough of the Lynn Canal. The ice field that carved southeastern Alaska's Inner Passage withdrew after the last Ice Age, but only as far as the outskirts of town. It broods 4,000 feet above Juneau, as if planning a pouncing return. Once the rugged gateway to the Alaskan frontier, Juneau is now a relatively affluent town of cozy shops and snug Victorian houses. Still, it's a speck of calm amid explosive, titanic forces: the vertical Chilkat mountain faces soaring above it, the crumpled blue blocks of the Mendenhall ice field bulging between peaks, the gales that come howling from the west to beat the water against the land.

We slip underwater in the protected cove, following a gentle incline of sand and gravel down to 30 feet where the canal wall broods over the black depths of the famed Inner Passage shipping lanes. As Chulyen the Raven probably knows, this is my maiden dry suit dive, and for a little while I'm flustered, busily chasing the air in the suit from my feet to my head. You need to pump a little air from your tank into a dry suit to avoid being shrink-wrapped by the pressure — a squeeze, they call it, and it can make you sing soprano — but if you puff in too much and it all goes to your feet, you can find yourself suspended upside down, without much remedy. But pretty soon I corral about the right amount of air around my midriff and achieve trim. In the classroom segment of the dry suit course, Lechelt promised that the suit would keep me toasty warm. In fact I'm refreshingly cool in the astringent 45-degree water, and absolutely bewitched by barnacles.

The shells of these jumbo cirripedia are as big as my neoprene-mittened fist, and the critters are reminiscent, in feeding, of the Addam's Family's handy servant, Thing. They're big enough to hand feed. Hell, they look big and dexterous enough to dial out for pizza. And there are hundreds of them in this colony, fringed fronds deftly rotating, catching hunks of organic detritus like fans at a baseball game snagging bags of peanuts.

We've come to Alaska in late summer, a fecund time of salmon spawns and plankton blooms, and fair to poor visibility. The first hard freeze will kill off the obscuring plankton and open the view to the winter average of 100 feet. But right now we're in the soup, the basic building broth that anchors the food chain, looking out for whatever prodigiously fattened apex feeders we might blunder into at close range: pods of orca; a dozen other species of whale; halibut the size of flattened Holstein steers; one-ton Steller sea lion bulls. Lechelt says they like to bluff charge divers — rushing out of the gloom and halting within inches of your mask, growling and blowing bubbles back at you.

The last 500 psi we reserve for milling with the siege of salmon in two to four feet of water. Like a herd of newly captured wild horses, several hundred mature silvers — or "humpies" — ceaselessly circle the narrow stream mouth, waiting for the urge or the courage to throw themselves onto freshwater trickling through the slippery stones. They take no note of us in their obsessive circling, bumping us, turning gloweringly aside. The yard-long males, hump-backed and hook-jawed, are gnarly masks of naked concupiscence, already rotting with lust like aquatic portraits of Dorian Gray.

Native Alaskans believed everyone is born with a *joncha*, a secret animal identity. Lechelt's joncha, I've decided, is the bear, because he eats so well, with such relish. A big, hearty, round-shouldered guy full of bonhomie, Lechelt is never more bearish than when he talks about seafood. You can practically hear the crab shells cracking when the gourmand summons up a perfect Juneau day: a leisurely morning of skiing at Eagle's Crest, followed by an afternoon of dry-suit seafood shopping in the sea — blizzards be damned — and finished off with a bearish beer commercial of scalded three-foot-long king crab legs and scallops the size of hockey pucks.

Lechelt's other passion is maritime history and the applied science of wreck diving. There are 60 catalogued wrecks within an hour's boat ride of Juneau; more than 700 registered in all Alaskan waters, ranging from Japanese junks to 19th century whalers to World War II mine-tenders, and countless others awaiting discovery. Onboard the *Shelby Ann* with captain Bud Storkel, Lechelt unrolls a plan of the TSS *Princess Kathleen* which collided with the mainland one foggy September morning in 1952. Everyone on board simply walked off into the trees, but the ship slid off the rocks later in the day and settled with her bow at 40 feet and her props down around 140 feet. Rumor has it she was scuttled for insurance, and the captain and first mate were both drunk — shades of the Exxon *Valdez*.

"There's a story that a salvage diver recovered, and then dropped, an emerald and gold crucifix that was an heirloom of a priest," Lechelt tells us. Also reputed to be in the hold are 40 cases of scotch — and a fortune in gold.

Twenty minutes out of harbor, Captain Bud nails the anchorage, and we follow the line down to the *Kathleen's* bow. "What you won't believe," Lechelt told us pre-dive, "is the sheer magnitude of this ship." When she comes into view at 30 feet, in an eerie green light, it's hard to grasp that we're looking at the work of man and not some natural feature of the channel. We follow the starboard rail down to 80 feet; the listing hull, encrusted with tube worms and heavily foliated with elephant ear kelp, plummets into darker, colder water. There's plenty of room to swim down inside her curved exhaust stacks, habitats now for clown nudibranchs and large beady-eyed prawns. I follow a school of rock bass into an open hatch and come upon the captain's head — his bathroom, that is. The commode is askew but intact, and so is the black and white mosaic tile floor. I polish a little section with my glove and it gleams bright as new.

The *Princess Kathleen*, made to order in Scotland for the Canadian Pacific Railway, once boasted two stained glass solariums, hammered brass ornaments and carved hardwood detailing, all in Native American motifs. She was a party ship, and a match in elegance for anything built in the Roaring Twenties. With Lechelt's detailed map we could launch a search for the scotch cached deep in the ship's bowels, but with the shaky viz and weird green light and the deathly cold (dry suits preserve your core warmth admirably but you're still keenly aware of the fatally freezing water) I'm already too spooked.

I'm thinking about the story Lechelt told us about the *Kathleen*'s sister ship, the *Princess Sophia*, which rests in 100 feet just 10 miles farther north along the Lynn Canal. Hers is a particularly tragic tale, one for the books — either Chulyen the Raven's or Jack London's. Making the season's last run from Skagway to Vancouver, the *Princess Sophia* was carrying an overload of passengers, many of whom were leaving Alaska and the Yukon for good, carrying their fortunes. After she ran aground on Vanderbilt Reef during a driving snowstorm on October 24, 1918, rescue vessels circled her in a gale for a whole night and a day, unable to offload anybody in the pounding storm surf. Sometime during the second night she slipped off the reef and went down, killing all aboard — 353 passengers and crew, and some 60 horses. It was the twilight of the Gold Rush, Chulyen's greatest prank.

We ascend through a ghostly flotilla of moon jellies. Throughout the dive we've been shadowed by thousands of coelenterates, drifting by like a slow hail of souls. Some are pinkie-nail-sized, some the size of a human head with tendrils 40 feet long. A large moon jelly has become entangled in one of the *Kathleen*'s forward mast stays and streams helplessly in the 5-knot current. Taking advantage of my dry suit mitts, I gather up a ropy bundle of tendrils and loose the beast into the stream, storing up good karma for the dives to come.

Robert Service, the poet laureate of the frozen north, wrote that God was tired when he made Alaska. Certainly, the 6,640-mile Alaskan coastline seems randomly intricate, convoluted like chaos itself. We're out in the Gulf of Alaska, off Kodiak Island, itself composed of dozens of islands and hundreds of peninsulas, the whole as busily crenulated with coves and pinnacles as one of its shaggy reef creatures.

Under windless, overcast conditions, pale clouds boiling down from pyramidal peaks to snag on towering Sitka spruces, captain Venlin Thenson pilots the 25-foot cabin cruiser, *The Shaman,* past abandoned

World War II gun emplacements on the rugged cliffs of Kodiak's Long Island as we head for one of his favorite pinnacle dives. Thensen's *joncha* is definitely the sea lion because, though he's a fine fishing guide and a humorous companion, he'd be happier if he were joining us underwater. Besides, he's just parallel parked *The Shaman* alongside an islet where two ton-and-a-half bull Steller sea lions lounge with their harem of 14 cows; alarmed by our approach, at least a dozen pups have sought higher ground near the pinnacle's guano-frosted crown. All at once, the cows spook, contorting like fat caterpillars and flopping into the sea. The bulls are barely bothered by the fuss. They glower at us over their massive shoulders and roar like lions — a shocking sound. We're close enough to smell the fish on their breath.

The pinnacle we're soon diving is really several peaks beginning at 30 feet and dropping to 80 feet at their base. The crevasses between peaks are plush with forests of enormous white anemones. To swim between these walls is to experience how tiny tropicals feel when they nestle in the anemones' stinging cells. We make pass after pass, mesmerized, as if strolling through mountain meadows of giant albino broccoli.

We're dealing with the same 30-foot viz as around Juneau — "lots of sea snow," as Thenson calls the soup of organic matter — but it's fine for atmospheric wide-angle views and outstanding for the close-in macro-observation this fabulously rich cold-water habitat deserves. Wherever you look, a thousand eyes look back at you. Wherever you place a hand, coon-striped shrimp flick free between your fingers, and hermit crabs trundle out from under your palm. Every other rock turns out to be a tattered Irish lord — a toad-faced sculpin — every other pebble is a decorator crab, its shell festooned with scraps of seaweed. I pick up a good-sized decorator crab, and discover a smaller kelp crab living on its back in the faux-kelp forest. And on the back of the smaller crab a tiny, translucent, tick-sized crab is keeping house. I let the colony drop with a creepy-crawly sensation akin to disgust — a crustacean fever dream.

Down at the pinnacle base lurks a four-foot lingcod, all teeth and bad disposition. Curious kelp greenlings have followed us down, and they nibble at our dry suits, trying to decide if we can be eaten. On the sandy bottom, manhole-cover-sized sunflower starfish sprawl over the pits they make as they dig for clams. These shaggy 18-legged brutes seem to have the texture of old stomped-on doormats, in decorator pastel shades of green and pink and blue. On closer inspection, the disheveled fuzziness reveals order — symmetrically clustered stipples as fine as otter's fur. I watch two as they copulate in their clam pit; it's slow and languorous love, 36 thighs intertwining, a million naked points of contact. The god who made these starfish wasn't tired, maybe just more than a bit mad.

In two days on Kodiak we dive a shallow wreck, try another pinnacle and kelp forest, and drive to a beach dive where the rusting stern of Calvin Coolidge's presidential yacht *San Diego* juts from the sand. Kodiak, the second largest island in the U.S. (only Hawaii is bigger), has a landmass equal to Connecticut, and nearly three-quarters the coastline of Florida. A measure of the island's underwater frontier status is that as a dive guide, Thenson has Kodiak all to himself.

I find the perfect airplane book for the turbulent flight to Homer: Alaskan folklorist Larry Kanuit's *Cheating Death*, 18 true-life stories of Frozen Doom's near-misses. This is Chulyen the Raven's old disastrous Alaska, with modern machinery added. There's a tale or two set in Kachemak Bay, on Cook Inlet, where our plane is headed. My favorite is a tasty yarn about a small boat, engine failure and 48 hours in 20-foot seas.

It's something to keep in mind as we motor out around the Homer Spit. Our guides, Cecil and Corrine Cheatwood, owners of C&C Aquatics, laugh when I mention Larry Kanuit's *Cheating Death*. Corrine says a friend once telephoned Cecil to tell him he was in the latest volume of the book — something about a wrestling match with a giant octopus. It turned out to be a different salvage diver, though it could've been Cecil. He's rassled 'pi before. Naturally, the Cheatwoods have their own death-defying stories. C&C Aquatics was first on the scene to assess damage in the Exxon *Valdez* disaster, which meant diving under three feet of oil slick, in and out of the cracked hull in zero viz.

Then there was the time when an ice sheet drifted over them during a winter recreational dive. "It would've been a disaster if we'd had a dive class with us," Corrine says. There's plenty of time for story-telling as we wait for slack tide. In Homer, life revolves around the swift and dynamic tide, and those who don't respect its power keep C&C Aquatics salvage department very busy with a constant supply of shipwrecks and lost or shattered gear.

Puttering about in the middle of Kachemak Bay, we sight a raft of some 20 sea otters. Otters hug one another as we approach, slip with well-oiled ease beneath the surface, pop up on the other side of the boat and return our curious stares. The sea otter is decidedly the Cheatwoods' *joncha*, because they are clever salvagers, both agile and tidily built, and Cecil admits he has a reputation for playing with big octopi.

Slack tide arrives at 8 p.m. — still plenty of daylight left — and we drop anchor on Corrine's Reef, so-named because Corrine likes this dive spot, and there's nobody else here to call it differently. Backrolling, we land in kelp and follow the swaying stalks down to 20 feet, to a flattened rock bed worn smooth by the tides. The sides of the reef are bushy with those enormous white anemones; one has captured a jellyfish and is slowly dismembering it — pulling it apart like so much cotton candy. Down at 60 feet on the clamshell-strewn bottom, it doesn't take long for Cecil to find an octopus. He gives chase over the cover-less bottom until the furiously backpedaling cephalopod inks him and slips away.

The viz down here is a downright claustrophobic 10 feet, and the water feels colder than Kodiak (it's 48F — about the same). That's probably just a function of the viz and my paranoia about the tides. I'm determined to stick close to Cecil, at least until I cross over a small canyon and see what looks like a sea cucumber the size of a man. It's warty and wrinkled and tubular, whatever it is, and as I come closer to investigate, it backs up, quite quickly, under a ledge. I gulp down about 250 psi coming to grips with the sight: nothing that ugly should be allowed to move that fast. Peering cautiously into its cave, I see two horror masks glaring back at me. They're wolf eels — and big ones — as grotesque as any medieval gargoyle.

Of course by now Cecil has disappeared. I'm lost in deadly waters, and suddenly it's Halloween to boot. I feel a tingling sensation in one of my hands. I've got a leaky glove, which translates almost instantly into numb fingers. When I surface and find the boat, and go to grab hold of the ladder, my chilled hand is completely useless — a little warning from the Raven. Motoring back to Homer, the Cheatwoods regale us with more Kachemak tall tales: of dives when the bottom is literally carpeted with halibut (Homer is the self-proclaimed "Halibut Capital of the World"); of the 200-pounder Corrine landed on rod and reel ("We gaffed it, harpooned it, and shot it with a pistol," she says); of pods of orca 20 strong hunting just outside the harbor.

It's 9:30 p.m. by now and still daylight, but an awesome bank of black clouds is slipping over the Kenai Mountains, about to close down the sunset over Cook Inlet — a promise of the grandeur and danger of the weather, and a foretaste of the coming winter darkness.

* * *

We meet Captain Dave in the Anchor Inn Bar in the very weird town of Whittier. Everything about Whittier is strange. To get there you drive your car onto a railway carriage, and ride in your car on the train into tunnels blasted through a mountain range until the track dead ends alongside a stunning fjord fed by plunging waterfalls. During World War II, the U.S. Army built a secret multistory barracks in this remote finger of Prince William Sound as a kind of Fortress of Solitude where we could stash President Roosevelt if we lost the war. Abandoned now, the derelict barrack rather sets the tone for the town.

"The population here is 50 percent born again Christian and 50 percent devout alcoholic," Don Moore, our Anchorage-based guide tells us. We cast our lot with the latter at the Anchor Inn where we're looking for a reliable boat with a functional captain. When Don asks if anyone can charter us a boat, literally everybody in the bar turns to us and says, "Yes!" We hire Captain Dave because he happens to be sitting next to Moore and because we can charter him by the hour, the half-day, the day, or the week. Hell, we can buy the boat outright — cheap, too!

And yes, he can take us to what's left of the spill, mostly scattered patches under several inches of sand. Dave's been in on the clean-up, made something over a hundred grand in a couple of months, and he gives us his take on the disaster. "We were like, come on oil! Come on into Whittier! We'll take our settlement money and move to South America where it's warm." But the wind blew the oil south, away from Whittier, and others got slicked, and then some got rich. This is part of the disaster too: the big oil money hangover.

In the morning we set out with Captain Dave on a true adventure dive: nobody knows where we're going or what we expect to find. We're just going to shoot sonar at the bottom and dive whatever virgin structures appear promising. An hour out of port we pick up on a cone-shaped protuberance rising steeply from several hundred feet to less than 30. We drop anchor and then plunge into the weird unknown.

For the first 20 feet we're pushing through a nearly opaque band of very cold vanilla-colored water, followed by a zone of azure. It's like diving through a slice of Neapolitan ice cream. Then the viz opens up on a blue-green dreamscape, a gently sloping hill planted with extraterrestrial life-forms by a farmer from Mars. Every three feet a translucent white plant-thing sprouts, three feet tall and as slender as a buggy whip; regularly interspersed between are stubbier intelligent ferns, gathering information about the planet from a very disadvantageous prospect. We follow the slope down to 120 feet, but that's all there is: a vast desert biculture of underwater R2D2s and C3POs.

I surface beside the boat after our final dive in Alaska, and I'm feeling pretty cocky for having survived. I hand up my 40-pound weight belt to Captain Dave. He hoists it up and then curses as he crushes his thumbnail between the lead plats.

"Look out!" Moore shouts.

I duck as the weights slip off the belt, whizzing by my head, disappearing down onto what I'll call Bucky's Bump, my namesake dive spot where I nearly got my noggin cracked and left something of my own behind. As for Moore, his *joncha*, obviously, is the eagle for his watchful eye. And Captain Dave? Well, he has a good laugh at that near miss, which was Chulyen's work, and his boat is called *The Raven*.

Spear Fishing

Like killer angels, black-hooded and armed to the teeth, we fold wings and plummet straight down on top of the wreck. How long has the old shrimp boat, all busted up and encrusted, lain undisturbed in these remote Marquesas? Fuckin' long enough! That's what I imagine Cal's thinking, Cal from West Palm by way of Jersey. It's his charter, really, along with a few long-time dive buddies. Over the past several years they've spent a fortune tracking the wily grouper, and they're good, I hear, *real* good, and hungry on this first dive of the trip. We've dropped down through a swirl of mackerel, horse-eye jack, and barracuda, to where schools of mutton snapper, dinner-party size, placidly loiter above the sand around the wreckage. It's like the Serengeti in the heyday of the Bwana — what do we shoot first?

As we hover among the herds, giant jewfish — two! three! four of them! — zoom out from cover, pectoral fins flaring, glowering, very pissed. Each torpedoing brute is surrounded by glimmering silversides, a minnow escort that matches every angry high-speed twist and turn. One hog-sized monster rushes up to me, brakes, sucks in a mouthful of its sycophants, and — BLEEAH! — spits them out dead or dying on the sand, as if to say, You looking for *game fish*, bitch?

But they're protected by law, and too big to shoot; they're not our prey. The jewfish decamp, but the mutton snapper remain, every one turned towards us six divers with the bland curiosity of the easily skewered. Hey! — Christian, the first mate of the sixty-foot deluxe charter boat Playmate, grabs my elbow. He's doing a frantic self-Moe, poking two fingers at his mask: Look! Where? There! *Where? There!!* Goddamn! It's a grouper, a big black grouper — Mycteroperca bonaci — a superb specimen of exactly what we're hunting for. It's damn well camouflaged, mottled, pale, black in name only when basking on coral rubble. Shoot it! Christian mimes, aiming his gun, making trigger waggles with a finger. Right! Right! But I've never shot a significant fish in my life. Don't want to wound it. Gotta get close. And it's just lying there, blubber-lipped, big eyes rotating. It could bolt at any second.

This is all happening a little too fast. One minute I'm bedding down in a bunk on a boat docked in Key West, and the next I'm waking up at dawn far out to sea above the Moffin Banks. *Moffin Banks?* "Yeah, Middle of Fuckin' Nowhere," the Captain, Jojo LaBounty, explained over bacon and eggs in the air-conditioned cabin. Now I'm wondering if this is the way it's going to be for the whole two-and-a-half-day charter — monsters of the deep performing aquatic extravaganzas, fat grouper as long as my leg passively awaiting the prong of my spear-point — as I fin a little closer, a little closer still, spear-gun extended at arm's length, not daring to breathe for fear the bubbles will spook the fish. When I'm so close I can practically poke it, I close my eyes and squeeze the trigger.

When you shoot a big fish at close range you can hear the spear's impact, almost feel it — a *thwack!* of crunching scales and bone. Instantly, the fish goes ballistic, exploding in a frenzy of futile evasive action, kicking up a cloud of sand or bits of coral. For a moment it's just a blur. Then, typically, it will pause, impaled, leaking blood — in the weird chromatics of depth, blood is green! — before beginning its desperate fight or flight. Grouper, being ambush predators and cubby-hole lovers, will dash for their coral fortresses, where many a fish and spear are lost.

These things, and much else, I'll learn later. But my first shot at a fish of consequence bonks harmlessly off the bottom, and it's Christian who goes ballistic. I can practically see steam rising from his hood as he contorts in frustration like Yosemite Sam. How could I have missed? Why did he ever let me try? For the duration of the dive we sulkily prowl around the reef near the wreck, Christian picking off snapper, making one great shot after another, nailing some on the fly after they've wised up and begun hastily retreating. He never misses. Meanwhile, I'm taking a few shots and missing every time; it's not as easy as the mate makes it look. Being the least experienced diver, I suck down my tank first and head for the surface, and Christian, charged with bringing the new guy back alive, shadows my ascent.

On board the Playmate, he's still shaking his shaved bald head. "If I see another fish like that I'm going to have to take the shot," he says. I nod, contrite. Yeah, yeah. Maybe ten minutes later the others begin popping up, unfurling "sausages" — inflatable signal tubes — and shrilling whistles to help Captain Jojo find them among the swells. One at a time they clamber aboard, handing off spear guns to Kathleen, cook and general mate, and each dragging over the transom a massive pot-bellied grouper with eyes the size of horses' eyes, gaping mouths armed with little pointy teeth, dark slick skin scarred with a jagged hole, bright white meat protruding from the exit wounds.

Captain Jojo, arms akimbo on the upper deck — he not only resembles (a little) the Skipper from "Gilligan's Island," he aspires to play him in the new reality-TV show — appraises the take. "Looks like you're top dog, Hollywood," he rasps, coining a nickname for John, a West Palm realtor with blond surfer good-looks.

I'm thinking *I* could've been top dog if I hadn't missed that fish. And Cal, mock-pissed, a feisty bantam rooster with a Rolex (debt consolidation is his bidness, but spear fishing is his passion) starts in on Jojo, ragging him about the dive site — "The visibility sucked! Nothin' down there but a bunch a rubble. Where're the ledges?" — and the Captain just chuckles, loving the abuse.

Welcome aboard the Playmate.

We do seven dives the first day, unprecedented in my recreational diving experience, but possible with a dive computer, pushing it to the no-decompression limit. Kathleen, Jojo, and Christian alternate as my dive buddies, and I learn plenty from each. Petite Kathleen has less trouble than I do hauling back the stout bands of rubber tubing to power-load her gun, and though she hasn't been hunting long she's far better at seeing fish than I am. The little fishes are everywhere, weaving in and out of coral crags and waving sea fans, but the big boys are few and well-hidden within the warp and woof of the dizzying pattern.

"Spear fishing is all in the eyes," Captain Jojo avers before we jump in for dive number three. Though a pragmatic old Key West Conch from his sun-bleached mane to his salt-cured toes — "It's my Portuguese blood; I'm a meat fisherman" — the Captain's philosophy of stalking big grouper smacks of the Taoist East, of Sun Tzu's "Art of War": "Act uninterested in them, and they'll be curious about you; you gotta box 'em in, but also leave 'em somewhere to go. Move slow like one of them big turtle they just saw."

Soon we're down about eighty feet, the Skipper and I, atop a vast coral plateau, and he's nimbly popping snapper and grouper, then hunkering down on the bottom to protect his back while he stuffs his kills into a black canvas bag "so the sharks can't see 'em."

"Might as well wear lead boots and just trample along on top of the reef," Cal says later, dissing Captain Jojo's technique out of the side of his mouth, while pretending to disdain the "LaBounty" that spills from the bag — including a twenty-odd pound black that had to be pursued, poked and pried from the tight coral confines to which it had retreated with the Captain's spear through its side. On this dive, everybody got his grouper except me, and Cal, who eschewed to shoot the medium-sized blackies he spotted. Cal's hunting style is to hover in a deadman's float high above a promising bit of bottom and just wait, peering down through the gloom with his peregrine eyes. His freezer at home is full, and all his friends' freezers are full of grouper fillets too. What he wants is the boat record, the monster grouper that's bigger than he is.

"No more of this crappy, scrappy, grabbly stuff, dammit! Find us some good bottom!" Cal baits the Captain.

As Jojo fires up the engines, Kathleen brings out a platter of fried grouper fingers that we wolf down with the sharpened appetites of the water-logged. Dive by dive, we're making westward for the Dry Tortugas and our night berth beside the 16 million brick hulk of Fort Jefferson. At dusk, with seabirds shrieking and wheeling against a sunset of purple, orange and green, we anchor in the calm lee for a good steak dinner, a bad Schwarzeneggar movie, and an early exhausted bed-time.

Early the next morning, cruising farther west, Captain Jojo finds virgin bottom above the Tortugas Banks, with potentially fish-flush ledges ranging from 65 to 135 feet. I'm kicking along the ledge with the first mate when he spots a pair of sizable hogfish. They're spectrally pale, tall-bodied, with banner-like dorsal fins and eponymous porcine snouts — very palatable, too. Christian signs for me to take the bigger of the two.

By this time, I've learned to lead the fish a bit, to anticipate the twitch; I've bagged a few and my hunting instinct has kicked in big-time. Gun-butt steadied in my left-hand palm, the long stock extended at right arm's length, I stalk, aim, fire: Got 'em! The hogfish thrashes, zooms to the end of the line connecting spear to gun, and somehow, despite the barbed spearhead, jerks free. Most unhappily punctured, it sails down over the ledge, finning feebly for the depths. By this time Christian is already stringing his kill through its eyeballs. Looking back at the mate for advice, I can read his mind by his gestures: What the fuck! Go get it!

I ought to have quick-loaded my gun, snapping back a single band, but I just grab the spear in hand and kick in pursuit, dragging the gun behind me, over the ledge, down through a frigid thermocline to the sandy bottom where I catch up to the wounded brute. Like Jack in "Lord of the Flies," I stab the beast, a savage thrust that goes clear through the thick body. Then, as Christian has taught me, I ascend some thirty feet to string my fish, taking the blood and bad vibes up with me so as not to spook any other fish in the area. That's when I see the shark, a seven foot reefie — the same ghostly blue as the deep sea — circling me, keeping a keen eye on the proceedings.

Nothing deterred, we continue the hunt along the top of the ledge. Suddenly a big yellowtail jack presents its broadside to me. Hello! *Bam!* It's my best shot of the trip, right behind the head, and a fish big enough to whirl me through the water and nearly bend my spear. I add it to my stringer which is a veritable crucible of oozing blood — and there're two sharks now, sizing us up like street toughs. Christian signals for me to come closer to him, and we hover back to back, watching the sharks circling nearer. Good thing Christian's packing heat: he unscrews his spear-head and swaps it with a .38 power-head. Not liking what he sees in the sharks' badass body language, the mate decides to take the fight to them, charging like a pit-bull, gun extended. *Kablam!!* Like a magic trick, before the sound waves settle both sharks instantly vanish, one dead-to-be, the other lessoned in diver harassment.

Back aboard the Playmate we've got a story to tell, and I'm top dog with my big Tortugas hog — until Cal surfaces with two hulking grouper.

"Who fired that powerhead?" he wants to know. "You scared off all the goddamn fish!"

Journey to God's Well

A burst of strange curses rises over the lip of that godforsaken Jamaican pit called God's Well.

"Bumbo!" one of our crew spits out from below. "Bumbo claat! Dem mad rass ants!"

Moments later, photographer Alex Kirkbride and our guide Delwin Rochester come scrambling over the rim of the sinkhole. "Did you hear them?" Delwin asks Alex. Delwin swears he could *hear* the ants bustling from their nest. "When they came out it made a roar like a crackling fire!"

I'm sorry I missed that: savage, virgin ants, waiting all history on a dark ledge, in a deep hole, under a damp log, in the steaming jungle — just waiting for some mad bastard to tread on them. Alex did the honors with his Soho combat boots.

Delwin, a young Jamaican entrepreneur who divides his time between the family tailoring business in Atlanta and their newly opened small resort called SeaRiv on Jamaica's undeveloped south coast, has never been all the way down to the forbidding waters of God's Well. But he's game to take us there in the name of adventure travel, SeaRiv's principal offering, along with the tranquility that precedes the arrival of reliable electricity, but seldom persists anywhere afterwards. And God's Well fits the adventure bill quite nicely. Aptly named, it is an awesome absence, a sheer-walled shout of space that opens up the limestone mountainside like the crater of a nuclear blast.

Insects shrill in the green heat. On the crumbly rim of the hole we crouch under low bushes with coils of rope, heaps of dive gear and dudes — lots of young dudes. To assist his local dive masters, Delwin has recruited a dozen porters from the nearby fishing village of Alligator Pond. Another 20 guys have apparently quit their jobs with the coastal road crew just to watch and see if we'll do something outstandingly stupid. Boys as young as eight, barefoot in dusty trousers, climb trees with pockets full of rocks, which they toss into the abyss, as boys must. We're hours from the nearest town, yet we've drawn a circus crowd.

The key to the descent — a scramble down the steep dirt slope, then a clamber along climbing roots to the rocky ledge with the ants and a lone sapling sturdy enough to rig a rope — lies in dividing the labor into minute portions, thus limiting the number of people arguing about a specific task to two or three. Just then an energetic labor dispute erupts, utterly undermining that plan. Dive master Leon, the most outspoken person I've ever met, is down on the ledge with the ant disposal team, being pummeled with advice and taunts from every man, youth, and stone-throwing lad. Leon answers each argument with passion, hitting high notes of anger and glee, lower tones of disgust and dismay, as if he stands alone against the enemies of Probity and Reason.

Soon, thin plumes of acrid smoke waft up over the edge of the sink, and the voices crescendo in satisfaction. The Jamaican crew is burning the ants out, smothering them with smoke and talk and laughter — the island's inexhaustible resources. I remove a cold Ting from the cooler, then sit down to wait some more. We hope to be underway by noon, when the sun heaves directly overhead, and God's Well will glow green and cloudy like a great cataracted eyeball.

* * *

There were times diving on Jamaica's wild south coast when I felt like a character in an H. Rider Haggard novel, some misguided adventurer pursuing a fabulous goal that demanded a lot of gear and a lot of cheap labor, and which would ultimately cost him his soul. This was never more true than when we drove the dirt streets of Alligator Pond with Delwin, recruiting a crew of porters for the God's Well expedition.

Geographically as far from both Kingston and Montego Bay as you can get, and temporally stuck in the 19th century, tiny Alligator Pond proper is a scant, dusty block dead-ending at the sea. Goats, chickens and scrawny blond dogs share the track with men and women balancing elaborate loads on their heads. The air is pungent with sea salt and smoke from open-air jerk stands and smoldering charcoal pits (Jamaica is a world leader in rate of deforestation) and the ganja of some unseen Rasta's spliff. Saturday morning, and SeaRiv's four-wheel-drive truck was the only vehicle on Main Street.

We took a side road that cut through pastures and vegetable plots out beyond the reach of electricity and telephones and indoor plumbing. In the dirt yards of tiny cement houses, children raced toy buses ingeniously fashioned from orange juice cartons and wooden spool wheels.

Seeing Alex and me in the cab of the truck, they gave chase, shrieking, "White man! White man!"

At a crossroads, Delwin stopped to work the grapevine, finding out who was up and about and interested in earning a few bucks. It was Delwin's shrewd policy to spread out the ecotourism dollar in small increments to as many pockets as possible. Though no one starved here — fish and fruit could be had for the picking — labor is as plentiful as currency is scarce. Indeed, I'd never seen so many people, mostly young men, just hanging out on corners and in four-stool rum stands, keeping watch for the main chance, or any diversion whatsoever, for that matter. The back of the truck swiftly filled with able-bodied gear-bearers ready to follow our whim with energy and abundant good humor. We sport divers, free of all burdens, would also be free to imagine that we were explorers, pocket Sir Richard Burtons in quest of Arawak idols or pirate gold at the bottom of God's Well. Here in the underbelly of Jamaica, a place of caves and springs and deserted black-sand beaches, there were no rules, no limits, and no checks on human folly.

Fully manned and provisioned, the God's Well expedition took off at devil-take-the-hindmost speed along the coastal road, scattering herds of goats and bursting through clouds of white butterflies. Beyond Gut River, one of half a dozen spring-fed streams that percolate out of the limestone mountains and meander to the sea through a morass of mangroves and reeds, the pavement abruptly ceased. We were blocked by an obstacle of some historic moment: a crew of 50 men attacking the bush with chainsaws and machetes and a bulldozer, opening the coastal road to traffic from Kingston. For better or worse, change was coming to Alligator Pond and the Long Bay Morass, the spring-fed refuge of the endangered manatee and the American crocodile.

* * *

At God's Well, after the incident of the ants, the rigging of the ropes went surprisingly quickly. Someone cut stakes and pounded them into the loose scree for footholds, eliminating the danger of the initial scramble down to the lower trees. It was a pleasure watching the crew work once they set to in earnest. They had played in these mountains throughout their boyhoods, and they took obvious pride in their mastery of this harsh, idiosyncratic karst country.

Soon tanks and gear bags were jouncing down the line to the ledge, and then in turn Delwin, Alex and I were lowered the final 30 feet by butt-sling, to a scrap of shingle at the water's edge. We landed right on top of the ant log which the crew had hurled down before us.

Across the green pool, a blindingly bright wall of limestone, hirsute with dangling linguini-like lianas, soared some 300 feet above us. A small crocodile, which had either fallen in or been flushed in through a cave, swam right for us, a miniature flagship of jungle menace. Rocks pelted down around it, and around us, too, as we eased into the water. As far as Delwin knew, only five divers had preceded us. The first two, a man and a woman, had become separated when the man experienced equipment failure. For some reason, the woman carried on alone into a cave and died there. The next three divers came from Florida to retrieve her body.

The sinkhole's lethal record was very much on our minds as we began the descent. For the first 30 feet, visibility was nil, the water a hot pea soup. At 50 feet we passed through a dramatic thermocline: temperature plummeted and the viz soared, revealing a stark, monochromatic spectacle. Along the dark sides of the sink little puffs of silt appeared, mini-explosions billowing in suspension, which we finally reasoned were the effects of stones still being thrown down from the peanut gallery. Below was a maze of ancient trees that had toppled into the sink over the course of centuries. God's Well was as cyclopic below as above: a narrowing funnel burrowing under the northern wall. We cleared the last of the deadfall trees at 140 feet, and continued down into the cavern zone. It was very cold, very dark under the mountain's brow.

At 158 feet we found the entrance to the cave and an abandoned diver's mask — a spooky memento mori. The cave looked like a killer, deep, tight, no more than four-feet-tall at the entrance, a mere wink in the stone, and silty. Hovering carefully, I tested the bottom with a finger and it plunged into a spongy black medium light as air that undulated like a sheet of gelatin as I tried to rise motionlessly away from it. One stray kick and it would be instant blackout. We wanted no part of that cave.

Still, we were far from disappointed with what we had seen and learned from the whole process, which was mainly that tourist divers could safely access God's Well, have a good spook, provide wages for a few, and provoke a great deal of local hilarity. We came up out of the cold, through the weird green water, and surfaced in the noonday heat — right next to the ant log, now bobbing on the water, still smoldering and teeming with shipwrecked ants. Yo ho ho! The ants had pursued us to the end, with a little help from the crew. Up on the rim of the sinkhole, the Jamaicans made the jungle loud with laughter.

On the drive back, Delwin pulled off the road beside a dense mangrove swamp and announced: "Gentlemen, the Suicide Run." Delwin hadn't actually done the Suicide Run, he admitted. He'd been waiting for some guinea pigs like Alex and me to test its amusement potential. Only the older, quieter of the two SeaRiv dive masters, Down (great name for a diver), had completed the two mile swim from the coastal road to the sea. Only Down knew the way. I didn't see any "run" at all, no water-course whatsoever — only a tangle of dark, interlocking roots, seemingly impenetrable. I had the powerful sensation that my leg was being pulled.

"You wanted to see crocodiles," Delwin said. "This looks like a good place for them."

The crew had worked hard and waited stoically in the heat while we dived God's Well. Now they showed off their skill at free-diving, letting off steam on the Suicide Run. They flashed and wriggled through the roots, setting a murderous pace. The Run became a race, something out of "Escape from Devil's Island." I would take a breath and dive, swimming sideways through hoops of roots and under sunken logs, pulling myself along hand over hand until I found a gap to come up through. All the while, the swimmer behind would be blowing exhalations like an angry walrus, trying to pass.

I surfaced once with a rubbery mangrove root wedged between my mask strap and my face, kebobbed like a chunk of jerked pork. I was out of the race by the time I disentangled myself. But there were strange sights to see: blue crabs among the detritus of the bottom, many pairs locked in copulation, their swimmerettes twirling like batons. Little freshwater minnows, navy blue and chrome, darted among mullet and African perch in the roots. The Run was both a spring and a swamp, combining cold clear water with prolific hatchery.

I didn't catch up until the entire pack stopped dead in its tracks. Half the crew had climbed high in the mangroves — in fins! Leon, the muscular orator, had climbed highest of all, and was warbling with laughter. Down, calmly clinging to a root, pointed toward the water: "Crocodile," he whispered. "He look too full in de belly to move."

Good thing, since we had swum right on top of the brute in barely six feet of water. I sucked in a breath and dove. It lay placid and still, bunked under the shelf of brush in its private gloom. Plump, coiled and powerful, its long distinctive snout was zippered tight with interlocking ivory, its pleated, prehistoric hide glowing the palest shade of blue. As big as a cow around the belly, the croc looked as potent as a living bomb. It finally spooked when Alex came too close with his camera, and vanished with a whip of its tail.

The sea, when at last we reached it, staggering up over a bar of black sand, felt hot as bathwater, and we lolled in the breakers soaking up warmth for the cold swim back to the truck.

We took a different route this time, through reeds, which proved just as remarkable as the mangroves. The tawny marsh grass spiked up 10 feet tall and floated in great island-mats. It was a world evocative of biblical times, of Moses in the bulrushes of the Nile, of the cradle of man. For long stretches the reeds completely closed off the waterway, and we had to dive under the barricades into dark water, looking for sapphire columns of light, ethereal zones of passage like the Star Trek transporter, where it was possible to beam up for a breath.

Back at SeaRiv long after dark, the chef and headwaiter, Uggers (great name for a giant, which he was) had dinner waiting: fried chicken and whole fish, which we fell upon with ravenous hunger. We ate in silence on the veranda, under a slow-twirling fan. The whole of SeaRiv, a big cement country house, seemed adrift in the black bush, as isolated in the darkness as a tramp steamer at sea. Images of the day kept coming back in vivid flashes. The entire amazing experience — God's Well, the mangroves, the reeds — had been just like being a kid again, when a day between darknesses is as long as any adult week, and everything is new and green and striving, and tumbles down upon you and your comrades in waves of terror and joy and you laugh, all cut up and bruised and caked in grime, until your ribs hurt from it. There was magic in this Jamaica, if it could take you back to that. All night I dreamed of caves and mazes, pursued by blue crocodiles.

The next day, everything fell apart. We planned to dive the reefs early to beat the wind, but the crew tried to launch the boat right in front of SeaRiv instead of farther east where they usually put in, and got the truck stuck in the sand up to the doors. While they waited and watched to see if the truck could be freed, the guys in the boat cruised back and forth until they ran out of gas. A wave swamped them and flooded the fuel line. In a matter of hours, Delwin's transportation had been reduced to a borrowed motorbike.

As a fledgling hotelier and dive operator with one foot in the business culture of Atlanta, and one foot in practically primeval Alligator Pond, Delwin has two powerful gods of disaster to propitiate. One is Murphy, who presides over mechanical failures. The other is Bredder Anansi, the native trickster, usually characterized as a spider. "The sneaky side of people," one Jamaican defined him for me. There's a ton of Murphy in the dive business, and plenty of Anansi in the fishing village. What Delwin was trying to do — ease Alligator Pond into the 20th century in time for the 21st, and awaken environmental consciousness among fishermen — required all the tact and diplomacy he could muster. It meant hiring locally and giving the crew enough rope to hang themselves.

"It's the only way they'll learn," Delwin told me. "I used to get all tense and angry whenever something went wrong. Now I just take a deep breath and get on with it."

Getting on with it this time meant chartering a local fisherman's traditional "canoe" the next morning. In exchange, Delwin had to offer Leon and Down's labor as spear fishermen on one of the dive sites to make up for the fisherman's loss of productivity — a dive operator's bargain with the devil.

The coral mounds and spur-and-groove formations offshore of Alligator Pond Beach are fished every day with line and trap, and lobsters are taken year-round in true frontier disregard for regulations. Yet the waters remain fishy, with lots of snapper and plentiful schools of grunts, spadefish and barracuda. The two coral mounds we dove, Saletsat and Drop-Drop, were veritable bug high-rises. I counted a hundred lobster in a quick census, and eventually lost interest in waving antennae. Both sites were near a solitary little sand cay miles out in Long Bay — a perfect cartoon desert island — where fishermen break for lunch and process their catches. The waste that washes into the water brings in Volkswagen-sized rays and bruiser nurse sharks. We saw the beady-eyed and barbeled bad boys on every dive, and watched dare-devil Down ride one by the tail.

Our last afternoon at SeaRiv we lunched with the fishermen on the spit and shared their cook-fire. We listened to the "thwack!" of the machete as they methodically hacked off the heads of countless lobsters, and we tasted fare from their mixed grill, an exotic sampling of what fish identification books usually classify as "odd-shaped swimmers."

Looking to shore we could see Delwin's domain in the blue haze of distance. The lay of the land looked like nothing so much as a lurking crocodile: Round Hill to the east was the bulbous tip of the snout, God's Well a missing molar, and the high plateau of Lover's Leap the bony ridge of the skull. It's a sleeping giant, smoldering with potential, and it could all vanish with a flick of the tail.

Diving the Yonaguni
Underwater Pyramid

Seated in a snug circle in the stern of the dive boat, we five Western-ers all bow ceremoniously to our respected dive-master Kanai-san who, gracefully kneeling on the Astroturf deck, has bowed to us, and who now returns our bows, so that we feel inclined to bow to her once again: ah so! Done bowing, we're all ears for the dive briefing — though I still find it difficult to tear my eyes away from the hundred-foot-tall cliffs that soar above the pitching boat. You'd be hard-pressed to imagine a more dramatic dive site. Here at the southern-most tip of Japan's Yonaguni Island, where the East China Sea surges and gnaws, powerful currents have undermined the massive mudstone cape so that it broods out over the foam like a giant face. Think Skull Island. Think Kong.

This would be a cool dive if there was nothing down below but rock spurs and fish — very cool, indeed, if its sapphire waters were populated by a swirl of breeding hammerhead sharks, which is what Kihachira Aratake, a local dive operator, was hoping to find when he first scouted the spot in March of 1986. What he found instead gave him goose-bumps of awe. He had back-rolled practically on top of an enormous pyramidal structure that began quite near the surface, and then plunged, by dis-tinct, terraced stages, to a depth of about a hundred feet. Immediately apparent was the hand of man — of many men! — in the uncanny regularity of the level terraces, in the perfect right angles of the steps that climbed to the top of the temple-like monolith. At the base of the structure there seemed to be a cobbled road that looped around it, and beyond the road a stacked-stone wall like the first line of defense in a fortress complex. Aratake was convinced that he had chanced upon the remnants of a lost civilization. He named the site Iseki — or "Ruins" — Point. As Aratake sought advice from experts, word spread of an un-derwater discovery in remote Yonaguni, potentially many millennia old, an Atlantis of the East.

In subsequent dives, new features were revealed — an arched en-trance way, twin obelisks, a turtle carving. These and other features of the Yonaguni "Monument" (as it is now locally known) Kanai has sketched for us on her erasable slate, pretty much previewing the entire dive in her chirpy, rapid-fire Japanese — translated for us *gaijin* by Lisa Slater, an adventurous 32-year-old Brit whose love of the language, culture, and especially the diving in the Ryukyu Archipelago (Okinawa and points south) led her to start a one-woman travel company, Open Coast. It's a thorough briefing, keeping Lisa plenty busy, including how we will enter— giant-striding *after* the count of three — and how we will come up — together, forming a pod at the surface, everyone holding on to each other. They are very conscientious divers, the Japanese.

"Let's go diving!" Kanai says at last, in English.

"Hai!"

We finish gearing up and fin-slap to the transom, all of us brimming with anticipation about what looms below, visible only as shifting patches of darkness in the bright blue.

"Ichi, ni, san … !"

We congregate on the bottom at about 60 feet in a world of giant stones. OK? Kanai signals. OK. OK? OK. OK? We're all OK. This then is "The Arch." Kanai has sketched it again on her slate, and gestures charmingly — part geisha, part Vanna White — towards the stacked stones. It's a crude arch at best, the five stacked stones impressively large but not seeming carved at all. Yet kicking through the narrow passage I feel a chill, like entering a gloomy tomb. Beyond rise the "Twin Towers," the matched obelisks. These do appear shaped — and very exactingly at that. Two perfect rectangles, more than 20 feet tall, they seem aligned, like the megaliths of Stonehenge, for some astrological purpose. In fact, the foremost expert on the Yonaguni Monument, Professor Masaaki Kimura of the University of the Ryukyus in Okinawa, believes the 4-inch gap between the obelisks may have channeled a shaft of sunlight signaling the autumn equinox.

Next we view "The Chapel," a platform on which is incised — or eroded — a dubious cross. Then we turn a corner and behold — with surprise, despite the briefing, and a measure of the same awe Kaharchira Aratake must have felt — the main Monument itself. It *is* an awesome sight: so massive, the stone so dark against the sea, the edges so uncannily carved. You immediately think of Mayan temples, the ziggurats of Sumer. It makes you dream of deep, deep time. And yet, like an optical illusion, the closer you get to it the more it changes. What seemed from a distance so apart from its surroundings seems from up close more of a piece, though certainly the most extreme geological expression of Yona-guni's bedrock stones. Kneeling on a terrace, sighting along a wall, I see the perfect edges blur. I touch the dense Brillo-like surface of encrusting sponges and algae and wonder: is it this growth which creates the illusion from afar of perfection, of artificially shaped edges? At the same time, the growth so obscures the face of the stone that any evidence of human craft would be difficult to find.

We spend a good twenty minutes kicking around the ruins, enjoying ideal conditions (the current can be wicked). I loiter at the Monument's summit, admiring the play of sunlight through crashing waves above "The Turtle." The mythology of Japan, according to Kimura, features magical guiding turtles, but this "carving" is a stretch. Could be any-thing, I'm thinking. On the other hand, if you were going to display a sacred loggerhead, this altar on the summit terrace would be just the place. Nearby is a cavity in the rock, maybe twenty feet deep and some-what rounded like a well. Professor Kimura calls this a tida hole — *tida* being the sun, and the hole the place from which it rises and disappears. Tida holes are features of other *gusuku* — which are palaces, fortresses and sacred sites all rolled into one — found in Japan. Another charming myth of the distant past.

Kanai has come to fetch me, pointing up. Soon we're gathered in our companionable pod on the surface, waiting while the boat backs up to us. The wind has come up, creating a feisty chop, and it's chilly aboard when we peel out of our wetsuits. One of the crew bustles about, distrib-uting hot barley tea in little silver cups. Ah! *Arigato!* Lisa Slater, visibly revved by the dive, can't believe how lucky our little group has been. Af-ter all we — Shelly and Michael, a married couple, both physicians, from D.C.; and Lee, Lisa's boyfriend, a film editor in L.A.; and me, the first dive journalist from the West to visit the ruins — arrived at Yonaguni (following three superlative days of diving in the nearby Yemana Islands) in a near gale. The weather has cleared right on schedule.

"So," Lisa asks me, beaming, "what do you think?"

For a blunt instrument some 500 feet long by 80 feet wide and eight stories tall, the Yonaguni Monument is an effective cutting tool: It seems invariably to divide its viewers into skeptics and believers. Our group splits right down the middle. Me, I'm a skeptic. For starters, I wonder what the monument is doing down *there* in the water instead of up on top of the cliff, which is where I would build *my* ziggurat. I would soon hear a theory countering that objection, via e-mail from Aratake-san, who compared the YUP (Yonaguni Underwater Pyramid) to the giant Buddhas of Afghanistan, carved into the rock face from forms suggested by nature — a pretty good theory. But for the moment I'm still under the spell of a highly qualified fellow skeptic, Boston University geologist Robert Schock.

Dr. Schock is doubly persuasive because he's both an academic and an iconoclast whose best-known work argues for the pre-dynastic antiquity of the Great Sphinx. Another of his books, "Voyage of the Pyramid Builders," credits our early civilizers with a much greater seafaring mobility than they are conventionally allowed. In short, pushing the clock back is a professional passion for Schock. If the YUP were man-made — or even somewhat altered by man — the work had to have been done while much of the oceans waters were still locked up in the glaciers of the last Ice Age, probably as much as 10,000 years ago. So he came to Yonaguni in 1997 hoping to find the smoking gun of a sophisticated antediluvian enterprise. Instead he found "a wonderful little island, and a fabulous place to dive." But nothing that couldn't be explained, "much more parsimoniously" — as he told me in a phone interview — "by natural processes." In fact, his hopes crumbled before he even got in the water, as he watched a typhoon tear away at the coast, and observed how the rock broke apart along horizontal bedding planes, creating those level terraces and vertical steps.

"As geologists, we're used to working with rocks that have incredible regularity," he told me. "If I want to find perfect angles, I'll look to minerals." Still, Schock feels the YUP is a fantastic structure, more exciting to him, from a geological point of view, than even the Grand Canyon. But not man-made. He won't believe it until somebody finds that smoking gun.

On the other hand, Professor Kimura can be equally convincing as he marshals his evidence: stone tools, post-holes, wedge marks on the stone, a stone tablet with incised markings recovered under a collapsed portion of the wall — to name just a few. Kimura's persuasiveness lies in his deep knowledge of Japanese anthropology, and that people's ancient and abiding love-affair with stone, whether as sacred mountains or megalithic shrines, or deftly manipulated garden sculpture. In one of his many expeditions to Yonaguni, beginning in 1992, he brought along traditional stone masons as consultants. At his Okinawa office, where his assistant serves me (and my translator) green tea on a patch of desk temporarily cleared of high stacks of papers, Professor Kimura tells me he was skeptical himself for the first five years of his research, and came around only reluctantly. It was the stone tablet that changed his mind. He opens a file cabinet and extracts a box in which, protected by bubble-wrap and swathed in purple cloth, lies a replica of the tablet. On it are carved a + sign, two os and a >. In Kimura's opinion, this is the smoking gun.

On my way out, the Professor takes me to a workshop across the hall to look at his newly completed scale model of the Monument. Ten years in the making, it is exactingly, obsessively, accurate. I can't help thinking of the Richard Dreyfus character in "Close Encounters" and his model of Devil's Tower. If this true believer sees a turtle carved on the summit, who am I to say I'm not the blind one. Kimura's parting words: "Until someone shows me proof that it's not man-made, I will believe that it is."

On our next to last night on Yonaguni, Lisa, Lee, and I go looking for evidence of the island's antiquity in the town's oldest bar. The proprietress, the town's oldest bar-keep, showers us with attention and serves us delicacies — enough sashimi for six, her special noodles — and brings us a listing of karaoke selections as thick as a Manhattan phonebook. This is actually our second bar, and it was the same thing at the first — little plates of fish and salads, cakes and candies, samples of the potent local saki, all arriving un-ordered. Japanese hospitality can be overwhelming, especially gastronomically.

Mostly, though, the Missus offers us talk, her life story. "This used to be a lonely island," she says. It's not exactly bustling now; we were the only ones on the street and it's by no means late. But point taken: Yonaguni is modern now, with some small factories, a big harbor project underway, a big hotel coming, they say. In her youth it was all rural; she was a farm girl who escaped that life by traveling to Okinawa where she worked and saved money. But she missed the island and so came back and opened this bar.

"But what about before then, in her parents and grandparents' day?" Lee wants to know. "Ask her where her ancestors came from."

"Ah, the old days," she says. "In the old days in Yonaguni there were only beautiful women and dogs. Then men came. When the men came they killed the dogs."

What?!

"I swear that's what she said," Lisa says.

But it's not entirely surprising. That day we toured the island with our dive guides, and wherever we stopped — at a cave high on the cliffs, by a pinnacle of rock in the sea, or a crack in the earth — we encountered more myth than history. There were obelisks elaborately inscribed, but in a Japanese either too archaic or too arcane for any of our group to read. And there was an ancient graveyard beside the sea, overlooking a gorgeous fringe of reef, where every tomb was a unique work of art, whether of recent vintage in flowing forms of cement, or of unknown antiquity, simple catacombs hewn into the bedrock, but so aptly carved they looked not just as if they had always been there, but as if they had always belonged.. Yonaguni is a place where history shades into mystery, and stone weathers into art — or back again into rock.

Before we have to leave Yonaguni we manage to do a couple more spectacular dives — one on a deepwater wall topped with a coral garden, a paradise for several varieties of "Nemos," as Kanai calls the clown fish; and one at a maze of bedrock spurs, full of caves and graceful arches reminiscent of those tombs. We make it back to Iseki Point one more time, too, the Gothic cliffs above, the black stone giant below. Again the bowing, the elaborate briefing (there are two new *gaijin,* a young couple from Scotland taking a resort course, no less; those two will be ushered through the ruins most carefully, practically carried, and they'll turn out to be believers). For me there'll be the moment of awe, and again the creeping doubt. And afterwards, shivering, the silver cup of hot barley tea — the whole experience a ritual I've come to love just as it ends.

Night Diving

There are two kinds of people at northern Florida's Emerald Sink after dark: those who get naked and jump out of trees, and those who put on rubber suits and go night scuba diving. There's not a lot of mingling amongst us. Mostly the two groups stalk circumspectly around each other's campfire at the sinkhole's rim, like two species of shore birds that can't eat each other's eggs and don't want to mate. Country music twangs from truck radios, goosed girls shriek in the dark, and sometimes a bandy-legged skinny-dipper will approach a group of divers suiting up on their tarp to peck at a particularly tasty-looking piece of scuba equipment and ask, "How much you pay for that?"

If it's a cave diver's complicated rig of redundant everything, the answer is "plenty." But most of us are just open-water divers packing the basic budget night-diving gear: a dependable, handheld D-battery-powered primary light; a smaller, clamp-on C-battery-powered backup light; and a glow-in-the-dark (chemiluminescent) light-stick, which will be attached to a sunken log at the sinkhole's center, marking a direct route to the surface.

Emerald Sink is shaped roughly like a flask. A thirty-foot-wide tube drops straight down sixty feet to the debris cone (where the sunken part of the sinkhole lies), and then opens up to a wider cavern angling down to 180 feet. My dive buddy and I like to putter around just below the summit of this black cone, drifting in and out of the cavern zone, probing our flashlights into cave entrances, and congratulating ourselves for not going into them. If Dracula were a kind of giant blind catfish, any one of these caves could be his castle.

There's a surprising amount of graffiti down here, mostly lovers' initials and fraternal insignia, though at a depth of eighty feet someone has gone to considerable trouble to carve this query in big block letters on the algae-darkened limestone: "WHAT ARE YOU LOOKING AT, ASSHOLE?"

Good question. If we were night diving in the ocean, on a reef or around a wreck, we might see shy nocturnal creatures openly foraging. Out of their hidey-holes octopuses would unravel, moray eels unreel and lobsters and other crustaceans creep forth in complete confidence. On the reef, divers' lights would blend a whole new palette of colors. Coral that appears dark blue by daylight becomes brilliant red by night, and the little purple gobies that flitted about it earlier would seem orange and sleep soundly on their side. Often in the ocean at night, you can swim through cosmic constellations of bioluminescent microorganisms — the famed phosphorescence that makes divers glow like velvet Elvises.

But Emerald Sink is just your basic freshwater swimming hole close to home, and, alas, there's not much to look at. Yet even when there's nothing to see — especially when there's nothing to see — night scuba diving offers a meditatively fruitful sensory-deprivation experience. As the mind soaks in the solution of darkness, it becomes susceptible to hypnagogic auditory hallucinations. Beyond the bubble and squeak of the regulator, you hear things: deeply internalized interlocutors waft up from the unconscious, clearing their throat and shaking their ship-wrecked cocktails from the other world. A few times during the séance atmosphere of a deep night dive at Emerald, I've heard the insistent ringing of a spiritualist's ectoplasmic telephone. And, I swear, one time I heard, down around 180 feet, where the narcosis kicks in, the distant flushing of the Devil's toilet.

On a night dive, once you've achieved neutral buoyancy, you can simply lie back on a black cushion, sighting up the telescopic tube of the sink at the dime-sized disc of the night sky. It glows faint and gray, like a Fifties TV set about to go on the fritz. On a good night you'll see a rippling moon looking back at you through the veins of thin black branches, and if you wait long enough, you're sure to see naked souls falling out of the trees, a veritable redneck Sistine Chapel of foreshortened bare limbs kicking up faraway clouds of turbulence as the angels toss them out of Heaven.

Everest at the Bottom of the Sea

You toss in your seaman's bunk and dream the oldest, oddest beach-comber's dream: Something has siphoned away all the waters of the seas, and you're taking a cold, damp hike down into the world's empty pool. Beer cans, busted pipes, concrete blocks, grocery carts, a Cadillac on its back, all four tires missing — every object casts a long, stark shadow on the puddled sand. With the Manhattan skyline and the Statue of Liberty behind you, you trek due east into the sunrise, following the toxic trough of the Hudson River's outflow — known to divers in these parts as the Mudhole — until you arrive, some miles out, at Wreck Valley.

You see whole fishing fleets asleep on their sides and about a million lobsters crawling around like giant cockroaches, waving confounded antennae in the thin air. Yeah, what a dump of history you see, a real Coney Island of catastrophes. The greatest human migration in the history of the world passed through here, first in a trickle of hard-asses, and then in that famous flood of huddled masses, Western man's main manifest destiny arcing across the northern ocean. The whole story is written in the ruins: in worm-ridden middens, mere stinking piles of mud; in tall ships chewed to fish-bone skeletons; five-hundred foot steel-plated cruisers plunked down on their guns; the battered cigar tubes of German U-boats; and sleek yachts scuttled alongside sunken tubs as humble as old boots.

You can't stop to poke around or fill your pockets with souvenirs. You're on a journey to the continent's edge, where perhaps the missing water still pours into the Atlantic abyss with the tremendous roar of a thousand Niagaras. Something waits there that might explain, and that must justify your presence in this absence, this scooped-out plain where no living soul belongs. And you know, with a sudden chill, that only your belief in the dream, the focus of your mind and your will on the possibility of the impossible, holds back the annihilating weight of the water.

You wake up in the dark and for a moment don't know where you are, until you hear the thrum of the diesel and feel the beam roll. Then you realize what awakened you was the abrupt decrease of noise, the engine throttling down, and the boat and the bunk you lie in subsiding into the swell, and you remember that you are on the open sea, drawing near to the wreck of the *Andrea Doria*. You feel the boat lean into a turn, cruise a little ways, and then turn again, and you surmise that up in the pilothouse, Captain Dan Crowell has begun to "mow the lawn," steering the sixty-foot exploration vessel the *Seeker* back and forth, taking her through a series of slow passes, sniffing for the *Doria*.

Crowell, whom you met last night when you hauled your gear aboard, is a big, rugged-looking guy, about six feet two inches in boat shoes, with sandy brown hair and a brush mustache. Only his large, slightly hooded eyes put a different spin on his otherwise gruff appearance; when he blinks into the green light of the sonar screen, he resembles a thoughtful sentinel owl. Another light glows in the wheelhouse: a personal computer, integral to the kind of technical diving Crowell loves.

The *Seeker*'s crew of five divvies up hour-and-a-half watches for the ten-hour trip from Montauk, Long Island, but Crowell will have been up all night in a state of tense vigilance. A veteran of fifty *Doria* trips, Crowell considers the hundred-mile cruise — both coming and going — to be the most dangerous part of the charter, beset by imminent peril of fog and storm and heavy shipping traffic. It's not for nothing that mariners call this patch of ocean where the *Andrea Doria* collided with another ocean liner the "Times Square of the Atlantic."

You feel the *Seeker*'s engines back down with a growl and can guess what Crowell is seeing now on the forward-looking sonar screen: a spattering of pixels, like the magnetic shavings on one of those draw-the-beard slates, coalescing into partial snapshots of the seven-hundred-foot liner. What the sonar renders is but a pallid gray portrait of the outsized hulk which, if it stood up on its stern on the bottom, 250 feet below, would tower nearly fifty stories above the *Seeker*, dripping and roaring like Godzilla. Most likely you're directly above her now, a proximity you feel in the pit of your stomach. As much as the physical wreck itself, it's the *Doria* legend you feel leaking upward through the *Seeker*'s hull like some kind of radiation.

"The Mount Everest of scuba diving," people call the wreck, in another useful catchphrase. Its badass rep is unique in the sport. Tell a fellow diver you've done the Great Barrier Reef or the Red Sea, they think you've got money. Tell 'em you've done the *Doria*, they know you've got balls. Remote enough to expose you to maritime horrors — the *Seeker* took a twenty-five foot wave over its bow on a return trip last summer — the *Doria*'s proximity to New York and New Jersey coasts has been a constant provocation for two generations. The epitome, in its day, of transatlantic style and a luxurious symbol of Italy's post-World War II recovery, the *Andrea Doria* has remained mostly intact and is still full of treasure: jewelry, art, an experimental automobile, bottles of wine — plus mementos of a bygone age, like brass shuffleboard numbers and silver and china place settings, not so much priceless in themselves but much coveted for the challenge of retrieving them.

But tempting as it is to the average wreck diver, nobody approaches the *Doria* casually. The minimum depth of a *Doria* dive is 180 feet, to the port side hull, well below the 130-foot limit of recreational diving. Several years of dedicated deep diving is considered a sane apprenticeship for those who make the attempt — that, plus a single-minded focus that subsumes social lives and drains bank accounts. Ten thousand dollars is about the minimum ante for the gear and the training and the dives you need to get under your belt. And that just gets you to the hull and hopefully back. For those who wish to penetrate the crumbling, maze-like interior, the most important quality is confidence bordering on hubris: trust in a lucid assessment of your own limitations and belief in your decision-making abilities, despite the knowledge that divers of equal if not superior skill have possessed those same beliefs and still perished.

Propped up on your elbows, you look out the salon windows and see the running lights of another boat maneuvering above the *Doria*. It's the *Wahoo*, owned by Steve Bielenda and a legend in its own right for its 1992 salvage of the seven-hundred-pound ceramic Gambone Panels, one of the *Doria*'s lost art masterpieces. Between Bielenda, a sixty-four-year-old native of Brooklyn, and Crowell, a transplanted southern Californian who's twenty years younger and has gradually assumed the lion's share of the *Doria* charter business, you have the old King of the Deep and the heir apparent. And there's no love lost between the generations.

"If these guys spent as much time getting proficient as they do avoiding things, they'd actually be pretty good," is Crowell's back-handed compliment to the whole "Yo, Vinny!" attitude of the New York-New Jersey old school of gorilla divers. Bielenda, for his part, has been more pointed in his comments on the tragedies of the 1998 and 1999 summer charter seasons, in which five divers died on the *Doria,* all from aboard the *Seeker.* "If it takes five deaths to make you the number-one *Doria* boat," Bielenda says, "then I'm happy being number two." He also takes exception to the *Seeker*'s volume of business — ten charters in one eight-week season. "There aren't enough truly qualified divers in the world to fill that many trips," Bielenda says.

To which Crowell's best response might be his piratical growl, "Ar-rgh!" which sums up his exasperation with the fractious politics of diving in the Northeast. He says he's rejected divers who've turned right around and booked a charter on the *Wahoo*. But hell, that's none of his business. His business is making the *Seeker*'s criteria for screening divers the most coherent in the business, which Crowell believes he has. Everyone diving the *Doria* from the *Seeker* has to be Tri-mix certified, a kind of doctoral degree of dive training that implies you know a good deal about physiology, decompression, and the effects of helium and oxygen and nitrogen on those first two. That, or be enrolled in a Tri-mix course and accompanied by an instructor, since, logically, where else are you gonna learn to dive a deep wreck except on a deep wreck?

As for the fatalities of the last two summer seasons — "five deaths in thirteen months" is the phrase that has been hammered into his mind — Crowell has been forthcoming with reporters looking for a smoking gun onboard the *Seeker* and with fellow divers concerned about mistakes they might avoid. "If you look at the fatalities individually, you'll see that they were coincidental more than anything else," Crowell has concluded. In a good season, during the fair-weather months from June to late August, the *Seeker* will put about two hundred divers on the *Doria*.

Nobody is more familiar with the cruel Darwinian exercise of hauling a body home from the *Doria* than Crowell himself, who has wept and cursed and finally moved on to the kind of gallows humor you need to cope. He'll tell you about his dismay at finding himself on a first-name basis with the paramedics that met the *Seeker* in Montauk after each of the five fatalities — how they tried to heft one body still in full gear, until Crowell reached down and unhooked the chest harness, lightening the load by an couple hundred pounds. Another they tried to fit into a body bag with the fins still on his feet.

But beyond their sobering effect on those who've made the awful ten-hour trip home with the dead, the accidents have not been spectacularly instructive. Christopher Murley, forty-four, from Cincinnati, had an outright medical accident, a heart attack on the surface. Vince Napoliello, a thirty-one-year-old bond salesman from Baltimore and a friend of Crowell's, "just a good, solid diver," was a physiological tragedy waiting to happen; his autopsy revealed a 90 percent obstructed coronary artery. Charlie McGurr? Another heart attack. And Richard Roost? A mature, skilled diver plain shit-out-of-luck, whose only mistake seems to have been a failure to remain conscious at depth, which is never guaranteed. Only the death of Craig Sicola, a New Jersey house builder, might fit the criticism leveled at the *Seeker* in Internet chat rooms and God knows where else — that a super competitive atmosphere, and a sort of taunting elitism projected by the *Seeker*'s captain and his regular crew, fueled the fatalities of the last two seasons.

Did Sicola, soloing on his second trip, overreach his abilities? Maybe so, but exploring the wreck, and yourself in the process, is the point of the trip.

"You might be paying your money and buying your ticket just like at Disney World, but everybody also knows this is a real expedition," says Crowell. "You've got roaring currents, low visibility, often horrible weather, and you're ten hours from help. We're pushing the limits out here."

All this you know because, like most of the guys on the charter, you're sort of a *Doria* buff … Well, maybe a bit of a nut. You wouldn't be out here if you weren't. A lot of the back story you know by heart. How on the night of July 25, 1956, the *Andrea Doria* (after the sixteenth-century Genoese admiral), 29,083 tons of *la dolce vita*, festively inbound for New York harbor, steamed out of an opaque fogbank at a near top speed of twenty-three knots and beheld the smaller, outbound Swedish liner *Stockholm* making straight for her. The ships had tracked each other on radar but lined up head-on at the last minute. The *Stockholm*'s bow, reinforced for ice-breaking in the North Sea, plunged thirty feet into the *Doria*'s side, ripping open a six-story gash. One *Doria* passenger, Linda Morgan, who became known as the miracle girl, flew from her bed in her nightgown and landed on the forward deck of the *Stockholm*, where she survived. Her sister, asleep in the bunk below, was crushed instantly. In all, fifty-one people died.

Eleven hours after the collision, the *Andrea Doria* went down under a froth of debris, settling onto the bottom on her wounded starboard side in 250 feet of cold, absinthe-green seawater. The very next day, Peter Gimbel, the department store heir (he hated like hell to be called that) and his partner, Joseph Fox, made the first scuba dive to the wreck, using primitive double hosed regulators. The wreck they visited was then considerably shallower (the boat has since collapsed somewhat internally and hunkered down into the pit the current is gouging) and uncannily pristine; curtains billowed through portholes, packed suitcases knocked around in tipped-over staterooms, and shoes floated in ether. That haunted-house view obsessed Gimbel, who returned, most famously, for a month-long siege in 1981. Employing a diving bell and saturation diving techniques, Gimbel and crew blowtorched through the first-class loading area doors, creating "Gimbel's Hole," a garage-door-sized aperture amidships, still the preferred entry into the wreck, and eventually raised the Bank of Rome safe. When Gimbel finished editing his film, *The Mystery of the Andrea Doria,* in an event worthy of Geraldo, the safe was opened on live TV. Stacks of water-logged cash were revealed, though much less than the hoped-for millions.

In retrospect, the "mystery" and the safe seem to have been invented after the fact to justify the diving. Gimbel was seeking something else. He had lost his twin brother to illness some years before, an experience that completely changed his life and made of him an explorer. He got lost in jungles, filmed great white sharks from the water. And it was while tethered by an umbilicus to a decosphere the divers called Mother, hacking through shattered walls and hauling out slimed stanchions in wretchedly confined space and inches of visibility, always cold, that Gimbel believed he encountered and narrowly escaped a "malevolent spirit," a spirit he came to believe inhabited the *Doria.*

But while Gimbel sought absolute mysteries in a strongbox, salvagers picked up other prizes — the *Andrea Doria*'s complement of fine art, such as the Renaissance-style life-sized bronze statue of Admiral Doria, which divers hack-sawed off at the ankles. The wreckage of the first-class gift shop has yielded trinkets of a craftsmanship that no longer exists today — like Steve Bielenda's favorite *Doria* artifact, a silver tea fob in the form of a locomotive with its leather thong still intact. A handful of Northeastern deep divers who knew one another on a first-name basis (when they were on speaking terms, that is) spread the word that it was actually fun to go down in the dark. And by degrees, diving the *Doria* and its two-hundred-foot-plus interior depths segued from a business risk to a risky adventure sport. In the late eighties and early nineties, there was a technical diving boom, marked by a proliferation of training agencies and a steady refinement of gear. Tanks got bigger, and mixed gases replaced regular compressed air as a "safer" means of diving at extreme depths.

Every winter, the North Atlantic storms give the wreck a rough shake, and new prizes tumble out, just waiting for the summer charters. The *Seeker* has been booked for up to three years in advance, its popularity founded on its reputation for bringing back artifacts. The most sought-after treasure is the seemingly inexhaustible china from the elaborate table settings for 1,706 passengers and crew. First-class china, with its distinctive maroon-and-gold bands, has the most juju, in the thoroughly codified scheme of things. It's a strange fetish, certainly, for guys who wouldn't ordinarily give a shit about the quality of a teacup and saucer. Bielenda and Crowell and their cronies have so much of the stuff that their homes look as if they were decorated by maiden aunts.

Yet you wouldn't mind a plate of your own, and all that it would stand for. You can see it in your mind's eye — your plate and the getting of it — just as you saw it last night on the cruise out, when someone popped one of Crowell's underwater videos into the VCR. The thirty-minute film, professionally done from opening theme to credits, ended beautifully with the *Seeker*'s divers fresh from their triumphs, still blushing in their drysuits like lobsters parboiled in adrenaline, holding up *Doria* china while Vivaldi plays. A vicarious victory whose emotions were overshadowed, you're sorry to say, by the scenes inside the *Doria*, and specifically by the shots of *Doria* china, gleaming bone-white in the black mud on the bottom of some busted metal closet who knew how far in or down how many blind passageways. Crowell had tracked it down with his camera and put a beam on it: fine Genoa china, stamped *ITALIA*, with a little blue crown. The merit badge of big boy diving, the artifact that says it best: I fuckin' did it — I dove da *Doria*! Your hand reaches out …

The cabin door opens and someone comes into the salon, just in time to cool your china fever. It's Crowell's partner, Jenn Samulski, who keeps the divers' records and cooks three squares a day. Samulski, an attractive blonde from Staten Island who has been down to the *Doria* herself, starts the coffee brewing, and eyes pop open, legs swing out over the sides of bunks, and the boat wakes up to sunrise on the open sea, light glinting off the steely surface and the metal rows of about sixty scuba tanks weighing down the stern.

On a twelve-diver charter, personalities range from obnoxiously extroverted to fanatically secretive — every type of Type A, each man a monster of his own methodology. But talk is easy when you have something humongous in common, and stories are the coin of the lifestyle. You know so-and-so? someone says around a mouthful of muffin. Wasn't he on that dive back in '95? And at once, you're swept away by a narrative, this one taking you to the wreck of the *Lusitania*, where an American, or a Brit maybe — somebody's acquaintance, somebody's friend — is diving with an Irish team. He gets entangled, this diver does, in his own exploration line, on the hull down at 280 feet. His line is just pooling all around him and he's thrashing, panicking, thinking — as everybody always does in a panic — that he has to get to the surface, like *right now*. So he inflates his buoyancy compensator (b.c.) to the max, and now he's like a balloon tied to all that tangled line, which the lift of the b.c. is pulling taut. He's got his knife out, and he's hacking away at the line. One of the Irish divers sees what's happening and swims over and grabs the guy by the legs just as the last line is cut. They both go rocketing for the surface, this diver and his pumped-up b.c. and the Irishman holding onto him by the knees. At 160 feet, the Irishman figures, Sorry, mate, I ain't dying with you, and has to let him go. So the diver flies up to the top and bursts internally from the violent change of depth and the pressurized gas, which makes a ruin of him.

Yeah, he should never have been diving with a line, someone points out, and a Florida cave diver and a guy from Jersey rehash the old debate — using line for exploration, the cave diver's practice, versus progressive penetration, visual memorization of the wreck and the ways out.

Meanwhile, a couple of the *Seeker*'s crew members have already been down to the wreck to set the hook. The rubber chase boat goes over the bow, emergency oxygen hoses are lowered off the port-side rail, and Crowell tosses out a leftover pancake to check the current. It slaps the dead-calm surface, spreading ripples, portals widening as it drifts aft. Because the *Doria* lies close to the downfall zone, where dense cold Atlantic water pours over the continental shelf and down into the Atlantic Trench, the tidal currents can be horrendously strong. Sometimes a boat anchored to the *Doria* will carve a wake as if it were underway, making five knots and going nowhere. An Olympic swimmer in a Speedo couldn't keep up with that treadmill, much less a diver in heavy gear. And sometimes the current is so strong, it'll snap a three-quarter-inch anchor line like rotten twine. But on this sunny July morning, already bright and heating up fast, Crowell blinks beneath the bill of his cap at the bobbing pancake and calculates the current at just a couple of knots — not too bad at all, if you're ready for it.

Crowell grins at the divers now crowded around him at the stern. "Pool's open," he says.

You can never get used to the weight. When you wrestle your arms into the harness of a set of doubles, two 120-cubic-foot-capacity steel tanks yoked together on metal plates, you feel like an ant, one of those leaf-cutter types compelled to heft a preposterous load. What you've put on is essentially a wearable submarine with its crushed neoprene dry-suit shell and its steel external lungs and glass-enclosed command center. Including a pony-sized emergency bottle bungee-strapped between the steel doubles and two decompression tanks clipped to your waist, you carry five tanks of gas and five regulators. You can barely touch your mittened hands together in front of you around all the survival gear, the lift bags, lights, reels, hoses, and instrument consoles. And yet for all its awkwardness on deck, a deep-diving rig is an amazing piece of technology, and if you don't love it at least a little you had better never put it on. It's the one thing you suppose you all have in common on this charter — stockbrokers, construction workers, high school teachers, cops — you're all Buck Rogers flying a personal ship through inner space.

The immediate downside is that you're slightly nauseated from reading your gauges in a four-foot swell, and inside your dry suit, in expedition-weight socks and polypropylene long johns, you're sweating bullets. The way the mind works, you're thinking, *To hell with this bobbing world of sunshine and gravity* — you can't wait to get wet and weightless. You strain up from the gearing platform hefting nearly two hundred pounds and duckwalk a couple of steps to the rail, your fins smacking the deck and treading on the fins of your buddies who are still gearing up.

Some of the experienced *Doria* divers from Crowell's crew grasp sawed-off garden rakes with duct-taped handles, tools they'll use to reach through rubble and haul in china from a known cache. Crowell gestures among them, offering directions through the *Doria's* interior maze. Your goal is just to touch the hull, peer into Gimbel's Hole. An orientation dive. You balance on the rail like old Humpty-Dumpty and crane your neck to see if all's clear on the indigo surface. Scuba lesson number one: Most accidents occur on the surface. There was a diver last summer, a seasoned tech diver, painstaking by reputation, on his way to a wreck off the North Carolina coast. Checked out his gear en route — gas on, take a breath, good, gas off — strapped it on at the site, went over the side and sank like a dirt dart. His buddies spent all morning looking for him everywhere except right under the boat, where he lay, drowned. He had never turned his breathing gas back on.

And there was a diver on the *Seeker* who went over the side and then lay sprawled on his back in the water, screaming, "Help! Help!" The fuck was the matter with the guy? Turns out he'd never been in a dry suit before and couldn't turn himself over. Crowell wheeled on the guy's instructor. "You brought him out here to make his first dry-suit dive on the *Doria*? Are ya *crazy*?" Then the instructor took an underwater scooter down with him, and he had to be rescued with the chase boat. *Arrgh*! Crowell laments that there are divers going from Open Water, the basic scuba course, to Tri-mix in just fifty dives; they're book-smart and experience-starved. And there are bad instructors and mad instructors, egomaniacal, guru-like instructors.

"You will dive only with me," Crowell says, parodying the Svengalis. "or else it's a thousand bucks for the cape with the clouds and the stars on it. Five hundred more and I'll throw in the wand."

"Just because you're certified don't make you qualified" is Steve Bielenda's motto, and it's the one thing the two captains can agree on.

You take a couple of breaths from each of your regs. Click your lights on and off. You press the inflator button and puff a little more gas into you buoyancy compensator, the flotation wings that surround your double 120s, and experience a tightening and a swelling up such as the Incredible Hulk must feel just before his buttons burst. Ready as you'll ever be, you plug your primary reg in your mouth and tip the world over … and hit the water with a concussive smack. At once, as you pop back up to the surface, before the bubbles cease seething between you and the image of the *Seeker*'s white wooden hull, rocking half in and half out of the water, you're in conflict with the current. You grab the granny line and it goes taut and the current dumps buckets of water between your arms and starts to rooster-tail around your tanks. This is two knots? You're breathing hard by the time you haul yourself hand over hand to the anchor line, and that's not good. Breath control is as important to deep divers as it is to yogis. At two hundred feet, just getting really excited could knock you out like a blow from a ball-peen hammer. As in kill you dead. So you float a moment on the surface, sighting down the parabola of the anchor line to the point where it vanishes into a brownish-blue gloom. Then you reach up to your inflator hose and press the other button, the one that sputters out gas from the b.c., and feel the big steel 120s reassert their mass, and calmly, feet first, letting the anchor line slide between your mitts, you start to sink.

For the thin air of Everest, which causes exhaustion universally and pulmonary and cerebral events (mountain sickness) seemingly randomly, consider the "thick" air you must breathe at 180 feet, the minimum depth of a dive to the *Doria*. Since water weighs sixty-four pounds per cubic foot (and is eight hundred times as dense as air), every foot of depth adds significantly to the weight of the water column above you.

You feel this weight as pressure in your ears and sinuses almost as soon as you submerge. Water pressure doesn't affect the gas locked in your noncompressible tanks, of course, until you breathe it. Then, breath by breath, thanks to the genius of the scuba regulator — Jacques Cousteau's great invention — the gas becomes ambient to the weight of the water pressing on your lungs. That's why breathing out of steel 120s pumped to a pressure of 7,000 psi isn't like drinking out of a fire hose, and also why you can kick around a shallow reef at twenty feet for an hour and a half, while at a hundred feet you'd suck the same tank dry in twenty minutes; you're inhaling many times more molecules per breath.

Unfortunately, it's not all the same to your body how many molecules of this gas or the other you suck into it. On the summit of Everest, too few molecules of oxygen makes you light-headed, stupid, and eventually dead. On the decks of the *Doria*, too many molecules of oxygen can cause a kind of electrical fire in your central nervous system. You lose consciousness, thrash about galvanically, and inevitably spit out your regulator and drown. A depth of 216 feet is generally accepted as the point at which oxygen in compressed air (which is 21 percent oxygen, 79 percent nitrogen) becomes toxic and will sooner or later (according to factors as infinitely variable as individual bodies) kill you. As for nitrogen, it has two dirty tricks it can play at high doses. It gets you high — just like the nitrous oxide that idiot adolescents huff and the dentist dispenses to distract you from a root canal — starting at about 130 feet for most people. "I am personally quite receptive to nitrogen rapture," Cousteau writes in *The Silent World*. "I like it and fear it like doom.

The fearsome thing is that, like any drunk, you're subject to mood swings, from happy to sad to hysterical and panicky when you confront the dumb thing you've just done, like getting lost inside a sunken ocean liner. The other bad thing nitrogen does is deny you permission to return immediately to the surface, every panicking person's solution to the trouble he's in. It's the excess molecules of nitrogen lurking in your body in the form of tiny bubbles that force you to creep back up to the surface at precise intervals determined by time and depth. On a typical *Doria* dive, you'll spend twenty-five minutes at around two hundred feet and decompress for sixty-five minutes at several stopping points, beginning at 110 feet. While you are hanging on to the anchor line, you're off-gassing nitrogen at a rate your body can tolerate. Violate deco and you are subject to symptoms ranging from a slight rash to severe pain to quadriplegia and death. The body copes poorly with big bubbles of nitrogen trying to fizz out through your capillaries and bulling through your spinal column, traumatizing nerves.

Enter Tri-mix, which simply replaces some of the oxygen and nitrogen in air with helium, giving you a life-sustaining gas with fewer molecules of those troublesome components of air. With Tri-mix, you can go deeper and stay longer and feel less narced. Still, even breathing Tri-mix at depth can be a high-wire act, owing to a third and final bad agent: carbon dioxide. The natural by-product of respiration also triggers the body's automatic desire to replenish oxygen. When you hyperventilate — take rapid, shallow breaths — you deprive yourself of CO_2 and fool the body into believing it doesn't need new oxygen. Breath-hold divers will hyperventilate before going down as a way to gain an extra minute or two of painless O_2 deprivation. But at depth (for reasons poorly understood), hypercapnia, the retention of CO_2 molecules, has the same "fool the brain" effect. It's a tasteless, odorless, warningless fast track to unconsciousness. One moment you are huffing and puffing against the current, and the next you are swimming in the stream of eternity.

Richard Roost, a forty-six-year-old scuba instructor from Ann Arbor, Michigan, one of the five *Doria* fatalities of the last two seasons, was highly skilled and physically fit. His body was recovered from the *Doria*'s first-class lounge, a large room full of shattered furniture deep in the wreck. It's a scary place, by all accounts, but Roost seemed to be floating in a state of perfect repose. Though he had sucked all the gas from his tanks, there was no sign that he had panicked. Crowell suspects that he simply "took a nap," a likely victim of hypercapnia.

So it is that you strive to sink with utter calm, pumping a bit of gas into your drysuit as you feel it begin to vacuum-seal itself to you, bumping a little gas into the b.c. to slow your rate of descent, seeking neutrality, not just in buoyancy but in spirit as well. Soon you've sunk into that zone where you can see neither surface nor bottom. It's an entrancing, mystical place — pure inner space. Things appear out of nowhere — huge, quick things that aren't there, blocks of blankness, hallucinations of blindness. Drifting, drifting ... reminds you of something Steve Bielenda told you: "The hard part is making your brain believe this is happening. But, hey, you know what: It really is happening!" You focus on the current-borne minutiae — sea snow, whale food, egg-drop soup — which whizzes by outside the glass of you mask like a sepia-colored silent movie of some poor sod sinking through a blizzard.

Your depth gauge reads 160 feet, and you hit the thermocline, the ocean's deep icebox layer. The water temp plunges to 45 degrees and immediately numbs your cheeks and lips. Your dry suit is compressed paper-thin; you don't know how long you can take the cold, and then something makes you forget about it completely: the *Doria*, the great dome of her hull falling away into obscurity, and the desolate rails vanishing in both directions, and a lifeboat davit waving a shred of trawler net like a hankie, and the toppled towers of her superstructure. And it's all true what they've said: you feel humbled and awed. You feel how thin your own audacity is before the gargantuan works of man. You land fins-first onto the steel plates, kicking up two little clouds of silt. Man on the moon.

You've studied the deck plans of the Grande Dame of the Sea — her intricacy and complexity and order rendered in fine architectural lines. But the *Doria* looks nothing like that now. Her great smokestack has tumbled down into the dark debris field on the sea floor. Her raked-back aluminum forecastle decks have melted like a Dali clock in the corrosive seawater. Her steel hull has begun to buckle under its own weight and the immense weight of water, pinching in and splintering the teak decking of the promenade, where you kick along, weaving in and out of shattered windows. Everything is moving: bands of water, now cloudy, now clear, through which a blue shark twists in and out of view; sea bass darting out to snatch at globs of matter stirred up by your fins. They swallow and spit and glower. Everywhere you shine your light inside, you see black dead ends and washed-out walls and waving white anemones like giant dandelions bowing in a breeze.

You rise up a few feet to take stock of your location and see that on her outer edges she is Queen of Snags, a harlot tarted up with torn nets, bristling with fishermen's monofilament and the anchor lines of dive boats that have had to cut and run from sudden storms. She's been grappled more times than Moby Dick, two generations of obsessed Ahabs finding in her sheer outrageous bulk the sinews of an inscrutable malice, a dragon to tilt against. In your solitude you sense the bleak bitch of something unspeakably larger still, something that shrinks the *Doria* down to the size of Steve Bielenda's toy-train tea fob: a hurricane of time blowing through the universe, devouring all things whole.

On the aft deck of the *Wahoo*, Steve Bielenda, still solid as a dock post in his early sixties, is kicked back in his metal folding-chair throne. He wears his white hair in a mullet cut and sports a gold earring. He was wild as a kid, by his own account, a wiseguy, wouldn't listen to nobody. The product of vocational schools, he learned auto mechanics and made a success of his own repair shop before he caught the scuba bug. Then he would go out with fishermen for a chance to dive — there weren't any dive boats then — and offered his services as a salvage diver, no job too small or too big. When he sold his shop and bought the *Wahoo*, it was the best and biggest boat in the business. Now, as the morning heats up, he's watching the bubbles rise and growling out *Doria* stories in his Brooklyn accent.

"When you say Mount Everest to somebody," he says, "you're sayin' something. Same with da *Doria*. It was a pinnacle wreck. It was something just to go there."

And go there he did — more than a hundred times. The first time in '81, with a serious *Doria* fanatic, Bill Campbell, who had commissioned a bronze plaque to commemorate the twenty-fifth anniversary of the sinking; and often with maritime scholar and salvager John Moyer, who won salvage rights to the *Doria* in federal court and hired the *Wahoo* in '92 to put a "tag" on the wreck — a tube of PVC pipe, sealed water-tight, holding the legal papers. Tanks were much smaller then, dinky steel 72's and aluminum 80's, compared with the now-state-of-the-art 120-cubic-foot-capacity tanks. "You got air, you got time," is how Bielenda puts it. And time was what they didn't have down at 180 feet on the hull. It was loot and scoot. Guys were just guessing at their decompression times, since the U.S. Navy Dive Tables expected that nobody would be stupid or desperate enough to make repetitive dives below 190 feet with scuba gear. "Extrapolating the tables" was what they called it: it was more like pick a lucky number and hope for the best. But Bielenda's quick to point out that in the first twenty-five years of diving the *Doria*, nobody died. Back then the players were all local amphibians, born and bred to cold-water diving and watermen to the nth degree. Swimming, water polo, skin diving, then scuba, then deep scuba — you learned to crawl before you walked in those days.

A thousand things you had to learn first. "You drive through a toll-booth at five miles an hour — no problem, right? Try it at fifty miles an hour. That hole gets real small! That's divin' da *Doria*. To dive da *Doria*, it's gotta be like writin' a song," the captain says, and he hops up from his chair and breaks into an odd little dance, shimmying his 212 pounds in a surprisingly nimble groove, tapping himself here, here, here — places a diver in trouble might find succor in his gear.

"And you oughta wear your mask strap under yer hood," he tells a diver who's gearing up. "There was this gal one time … " and Bielenda launches into the story about how he saved Sally Wahrmann's life with that lesson.

She was down in Gimbel's Hole, just inside it and heading for the gift shop, when this great big guy — John Ornsby was his name, one of the early *Doria* fatalities — comes flying down into the hole after her and just clobbers her. "He rips her mask off and goes roaring away in a panic," Bielenda says. "But see, she has her mask under her hood like I taught her, so she doesn't lose it. It's still right there around her neck."

The blow knocked Wahrmann nearly to the bottom of the wreck, where an obstruction finally stopped her fall seven sideways stories down. But she never panicked, and with her mask back on and cleared, she could find her way out towards the tiny green speck of light that was Gimbel's Hole, the way back to the world. "She climbs up onto the boat and gives me a big kiss. 'Steve,' she says, 'you just saved my life.'"

As for Ornsby, a Florida breath-hold diver of some renown, his banzai descent into Gimbel's Hole was never explained, but he was found dead not far from the entrance, all tangled up in cables as if a giant spider had been at him. It took four divers with cable cutters two dives each to cut the body free. Bielenda has been lost inside of wrecks and has found his way out by a hairbreadth. He and the *Wahoo* have been chased by hurricanes. One time he had divers down on the *Doria* when a blow came up. He was letting out anchor line as fast as he could, and the divers, who were into decompression, were scrambling up the line hand over hand to hold their depth. The swells rose up to fifteen feet, and Bielenda could see the divers in the swells hanging on to the anchor line, ten feet underwater but looking down into the *Wahoo*! A *Doria* sleigh ride — that's the kind of memories the *Doria*'s given him. Strange sights indeed. He knows he's getting too old for the rigors of depth, but he's not ready to let go of the *Doria* yet, not while they still have their hooks in each other.

Up in the pilothouse of the *Seeker*, Dan Crowell is fitting his video camera into its watertight case, getting ready to go down and shoot some footage inside the wreck. He tries to make at least one dive every charter trip, and he never dives without his camera anymore if he can help it.

The more you learn about Crowell, the more impressed you are. He's a voracious autodidact who sucks up expertise like a sponge. He has worked as a commercial artist, a professional builder, a commercial diver, and a technical scuba instructor, as well as a charter captain. His passion now is shooting underwater video, making images of shipwrecks at extreme depths. His footage of the *Britannic* was shot at a whopping 400 feet. When Crowell made his first *Doria* dive in 1990, a depth of 200 feet was still Mach I, a real psychological and physical barrier. He remembers kneeling in the silt inside Gimbel's Hole at 210 feet and scooping up china plates while he hummed the theme from *Indiana Jones,* "and time was that great big boulder coming at you."

In '91, Crowell didn't even own a computer, but all that changed with the advent of affordable software that allowed divers to enter any combination of gases and get back a theoretically safe deco schedule for any depth. "In a matter of months, we went from rubbing sticks together to flicking a Bic," Crowell says. It was the aggressive use of computers — and the willingness to push the limits — that separated the *Seeker* from the competition. When the colorful Bill Nagle, the boat's previous captain, died of his excesses in `93, Crowell came up with the cash to buy the *Seeker.* He'd made the money in the harsh world of hard-hat diving.

Picture Crowell in his impermeable commercial diver's suit, with its hose-fed air supply and screw-down lid, slowly submerging in black, freezing water at some hellish industrial waterfront wasteland. The metaphorical ball cock is stuck and somebody's gotta go down and unstick it. Hacksaw it, blast it, use a lift bag and chains — the fuck cares how he does it? Imagine him slogging through thigh-high toxic sludge hefting a wrench the size of a dinosaur bone. His eyes are closed — can't see a damn thing down there anyway — and he's humming a tune to himself, working purely by touch, in three-fingered neoprene mitts. Think of him blind as a mole and you'll see why he loves the camera's eye so much, and you'll believe him when he says he's never been scared on the *Andrea Doria.*

"Well, maybe once," Crowell admits. "I was diving on air and I was pretty narced, and I knew it. I started looking around and realized I had no idea where I was." He was deep inside the blacked-out maze of the wreck's interior, where every breath dislodges blinding swirls of glittering rust and silt. "But it just lasted a few seconds. When you're in those places, you're seeing things in postage-stamp-sized pieces. You need to pull back and look at the bigger picture — which is about eight and half by eleven inches." Crowell found his way out, reconstructing his dive, as it were, page by page.

You've always thought the way water blurs vision is an apt symbol of a greater blurring, that of the mind in the world. Being matter, we are buried in matter — we are buried alive. This is an idea you first encountered intuitively in the stories of Edgar Allan Poe. Madman! Don't you see? cries Usher, before his eponymous house crashes down on top of him. And the nameless penitent in "The Pit and the Pendulum" first creeps blindly around the abyss, and then confronts the razor's edge of time. He might well be looking into Gimbel's Hole and at the digital readout on his console; he is literature's first extreme diver immersed in existential fear of the impossible present moment. But the diver's mask is also a miraculous extra inch of perspective; it puts you at a certain remove from reality, even as you strike a Mesphistophelian bargain with physics and the physical world.

You're twelve minutes into your planned twenty-five-minute bottom time when the current suddenly kicks up. It's as if God has thrown the switch — *ka-chung!* — on a conveyor belt miles wide and fathoms thick. You see loose sheets of metal on the hull sucking in and blowing out, just fluttering, as if the whole wreck were breathing. If you let go, you would be whisked away into open sea, a mote in a maelstrom. The current carries with it a brown band of bad visibility, extra cold, direly menacing. Something has begun to clang against the hull, tolling like a bell. Perhaps, topside, it has begun to blow. Keep your shit together. Control your breath. Don't fuck up. And don't dream that things might be otherwise, or it'll be the last dream you know. Otherwise? Shit ... this is it. Do something. Act. Now! You're going to have to fight your way back to the anchor line, fight to hold onto it for the whole sixty-five minutes of your deco. And then fight to get back into the boat, with the steel ladder rising and plunging like a cudgel. What was moments ago a piece of cake has changed in a heartbeat to a life-or-death situation.

Then you see Dan Crowell, arrowing down into Gimbel's Hole with his video camera glued to his eyes. You watch the camera light dwindle down to 200 feet, 210, then he turns right and disappears inside the wreck. Do you follow him, knowing it is precisely that — foolish emulation — that kills divers here? Consider the case of Craig Sicola, a talented, aggressive diver. On his charter in the summer of '98, he saw the crew of the *Seeker* bring up china, lots of it. He wanted china himself, and if he'd waited, he would've gotten it the easy way. Crowell offered to run a line to a known cache — no problem, china for everybody. But it wouldn't have been the same. Maybe what he wanted had less to do with plates than with status, status within an elite. He must've felt he'd worked his way up to the top of his sport only to see the pinnacle recede again. So he studied the *Doria* plans posted in the *Seeker*'s cabin and deduced where china ought to be — his china — and jumped in alone to get it. He came so close to pulling it off, too.

Dropping down into Gimbel's Hole, he found himself in the first-class foyer, where well-dressed passengers once made small talk and smoked as they waited to be called to dinner. He finessed the narrow passageway that led to the first-class dining room, a huge, curving space that spans the width of the *Doria*. He kicked his way across that room, playing his light off lumber piles and shattered tables. Down another corridor leading farther back toward the stern, he encountered a jumble of busted walls, which may have been a kitchen — and he found his china. He loaded up his goody bag, stirring up storms of silt as the plates came loose from the muck. He checked his time and gas supply — hurry now, hurry — and began his journey back. Only he must have missed the passage as he recrossed the dining room. Easy to do: Gain or lose a few feet in depth and you hit blank wall. He would've taken in a great gulp of gas then — you do that when you're lost; your heart goes wild. Maybe the exit is inches away at the edge of vision, or maybe you've got yourself all turned around and have killed yourself, with ten minutes to think about it.

Sicola managed to find his way out, but by then he must've been running late on his deco schedule. With no time to return to the anchor line, he unclipped his emergency ascent reel and tied a line off to the wreck. Which was when he made mistake number two. He either became entangled in the line, still too deep to stop, and had to cut himself free, or else the line broke as he ascended. Either way, he rocketed to the surface too fast and died of an embolism. Mercifully, though, right up to the last second, Sicola must have believed he was taking correct and decisive action to save himself. Which, in fact, is exactly what he was doing.

But with a margin of error so slender, you have to wonder: Where the hell does someone like Crowell get the sack to make fifty turns inside that maze? How can he swim through curtains of dangling cables, twisting through blown-out walls, choosing stairways that are now passages, and taking passages that are now like elevator shafts, one after another, as relentlessly as one of the blue sharks that school about the wreck? By progressive penetration, he has only gone as far at a time as his memory has permitted. Only now he holds in his mind a model of the ship — and he can rotate that model in his mind and orient himself toward up, down, out. He's been all the way through the *Doria* and out the other side, through the gash that sank her, and he brought back the images. This is what it looks like; this is what you see.

But how does it feel? What's it like to know you are in a story that you will either retell a hundred times or never tell? You decide to drop down into the black hole. No, you don't decide; you just do it. Why? You just do. A little ways, to explore the wreck and your courage, what you came down here to do. What is it like? Nothing under your fins now for eighty feet but the mass and complexity of the machine on all sides — what was once luminous and magical changed to dreary chaos. Drifting down past the cables that killed John Ornsby, rusty steel lianas where a wall has collapsed. Dropping too fast now, you pump air into your b.c., kick up and bash your tanks into a pipe, swing one arm and hit a cable, rust particles raining down. You've never felt your attention so assaulted: it is everything at once, from all directions, and from inside, too. You grab the cable and hang, catching your breath — bubble and hiss, bubble and hiss. Your light, a beam of dancing motes, plays down a battered passageway, where metal steps on the left-hand wall lead to a vertical landing, then disappear behind a low, sponge-encrusted wall that was once a ceiling. That's the way inside the *Doria*.

There is something familiar about that tunnel, something the body knows. All your travels, your daily commutes, the Brownian motion of your comings and goings in the world, straining after desires, reaching for your beloved — they've all been just an approach to this one hard turn. You can feel it, the spine arching to make the corner, a bow that shoots the arrow of time. In the final terror, with your gauges ticking and your gas running low, as dead end leads to dead end and the last corridor stretches out beyond time, does the mind impose its own order, seizing the confusion of busted pipes and jagged edges and forcing them into a logical grid, which you can then follow down to the bottom of the wreck and out — in a gust of light and love — through the wound in her side? Where you find yourself standing up to your waist in water, in the pit the current has gouged to be the grave of the *Andrea Doria*. Seagulls screech in the air as you take off your gear piece by piece and, much lightened, begin to walk back to New York across the sandy plane. And it comes as no surprise at all to look up and behold the *Seeker* flying above you, sailing on clouds. On the stern deck, the divers are celebrating, like rubber-suited angels, breaking out beers and cigars and holding up plates to be redeemed by the sun.

About the Author

BUCKY McMAHON was born in Atlanta, Georgia in 1955, the youngest of four siblings, and doubtless the beneficiary of the Roman Catholic ban on birth control. Nevertheless, a certain winsome helplessness and beaver-like dentition (christened Michael, he was soon known as Bucky) preserved him through the "dark years" until the sudden eruption of consciousness — or memory, at least — chasing a butterfly, net cocked overhead, into screeching traffic in Coral Gables, Florida. His other family nickname, acquired soon after, was "Nature Boy," for the many small animals he captured and brought home to be his totems.

In 1963 the family relocated to Neptune Beach, where the young dude became a fanatical surfer and tireless player of pick-up sports of all kinds. He did not apply himself academically, attended college reluctantly, and affects to remember much of this poorly. A modestly gifted visual artist, his first attempt at a career, after dropping out of college, was as a stone carver. This was a terrible idea! How he suffered! Yet, not so much really.

Finally, after a series of Raymond Carver-esque dead-end jobs, complicated by not-quite-Carver-esque drinking, he declared a "do-over," returned to college, and, paying for the classes himself, actually attended them faithfully. While a graduate student at the Florida State University Creative Writing Department, he began publishing short fiction, a comic strip (*Fat Rabbit*, with Tim Hoomes), as well as a weekly humor column, "Barmadillo," for the *Tallahassee Democrat*.

In 1992, he published his first feature article for *Outside* magazine. That was the beginning of a long, strange career in the travel/adventure writing biz, the best of which is collected here. His yarns have been anthologized in the *Best American* series, once for Travel and once for Sports. A certain sentence, long and spiraling, and right on the gleeful brink of syntactical smashup, was chosen as one of the 70 greatest sentences by *Esquire* magazine (along with efforts from old friends Ernest "Papa" Hemingway and Scottie Fitzgerald). In 2005 he was awarded a novelty plaque by his sister, Molly, which reads, "If you haven't grown up by age fifty, you don't have to."

An absolutely magical writer, Bucky McMahon is one of the greatest to have ever stared at a blank page. In a cliché-ridden world, each story by Bucky is a miracle of discovery. He sees in the dark and finds beauty where most writers wouldn't dare to look. A character is never more human than when he is in these good hands. And, a reader will never have a better guide across these landscapes.

— *Mark Warren*

Bucky McMahon is a word wizard. These essays take you deep underwater, slogging through the swamp, brachiating through the jungle, luffing past the lava flow, yawning in the classroom, yo-yoing on the open sea; and now and again just for good measure surfing the psychic cosmos. A humble heart and a fine intellect are here coupled to a flair for ecstasy, and as he says of Wakulla, mother of all springs, it is good, it is good, it is good.

— *Janet Burroway*

Climate change is too vast for most of us to believe. The Gulf Stream might as well be fairy tale. But when Bucky McMahon jumps into a life raft 50 miles from Miami and floats alone through night and day, trying to grasp what the Gulf Stream really is, trying to experience it, we see the problem. In the best fiction, a writer finds a moment that reveals a life, distills it. In the best magazine writing, a writer finds this moment for a culture and time. That's Bucky McMahon's genius. He's funny and light, and you rip right along enjoying his tale, but then suddenly you realize he's done something important.

— *David Vann*